TUTORIALS IN LEARNING AND MEMORY

ESSAYS IN HONOR OF GORDON BOWER

BI 0559805 2

TUTORIALS IN LEARNING AND MEMORY

ESSAYS IN HONOR OF GORDON BOWER

EDITED BY John R. Anderson
Carnegie-Mellon University

AND

Stephen M. Kosslyn
Johns Hopkins University

W. H. FREEMAN AND COMPANY
San Francisco • New York

Library of Congress Cataloging in Publication Data
Main entry under title:

Tutorials in learning and memory.

Includes bibliographies and index.
Contents: Learning and memory in infants / Gary M. Olson—Acquiring expertise / Alan M. Lesgold—Spreading activation / John R. Anderson—[etc.]
1. Learning, Psychology of—Addresses, essays, lectures. 2. Memory—Addresses, essays, lectures. 3. Bower, Gordon H. I. Bower, Gordon H. II. Anderson, John Robert, 1947– . III. Kosslyn, Stephen Michael, 1948–
BF318.T87 1984 153 83-20684
ISBN 0-7167-1570-8
ISBN 0-7167-1571-6 (pbk.)

Printed in the United States of America

1 2 3 4 5 6 7 8 9 0

CONTENTS

PREFACE

This book contains a series of essays by psychologists who were students of Gordon H. Bower during the period from 1967 to 1978. We all feel a great intellectual debt to Gordon, and we wish to thank him in a way that, as a teacher, he would appreciate—by serving the education of current graduate students. Thus, we have put together a set of state-of-the-art tutorials on topics in the area of learning and memory (broadly defined). This volume is a tribute commemorating Gordon's 50th birthday, but we don't want to imply that it is some sort of capstone to the teaching aspect of his career—far from it. Gordon has had a generation of graduate students since we passed through Stanford, and he has many more waiting in the wings. (It should also be noted he produced a generation of research psychologists before any of us arrived at Stanford). We would not be surprised if on some other birthday another crop of Bower students produce a second volume. In this preface, we would like to record our impressions of Gordon Bower during our period at Stanford.

To truly understand Gordon Bower, one must know something of his origins. Gordon grew up in a tiny village in Appalachia, where he was a star high school athlete. He was selected to all-state teams in both baseball and basketball. He attended college on a baseball scholarship and struggled hard with the decision of whether or not to play professional baseball, fortunately (for us) deciding in favor of psychology. This is not the sort of beginning one would associate with one who holds a distinguished chair in psychology at Stanford University, but it somehow led to the deep intellectual commitments that are now part of the core of Gordon's personality.

Gordon never tried to hide the rough and rustic world of his youth—but we often suspected that he exaggerated the jock aspects of his Appalachian origins. To put it politely, Gordon was "gruff." His conversation was peppered with many colorful and forceful phrases that cannot be repeated here. With that gruff earthiness, however, he brought a depth of intellectual concern that served to inspire his students. Indeed, he brought a commonsense attitude to research, an approach that made the science of psychology seem all the more pure. The name of the game was theory and experimentation, rather than the political intrigues of academia. This no-nonsense approach led one fellow, but more junior, faculty member to refer to Gordon as the John Wayne of psychology.

Gordon has an international reputation for identifying weak intellectual endeavors. Many a colloquium speaker at Stanford or at conferences can attest to the incisive nature of his critical questions. It is probably relevant that when he played baseball, Gordon was a pitcher. We suspect that he viewed intellectual debate very much like a pitcher probing for a batter's weaknesses. Graduate students coming to work with Gordon often felt like rookie batters facing the big league pitcher. We all struck out many times, but by confronting the "pro," we all learned to sharpen our intellectual batting eye.

Gordon was at his toughest during the 1960s, mellowing a little with the passing years. His part of an interaction tended to be brusque, direct, incisive, and often bawdy. His students soon discovered, however, that under that harsh exterior beat the proverbial heart of gold. But the gruff exterior is what they first encountered. And there was one message that the gruffness made clear—intellectual nonsense was not to be tolerated.

These were hard times in academia. The war in Vietnam was at its height. The counterculture was also at its height. The campus was often filled with protests and tear gas, and there was much emphasis on encounter group experiences in "finding oneself." Some graduate students lost their way in that world, but Gordon did his best to keep us on a sensible intellectual course. Besides identifying intellectual nonsense, he had the ability to inspire his students with ideas. One often left a meeting with Gordon or one of his research presentation, truly passionate about the issues in psychology. Students who convinced Bower to be their advisor counted themselves especially lucky.

When Alan Lesgold and Gary Olson arrived at Stanford in 1967, and John Anderson in 1968, each intended to specialize in mathematical psychology. The psychology department was then dispersed across the campus, and Gordon had a small office in the basement of Cubberly Hall. However, the intellectual center of this world was Ventura Hall, where a seminar on mathematical psychology was held every Friday afternoon. That was where Gordon Bower "educated" graduate students on the fine points of scientific analysis and argumentation. There was a special seat at the end of the seminar table reserved for Gordon, so that he could face the speaker directly. No one else took that seat, even if Gordon was late and there was standing room only. Once, Gordon found an occupant in his chair, and gave a comic "humpf," it was quickly vacated.

Gordon has always excelled at seeing the shortcomings of existing approaches and identifying the promise of new techniques. He played the key role in leading his students (and perhaps the department) from mathematical psychology to cognitive psychology. Gordon explained to his students that there were interesting psychological phenomena that mathematical psychology could not handle and that they had better learn computer simulation techniques.

Gordon was very demanding of his students and insisted that they keep their productivity high. Each student was expected to finish at least one project every quarter. He would not tolerate a student getting bogged down in some intellectual problem. His way of jarring a student out of such intellectual constipation was to make a comment like, "Well, if you can't come up with any good ideas right now, at least do an experiment so you can observe subjects learning." We learned the importance of empirical findings in guiding theory and the danger of becoming too autistic in one's theorizing. However, Gordon also stressed the value of the good idea and clear thinking about an issue. When John Anderson timidly asked for a first-year evaluation, Gordon replied, "You're not doing badly, but you should try to come up with more good ideas." After a particularly disastrous seminar presentation, Stephen Kosslyn shuffled into Gordon's office and was told, "You can't just give 'em a lick and a promise. You've got to have the theory carefully worked out before you go talk about it."

In the late 60s, Gordon had his scare from lung cancer. Nothing came of it, except that he gave up smoking. None of his students knew about his worries until after the diagnosis was found to be a false alarm. During that period Gordon may have been a bit harsher, but his stress was not apparent in either his own intellectual productivity or that of his students.

In the early 70s, things changed rapidly at Stanford. Bill Estes left the faculty; Roger Shepard joined it in 1970, followed shortly by Herb Clark and Ed Smith. The whole department moved to Jordan Hall, and the Ventura seminar was transformed into the Friday seminar, which now included all of the faculty and students in experimental psychology. The mathematical content gradually decreased and the seminar began to focus on cognitive psychology. When Lesgold, Olson, and Anderson received their doctorates in the early 70s, each considered himself a cognitive psychologist, rather than a mathematical psychologist.

So, by the time Stephen Kosslyn arrived in 1970, and Arnie Glass and Perry Thorndyke in 1971, psychology at Stanford had already undergone major changes. The department was housed under a single roof, many more students were working on cognition, and computer simulation was on everyone's mind. The remnants of verbal learning and mathematical psychology were disappearing. Semantic memory and mental imagery were new topics, and Kosslyn, Glass, and Thorndyke were soon joined by Keith Holyoak in pursuing these exciting areas of research. Gordon served to lead us from the world of verbal learning to semantic memory, and very early recognized the importance of artificial intelligence for psychology.

The mid-70s found further transformations in Gordon Bower. The Vietnam war ended and the counterculture transformed itself into the "me" generation, but Gordon continued pursuing the best intellectual topics around. His interests expanded to supervising dissertation research on individual differences by Robert Sternberg and doctoral work on motor programs by David Rosenbaum. His own research interest turned more and more to story processing. Again, Gordon led the way at Stanford in a new shift in research. John Black remembers a chance conversation with Gordon in the men's room in which he was convinced to work with Gordon on story processing.

As the years rolled by there was also a gradual transformation in Gordon's personality and his style of teaching and supervising research. He became less and less the critic and more and more the supporter. At the 1977 Carnegie Symposium Gordon was asked to critique the papers; he did so, but then ended his comments with a criticism of criticism, issuing a call for intellectual "cheerleaders." Gordon became more and more of a father figure to his students. However, he played his new role with the same Appalachian color that he had brought to his former role. He took to referring to his graduate students with phrases like "young fellers" and "whippersnappers," and after a presentation at a Friday seminar, his question might take a much kinder tack, such as "Now, what simple summary can I take home to Grandmother?"

Gordon has been a great source of professional support for his students. He bothered to listen to our half-baked ideas, to attempt to understand them, and of course, to criticize or sharpen them. (He even did this for staff members, once writing a detailed critique of a newspaper article on ESP for a secretary.) Gordon's ability to take your ideas, expand on them, refine and recast them better than you could was legendary. Many of us received enormous aid in rewriting our papers. Often we got a paper (or dissertation) back completely rewritten; many of these papers were published without Gordon's name on them. Both he and his wife Sharon expended great effort in helping students become better public speakers. Not only were seminar presentations criticized thoughtfully, but often personal feedback on public speaking was given to the aspiring candidate before he gave a talk as part of a job interview. All of us had our communication skills improved by studying with Gordon; however, his own abilities in this domain remain something very special—an ideal toward which we all still strive.

Gordon also cared about the personal lives of his students. He empathized with the ups and downs of their love lives and marriages, although he wisely did not interfere. Many of us suffered crises of confidence and motivation, defects of personality, and family disasters which he helped us struggle through. He lent some of us money when we needed it, and even gave Arnie Glass his wedding. He took it as his special mission to see that each student made it through the program with an improved self-image. John Anderson remembers when he missed a deadline on the HAM book because he had spent the whole day in San Francisco with Lynne Reder, whom he had just started dating. He apologized to Gordon, who responded, "Don't worry, John, the world can wait another day for HAM."

But beyond all such personal concerns, intellectual issues remained foremost in Gordon's mind. At one Friday seminar Arnie Glass offered the audience the choice of hearing about either his research or his fabulous comic book collection. Everyone voted for the comic books, except the man at the end of the table. Arnie concluded, "Well, after taking a weighted vote, I think that I should talk about my research."

While it may not have extended to comic books, Gordon had very diverse interests. Besides mathematical and cognitive psychology, he maintained an active interest in comparative and physiological psychology, personality theory and behavior therapy, hypnosis, aging, and drugs. Studying with Gordon, one never lost the feeling of being part of a larger field. His enormous breadth of expertise also enabled him to advise students on an equally wide range of research topics, as should be evident in the following brief sketches of our research with him.

Alan Lesgold began his work with Gordon on verbal learning, eventually focusing on the way information could be organized into structures in memory. Gary Olson was initially interested in verbal learning, then psycholinguistics, and found Gordon always interested in learning new material as the need arose. John Anderson began to work on a series of experiments on the categorical nature of free recall. Gordon kept prodding him until he developed the FRAN model. A series of experiments Gordon "urged" on John led to a more general theory of free recall, while another series led to a theory of sentence memory and finally to a jointly authored book,

Human Associative Memory (1973), which was heavily inspired by developments in linguistics and artificial intelligence.

Fortuitously, when Stephen Kosslyn arrived Gordon had just finished a draft of a review paper on mental imagery and thus had been thinking about the topic in some depth. Although Gordon was not particularly interested in children (as objects of psychological study), he was willing to collaborate with Stephen in an investigation of whether children used imagery in their thinking more than adults.

Arnie Glass and Gordon Bower published in fields as diverse as semantic memory and Gestalt factors in perceptual memory. Gordon and Arnie also had a common interest in drugs and the mind, and were the only members of the psychology department to attend a seminar on the topic that required going across town to the VA. Perry Thorndyke came to Stanford fully committed to approaching psychology from the perspective of artificial intelligence. Gordon was sympathetic to this approach, which required him to let up slightly on his long-standing bias toward early and continuous outflow of empirical results. Instead, he encouraged Perry's interest in psycholinguistics, actively consulting in his empirical studies of memory for verbs, sentence processing, and narrative recall.

When Keith Holyoak first arrived at Stanford, Gordon promptly set him to work looking at effects of semantic interpretation on recognition memory for naturalistic sounds (e.g., a sound initially interpreted as a heartbeat is not recognized later if it is subsequently interpreted as a bouncing ball). This experiment was completed in Holyoak's first quarter; Gordon wrote it up and it was promptly accepted for publication in the *Journal of Experimental Psychology*. Holyoak reports that this was his first publication at Stanford and the only one ever accepted without revision—and that he didn't write a word of it.

Bob Sternberg arrived at Stanford with a firm idea of what line of research he wanted to pursue. Although Gordon was not especially interested in the nature of individual differences in intellectual function, he believed the topic was well worth investigating and that Bob was capable of doing so. As usual, Gordon put his money where his mouth was and supported Bob's research through his dissertation, even though the work produced little direct benefit to Gordon's research. David Rosenbaum also pursued an independent course of research. The study of motor control was not one of the topics that most fascinated Gordon, but he characteristically supported David's interests and provided his usual in-depth reflections about the work and its future.

When John Black arrived at Stanford, Gordon was deeply into a "new wave" of investigations of how large clusters of information are organized in memory. Unlike the early work in verbal learning, the new work was heavily inspired by recent developments in artificial intelligence (AI). Gordon was interested in the nature of the schemas used to comprehend and remember highly structured information. John and Gordon published a number of collaborative papers on the use of narrative schemas during story comprehension and recollection.

Although we could have organized this book in several ways, we chose to order the chapters chronologically, in terms of the year the author finished his doctorate. This organization allows the reader to see changes in research emphases that have occurred since the time the authors were students. Some of the trends over the years are obvious—for example, the movement from verbal learning to AI-inspired work. Some of us have continued along the same track Gordon helped us set down, whereas others have gone off in entirely new directions. But in all cases, we carry with us a splinter of Gordon's integrity, respect, and love for good science. It is clear to us that our work and our lives still bear the mark of our experience with Gordon. It is as if the rolling stone never completely leaves behind the influence of the forces that guided its initial movement.

TUTORIALS IN LEARNING AND MEMORY

ESSAYS IN HONOR OF GORDON BOWER

1

LEARNING AND MEMORY IN INFANTS

Gary M. Olson
University of Michigan

In its modern revival, covering the past 25 years or so, the study of learning and memory has tended to focus on the young adult. An enormous data base has emerged for this population, which consists largely of college freshmen and sophomores, and sophisticated theories have been developed to account for these findings. Most of the chapters in this volume testify to the richness and sophistication of this primary body of literature on learning and memory.

During the past 15 years, however, increased attention has been given to studies of the processes of learning and memory across a much wider age range. The major focus has been the study of grade-school children, and following an intensive decade or so of research, there now exists a great deal of data on learning and memory in this age group (see, e.g., the recent review by Brown, Bransford, Ferrara, & Campione, 1983). There are also growing data bases on infants and preschool children, as well as on changes in the adult in the later years of the life span. Taken as a whole, these investigations promise to reveal the progress of learning and memory skills across the full life of the human organism, adding substantial perspective to our general understanding of these basic abilities.

Preparation of this chapter was supported by a Research Career Development Award (HD 00169) and a research grant (HD 10486) from the National Institute of Child Health and Human Development.

The study of learning and memory in infants is especially exciting for several reasons. First, it allows us to trace the ontogenesis of learning and memory skills from their very beginning. Second, basic questions about the relative contributions of maturation and experience can be addressed by discovering what kinds of skills the infant enters the world with and how these skills develop during the very early postnatal months, when an enormous amount of neural maturation occurs. Third, infants offer a unique view of the nonverbal human. Almost all we know about learning and memory in older children and adults indicates that verbal, symbolic skills play a dominant role in all human cognition. The infant, however, simply does not yet possess these skills. Of course, the issue of what learning and memory is like without language is confounded by the fact that infants, while nonverbal, are also immature. While important data about nonverbal processing can still be collected, this immaturity limits what we can learn about adult nonverbal information processing from infant studies. Fourth, and finally, the comparative study of learning and memory has also flourished recently (Spear & Campbell, 1979; Tighe & Leaton, 1976), and by studying nonverbal animals, the preverbal infant, and the verbal child and adult, we can gain a better perspective on the phylogenetic as well as ontogenetic basis of learning and memory abilities.

In this chapter I will provide a brief introduction to the psychology of learning and memory in infants. I have two goals: first, to describe the methods that are used for studying the infant's information processing abilities; second, to illustrate the application of these methods to the study of a specific theoretical issue, perceptual classification. Research on this particular topic is recent and has important implications for the study of information processing skills and their development. There is a far vaster literature on infant learning and memory than can possibly be covered in this brief tutorial chapter, but I have reviewed this research in greater detail elsewhere (Olson, 1976; Olson & Sherman, 1983a; in press, b; Olson & Strauss, in press).

METHODS FOR STUDYING LEARNING AND MEMORY IN INFANTS

Almost all that the infant does has the potential for revealing information about learning and memory abilities. However, in this chapter I will confine myself to those behaviors that have been used extensively by investigators to study such abilities, namely, conditioning and habituation tasks. My purpose in reviewing these methods is to show how one can ask questions about the infant's learning and memory abilities. I have chosen to focus on methodology for two reasons. First, the methods available for studying infants are less familiar to most students of learning and memory than those described in other chapters in this book. Second, as research on infancy becomes more widely known, it is important that readers possess sufficient critical skills to be able to evaluate what they read. To be frank, the field of infancy research has been plagued by poorly designed and inadequately controlled experiments. But these very studies often receive widespread attention because of their sensational claims. It is essential to know how to differentiate a carefully conducted study from one that has serious design or procedural flaws.

Most research on infant learning and memory has been conducted since the mid-1960s. Because this work began when very little was known about the infant's abilities, the research has been dominated by basic descriptive questions. Can infants learn and remember? Under what conditions? What can they do at different ages? Infancy research is difficult to conduct, so only modest gains have been made in addressing these basic questions.

The methods described here are far more important in a broader sense than merely a set of techniques for studying learning and memory. Because all of them permit the investigator to ask questions about discrimination and generalization, they have been used to study a broad range of questions concerning the sensory, perceptual, and conceptual abilities of infants. Indeed, although these procedures are *prima facie* learning methods, they are among the major means used to study all kinds of infant perceptual and cognitive capacities.

Conditioning Paradigms

The psychology of learning from the 1930s through the 1950s was dominated by the study of conditioning, predominantly with animal subjects. There were a few studies of conditioning in infants conducted during this period (Marquis, 1931; Wenger, 1936; Wickens & Wickens, 1940), although they each had serious methodological flaws. There is also a more recent literature on conditioning in infants, and though conditioning techniques have not been as widely used as habituation, they are common enough for us to examine some of them.

Classical Conditioning

Although there are many variations to the basic procedure, classical conditioning consists in essence of the transfer of stimulus control from a stimulus which reliably elicits a reflex to one which was previously neutral. There are several components to the classical conditioning paradigm. First, there must be an initial pattern of stimulus control in which one stimulus, called the unconditioned stimulus (UCS), reliably elicits an identifiable unconditioned response (UCR), while a second, called the conditioned stimulus (CS), does not elicit the response. Typically, simple reflexes like salivation in response to the smell or sight of food, an eye-blink in response to an air puff, and heart-rate changes in response to a loud tone or a bright light are studied. The UCS and CS are presented in close temporal sequence during the *acquisition* phase of the experiment, optimally, with the CS preceding the UCS. After acquisition, an *extinction* phase is presented, in which the CS is presented alone. The occurrence of responses to the CS during this extinction phase is the main indicator of conditioning, that is, that a conditioned response (CR) can be elicited. If the extinction phase continues without further presentations of the UCS, the response will eventually cease to occur.

Classical conditioning is one of the basic forms of learning, and since Pavlov's initial investigations, it has been studied extensively. Most theorists recognize it as only one of a variety of forms of learning, but it is of special interest because of its phylogenetic generality. Classical conditioning is largely confined to psychophysiological reflexes, and it provides a means of studying learning and memory in organisms who have limited response repertoires, such as the nonverbal and physically immature infant. Traditionally, classical conditioning has been thought of as a simple form of learning that follows elementary connectionist principles. Those familiar with the full range of classical conditioning phenomena and the modern expectancy theories that have arisen to explain these phenomena (see, e.g., Rescorla & Wagner, 1972; Wagner & Rescorla, 1972) would now find this attribution simplistic and misleading.

As in any of the experimental learning paradigms, it is important to differentiate various forms of pseudolearning from true learning. Repeatedly presenting a stimulus can make the occurrence of a response more likely because of sensitization of the response rather than being due to transfer of stimulus control.[1] In order to rule out this confounding factor, a control group is presented the UCS the same number of times as the experimental group, but either without any presentation of the to-be-conditioned stimulus or with the CS and UCS presented in a random, unpaired fashion. Wickens and Wickens (1940) found that a group of infants who were presented with the UCS alone exhibited as many conditioned re-

[1]Sensitization refers to an *increase* in response magnitude as a function of mere repetition of a stimulus. It is the opposite of habituation, which will be discussed later in this chapter.

sponses on a test trial as did those who had been given paired presentations of the CS and UCS. This finding implies that the responses occurring on the test trials were due to sensitization rather than to a transfer of stimulus control to the CS.

On the basis of a new conceptualization of the conditioning paradigm, Rescorla (1967, 1972) argued that the UCS presented alone was not a good control for sensitization effects. He observed that in a classical conditioning paradigm the CS acquires informational value during the course of acquisition; that is, it comes to predict the occurrence of the UCS. From this point of view, the important characteristic of the relationship between the CS and UCS is their *correlation*. In the typical paradigm, these have a perfect positive correlation during acquisition. Each time the CS occurs, the UCS occurs. However, presenting the UCS without the CS has a perfect negative correlation, which is also relevant to the organism as information. A better control would be to present the CS and UCS throughout the acquisition phase but with no temporal correlation in their occurrence. In this way, both the experimental and the control groups would have the same number of presentations of the CS and UCS. For experimental subjects, the CS would always predict the occurrence of the UCS, while for control subjects the CS would have no informational value.

An example of a classical conditioning study conducted with infants is one of the experiments reported by Brackbill, Fitzgerald, and Lintz (1967). These investigators examined the conditioning of both pupil dilation and pupil constriction in response to two CSs: a fixed time interval and a tone. In a third condition, these two CSs were combined. The UCS for pupil dilation was a change in illumination from the light to dark, while for constriction it was a change from dark to light. For the temporal CS for conditioning of dilation, the light remained on for 20 seconds and then went off for 4 seconds in a continuous cycle. The complementary arrangement—a continuous cycle of light off for 20 seconds and on for 4 seconds—was used for conditioning of constriction. A test trial consisted of withholding the UCS (change in illumination), that is either leaving the light on or off at the end of 20 seconds. The occurrence of the appropriate pupillary response on such test trials was an indication of successful conditioning. For conditioning with the tone plus a time interval, a brief complex sound was presented 1.5 seconds prior to the switch in illumination during the conditioning trials. During test trials, the tone appeared in the same position relative to the time interval but there was no change in illumination. Finally, for conditioning with the tone alone, the sound again appeared 1.5 seconds prior to a change in illumination during conditioning, but now the intervals varied from 10 to 30 seconds, with an average of 20 seconds. Test trials again consisted of presenting the tone alone.

Two control groups were used. In one, the light onset or offset occurred at random intervals ranging from 10 to 30 seconds, with an average of 20 seconds. This is a pseudoconditioning control for the time CS. A second control group was presented the sound CS concurrently with the change in illumination UCS. (In general, presenting the CS and the UCS concurrently, as opposed to having the CS precede the UCS, is ineffective in producing conditioning. This is clearly not quite the zero correlation control recommended by Rescorla, but it does provide a check on the tendency of the CS to potentiate the CR.)

This study was run with infants whose ages averaged 53.3 days (range-26 to 86 days). Four subjects were run in each of the three CS conditions for both dilation and constriction. All subjects in the time and the time-plus-sound groups showed conditioning: significant dilation for the dilation groups, significant constriction for the constriction groups. No subjects in the sound-alone group showed conditioning, nor did any subjects in either of the control groups. Interestingly, the time-plus-sound group conditioned to dilate their pupils showed significantly greater dilation than the time-only group, whereas the time-plus-sound group conditioned to constrict showed significantly less constriction than the time-only group for constriction.

These results show that a simple psychophysiological response—pupil dilation—can be classically conditioned to a temporal stimuli. The design of the experiment is especially elegant in that the pupillary response can go in either direction, and the response was conditioned in each direction. It is also significant that the sound-only group showed no evidence of conditioning. This pattern of findings is typical of the infant classical conditioning literature: some CS–UCS combinations have produced successful conditioning, whereas others have proven resistant to conditioning. Reviewing such data Fitzgerald and Brackbill (1976) and Sameroff and Cavanagh (1979) concluded that infant classical conditioning supports the idea that there are certain *constraints* on learning. That is, the infant is biologically predisposed to notice some stimulus-response correlations and not others. This concept has received extensive discussion in the general literature on conditioning (Hinde & Stevenson-Hinde, 1973; Seligman, 1970).

Operant Conditioning

In operant conditioning, behavior is controlled by the presentation of reinforcement when specific stimulus-response pairs occur. A spontaneously emitted behavior is followed by a reinforcing event, that is, a positive or negative outcome. (A positive outcome is the *occurrence* of something good or the *cessation* of something bad. A negative outcome is just the opposite.) The first form of reinforcement tends to increase the probability of occurrence of the response, whereas the latter tends to decrease it. Typically, the reinforcement is presented along with a neutral stimulus, so that later the strength of the conditioned response can be measured by presenting this stimulus alone.

The key feature of the operant conditioning paradigm is the *contingency* between the emitted behavior and the reinforcement. Thus, control conditions in an operant conditioning experiment must break this contingency in one of several ways. Merely omitting the reinforcement allows the investigator to observe the changes in the rate of the to-be-conditioned response that would occur anyway. Presenting the reinforcing stimulus in a noncontingent fashion (usually randomly) reveals the extent to which the reinforcing stimulus itself tends to produce the behavior of interest. Probabilistic relationships between the reinforcer and the response—called partial reinforcement—yield effective learning, though typically at a slower rate than steady reinforcement of the response.

There is an extensive literature on operant conditioning in infants, including a large number of review articles (Kessen, Haith, & Salapatek, 1970; Rovee-Collier & Lipsitt, 1980; Rovee-Collier & Gekoski, 1979; Sameroff & Cavanagh, 1979). Although many conceptual and methodological issues are pertinent to this paradigm, my goal here is to introduce the operant conditioning paradigm that is typically used with infants and to highlight briefly some of the major methodological issues.

A large number of stimuli and wide variety of behaviors have been examined in infant operant conditioning. For instance, early studies by Papousek (1959, 1961, 1967) examined head turns in response to auditory and visual stimuli, with food often used as the reinforcer. Investigators have also used complex visual or visual-auditory events as reinforcers for head turns (Fagen, 1977). Both nutritive (Sameroff, 1968, 1972) and non-nutritive (Siqueland & DeLucia, 1969) sucking have been studied, with many different types of reinforcing stimuli. More recently, Rovee-Collier and her colleagues have conducted a wide range of studies examining reinforcement of infant foot kicks (Fagen & Rovee, 1976; Rovee & Fagen, 1976; Rovee & Rovee, 1969; Rovee-Collier, Sullivan, Enright, Lucas, & Fagen, 1980; Sullivan, Rovee-Collier, & Tynes, 1979). Finally, starting with a classic study by Rheingold, Gewirtz, and Ross (1959), there has been a continuing interest in the operant conditioning of infant vocalizations with social reinforcement.

To make our discussion more concrete, let us consider one representative infant study, that by Rovee and Rovee (1969). This study used the technique of conjugate reinforcement, in which reinforcement is continuously available, but its intensity depends directly upon the rate of response. This variant of the operant conditioning paradigm has been extremely popular in recent infant research.

In the Rovee and Rovee study, 10-week-old infants were tested in their cribs at home. A mobile that the infants had seen on their cribs at least 6 weeks was hung at the foot of the crib. For the experimental group of six infants, a soft silk cord linked the infant's left ankle to the mobile. Thus, infant foot or leg movements would cause the mobile to move.

The experimental group received 27 minutes of testing. During the first 3 minutes, the cord was attached to the foot but not to the mobile, and the baseline rate of foot kicking was assessed. Then there was a 15-minute acquisition period with the cord attached to both the infant's foot and to the mobile. Finally, there was a 5-minute extinction period during which the cord was once again unattached from the mobile. Two minutes intervened between each part of the experiment to allow preparation for the next phase.

Two control groups were used. In the first, six infants received the same 27 minutes of testing, except that the cord was never attached to the foot. However, during the acquisition phase, the mobile was moved by the experimenter to mimic what happened during the experimental group's acquisition phase. This provided noncontingent visual stimulation.[2] A second control group received the same series of presentations as the first one, but had the cord attached to their ankle so they could feel the movement of the cord, as well as see the experimenter's movements of the mobile.

Figure 1-1 shows the results. The dependent variable was the averge number of foot kicks by the infants per minute during each phase of the experiment. Note that a moderate rate of foot kicking occurred for all three groups during the 3-minute baseline period. However, during the acquisition period, only the group whose foot kicks controlled the mobile increased their rate of responding. During the extinction period, when foot kicks for the experimental group no longer controlled the mobile, the rate of responding fell off, coming to be indistinguishable from that of either control group. On the other hand, neither control group showed any change in the rate of foot kicks across the testing session. The noncontingent stimulation provided during the acquisition phase had no effect on their response rate. This is the classic pattern of behavior for an operant conditioning experiment. The reinforcement provided during the

[2]It is understood that this is not an ideal control for visual feedback because of the very real possibility of experimenter bias affecting the nature and timing of the mobile movements.

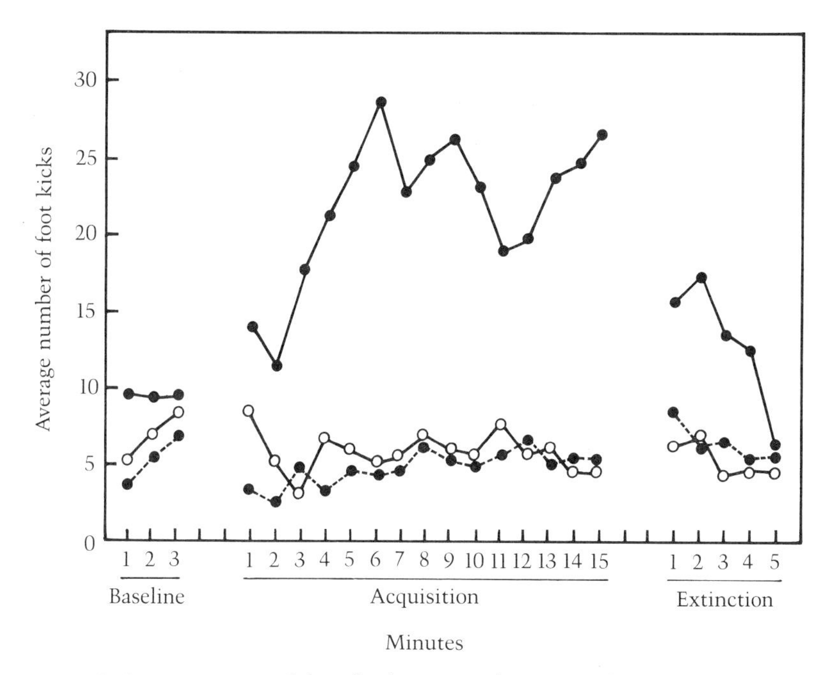

FIGURE 1–1 Mean rate of foot kicking as a function of reinforcement condition in the study by Rovee and Rovee (1969). Each point represents 1 minute of observation. The solid line with filled circles is the experimental group. The solid line with open circles is the visual-somesthetic control group and the dashed line is the visual only control.

acquisition phase influenced the rate of responding, specifically because there was a contingent relation between the infant's behavior and the occurrence of the reinforcing event.

There are of course many issues of control and methodological detail that complicate the use of a specific paradigm, and operant conditioning with infants is no exception. The review articles cited earlier, along with Olson and Sherman (1983) are appropriate sources for further details.

Savings and Reinstatement in Conditioning

If something has been partially or completely learned, a later learning experience with it ought to lead to *savings* in relearning. The best example of such effects is the *reinstatement* effect in long-term memory for conditioned foot kicks demonstrated by Rovee-Collier et al. (1980). Three-month-old infants were conditioned using the foot-kick procedure just described. Following short retention intervals, on the order of 24 hours or so, such infants would readily show retention on a nonreinforced test at the beginning of a second session. However, over very long intervals, such as several weeks, no evidence of retention was found. These investigators found that if they gave the infants a brief exposure to the reinforcing mobile 24 hours prior to the retention test, they could obtain evidence of significant retention over intervals as long as 4 weeks for infants who were 3 months old at the time of original training. Such long-term retention could not be demonstrated without the reinstatement procedure nor was the reinstatement experience sufficient by itself to produce learning.

Savings or reinstatement effects are especially useful when studying retention over long intervals or after brief familiarization experiences. Investigators of learning and memory have long viewed savings in relearning as an especially sensitive measure of memory effects (Nelson, 1971). Though the techniques have not been widely used yet with conditioning with infants, the study by Rovee-Collier et al. (1980) suggests that it is an informative method for evaluating the limiting conditions of infant learning and memory.

Summary

Conditioning tasks were the earliest experimental methods used to study infant learning. Though they have not been as popular as habituation during the 1970s and '80s, they are still useful methods for uncovering infant information processing skills. Operant conditioning in particular is an extremely attractive task for studies of learning, memory, and discrimination where distinctive stimulus-response contingencies have an important methodological or conceptual role.

Learning and Memory Tasks Based on Shifts of Attention

Infant attention has been extensively studied, using a broad range of methods (for a review, see Olson and Sherman, 1983). A variety of psychophysiological and behavioral measures are available, and infant attention is influenced by many factors of interest to investigators. One such factor is familiarity. Other things being equal, novel stimuli elicit more attention than familiar ones. In general, attention to stimuli *habituates* as the stimuli are presented repeatedly. Habituation is a simple and reliable phenomenon, easy to measure and evident in many domains. The explosion of research on infant perception, learning, memory, and cognition in the past 15 years has been due in large part to the use of the habituation paradigm.

In this section I will focus my discussion of habituation phenomena on tasks involving visual stimuli. Thus, it will be useful to know how visual attention is typically measured in infants. Figure

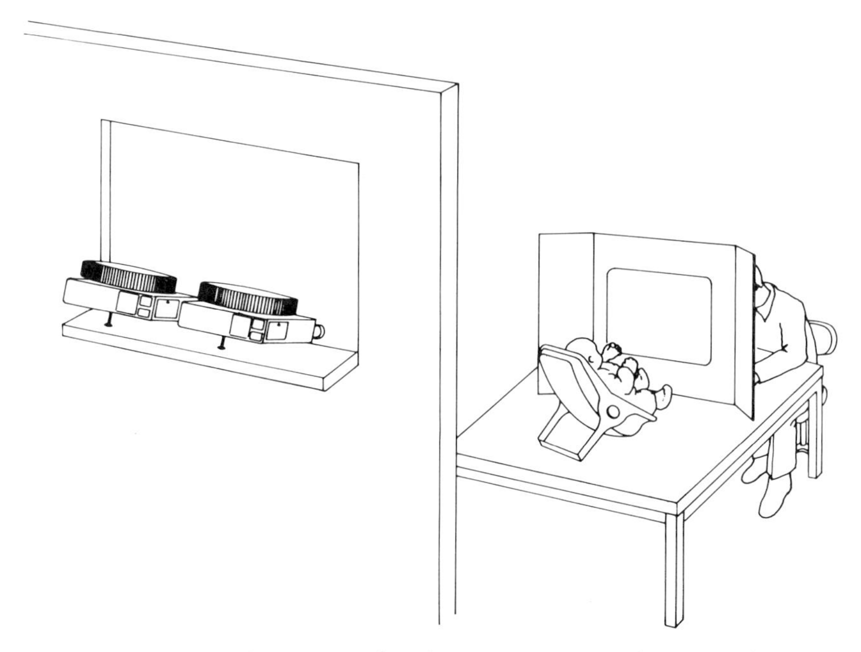

FIGURE 1–2 Typical apparatus for observing corneal reflections of stimuli in infants. Stimuli are projected onto the screen in front of the infant in a darkened room. The observer watches the infant's eyes through a small peephole in the screen. There are two peepholes, so that interobserver reliability can be monitored.

1-2 shows a typical laboratory apparatus. Infants are shown visual stimuli on a screen, and an observer views the infant through a small peephole in the screen. The stimuli can be seen reflected in the infant's eyes, as shown in Figure 1-3. The stimulus that is superimposed over the infant's pupils is assumed to be what the infant is looking at. This simple and reliable method has been used extensively to measure infant visual attention.

FIGURE 1–3 Observer's view of the reflection of stimuli on the infant's cornea.

There are many specific ways in which habituation phenomena can be used in the laboratory. However, in actual practice, two broad classes of methods have been used—the habituation task and the paired-comparison task.

The Habituation Task

The logic of habituation is simple. A stimulus is presented and some measure of orientation or attention to it is monitored. Initially, the infant will attend quite readily to the stimulus because it is a novel event. If the stimulus is presented a number of times in succession, or if it is made available for an extended period of time, the infant's attention wanes. The process was first clearly stated by Sokolov (1963): the level of attention to the stimulus is due to the extent to which the current perceptual trace of it matches traces that are available in memory. The link to memory is the assumption that the different pattern of attending to the stumulus early and late in the series of presentations is because the infant remembers the stimulus. Of course, there are many factors other than familiarity that affect the level of attention to stimuli. Methodological advances in the study of habituation have led to greater sophistication in how to distinguish among these various factors.

Early attempts to measure infant habituation were often plagued by incomplete controls. In a major analysis of habituation, Jeffrey and Cohen (1971) described the issues of control and method that are pertinent to using habituation tasks with infant subjects. Habituation tasks are defined by several basic components. The most basic one is the *trial*, the series of discrete presentations of the stimuli. Trials in turn are comprised of two broad classes: *familiarization* trials and *posthabituation* trials. The familiarization trials are those in which the stimulus or stimuli whose habituation is being measured are presented. Habituation is the decline in attentiveness over the course of these familiarization trials. On the posthabituation trials, a further series of presentations of familiar and novel stimuli is used to ensure that the lowered level of attentiveness is specific to repeated presentation of the familiar stimuli. This specific finding is revealed in posthabituation trials by significantly greater attentiveness to novel stimuli than to the familiar ones.

The role of the posthabituation trials is crucial. A decline in attentiveness across a series of familiarization trials could arise for a number of reasons. For instance, the infant might change *state*—become drowsy or irritable, for example. Some general type of receptor or effector fatigue could also occur. These general changes in the infant's responsiveness have a different conceptual status than a specific loss of attentiveness due to the formation of a memory trace. If the decline in attentiveness is due to general factors, the novel and familiar stimuli ought to be attended to at roughly equal levels, whereas if a memory trace has been established and the infant is still capable of being attentive, the novel stimulus ought to elicit significantly greater attention than the familiar one.

Even this control is not sufficient. Stimuli are not equal in their power to elicit attention due to factors other than their relative novelty. To take an example, a gray patch and a moving, talking face are going to elicit extremely different amounts of visual attention from an infant who has seen neither before. If we presented the gray patch during the familiarization trials and then found greater looking toward the face when we presented it as a novel stimulus, we would not have a very convincing argument against nonspecific changes in attention. Thus, greater looking toward the novel stimulus on a posthabituation trial does not guarantee that the decline in looking during familiarization is an indication of memory for the habituated stimulus. Two remedies are available for this problem of differences in stimulus strength. One is to measure the preferences for the stimuli independent of the habituation experiment. This could be done by presenting the stimuli to subjects who had seen neither before, in order to measure their relative strengths of eliciting attention. The other remedy is to counterbalance stimuli so that any particular stimulus serves equally often as an old and a novel stimulus in the overall design of the habituation experiment. Counterbalancing means that *net* effects in the group of subjects run in any condition could not be due to stimulus preferences.

The traditional way of running an habituation task with infants is to use what is called a fixed-trials procedure. Each trial consists of the presentation of the stimulus to be habituated for a specified interval of time. The level of attention during this interval is the basic dependent variable. A fixed number of such trials are presented during the familarization phase, and the decline in attentiveness is measured by an analysis of variance with trials as a factor. The ideal posthabituation sequence would have at least one novel stimulus followed by at least one further presentation of the familiar stimulus.

During the 1970s, a new variant of the habituation task became popular. The *infant-control procedure* (Cohen & Gelber, 1975; Horowitz, Paden, Bhana, & Self, 1972) introduced several important procedural changes. First, the nature of individual trials was altered to consist of one unlimited look by the infant. Second, the familiarization portion was run to a *criterion of habituation* rather than for a fixed number of trials. And third, because of the use of a preselected criterion, some new issues pertaining to the posthabituation trials arose. The infant-control habituation task has become popular because of a number of conceptual, analytic, and procedural advantages this paradigm has over the standard fixed-trial procedure. But there are also potential pitfalls. All of these matters are discussed in detail in Olson and Sherman (1983).

A concrete example of an infant habituation experiment using this new technique comes from my laboratory work. One hundred and twenty 4-month-old infants completed an infant-control habituation task using visual stimuli.[3] During familiarization, habituation was defined by a criterion of three trials in a row in which the infant attended for less than 3.15 seconds. Three different stimuli were used: (a) Checkerboard: a 6 × 6 checkerboard composed of red and yellow squares; (b) Fabric Swatch: a square piece of fabric composed of a fine check of blue and white, with several orange, yellow, and white flowers superimposed irregularly; and (c) Hearts Pattern: a square, horizontally and vertically symmetrical pattern of 18 small yellow hearts on a black background. These three stimuli were photographed and projected on a screen in the apparatus shown in Figure 1.2. For each infant one of the stimuli was used as the repeating pattern and the other two were used as the new patterns presented on the postcriterion trials. A fully counterbalanced design was used. When the criterion of habituation was met, a six-trial postcriterion square was presented. This consisted of two more presentations of the old stimulus, two trials of novel stimuli, and finally, two more trials of the old stimulus.

The mean number of trials to criterion varied significantly as a function of stimulus. Habituation occurred most rapidly to the Checkerboard (9.6 trials) and most slowly to the Fabric Swatch (14.5 trials), with the Hearts Pattern intermediate (12.3 trials). On the postcriterion trials (Table 1.1), looking was not significantly different from the criterion level on the first two trials, showed significant increases on trials 3 and 4 when the two novel stimuli were presented, and showed a significant decline on the final two trials when the old stimuli were presented again. This pattern of recovery and rehabituation of looking on the postcriterion trials, in combination with the fact that all infants reached a predefined criterion, indicates that habituation occurred for each of the stimulus patterns.

Since visual habituation has been the most widely studied experimental task with infants, there now exists a vast literature using infants of many ages, as well as different types of stimuli, experimental designs, and specific procedures (see, e.g., Jeffrey & Cohen, 1971; Cohen & Gelber, 1975; Cohen, 1976; Olson, 1976; and Olson & Sherman, 1983).

[3]As is typical in infant research, in order to get 120 subjects in the full design an additional 61 subjects had to be run. The majority of these additional subjects were lost because of fussiness which prevented completion of the session.

TABLE 1-1 Postcriterion Performance in a Typical Infant Control Habituation Task

	Trial					
Stimulus	Old	Old	New_1	New_2	Old	Old
Checkerboard						
Mean	2.76	2.39	12.41	9.00	4.62	2.93
SD	1.59	1.54	12.90	9.01	5.14	1.73
Fabric Swatch						
Mean	2.68	2.89	8.50	7.78	4.17	3.49
SD	1.76	1.95	6.71	5.73	3.08	2.83
Hearts Pattern						
Mean	2.58	3.18	8.64	7.84	3.13	2.45
SD	1.45	2.29	5.71	6.46	1.59	1.62

Note: $N = 40$ for each stimulus.

The Paired-Comparison Task

Fagan (1970), using an idea first reported by Fantz (1964), developed a special adaptation of the habituation procedure which has proven to be quite useful in studying infant visual memory. The infant is exposed to a visual stimulus and then is tested for retention by being presented two stimuli simultaneously, the old one and a new one. Relatively greater time spent looking toward the new stimulus implies retention of the old stimulus. (Reliably more looking toward the old stimulus could also be used to infer retention in a properly counterbalanced design, but in practice infants of all ages usually look longer at the novel stimulus.)

Though it is tempting to view this procedure as an analogue of the forced-choice recognition test used in memory research, this would be inappropriate, since there is no notion of "correct choice" for an infant guiding its own selection of stimuli. Rather, the paired-comparison task is more analogous to a choice or preference task. In principle, formal techniques used to analyze choice or preference data could be applied to paired-comparison data (Thomas, 1973), but this has rarely been done.

As with the habituation task, behavior in the paired-comparison task has multiple determinants. Figure 1-4 summarizes the kinds of factors which might govern an infant's choice between two stimuli, *A* and *B*. The relative novelty-familiarity of the stimuli is of primary importance. In order to measure memory effects independent of the other determinants of choice, investigators typically do two things: (a) they choose stimuli which infants look at about equally often prior to familiarization with one of them; and (b) they counterbalance stimulus assignments over subjects, so that equal

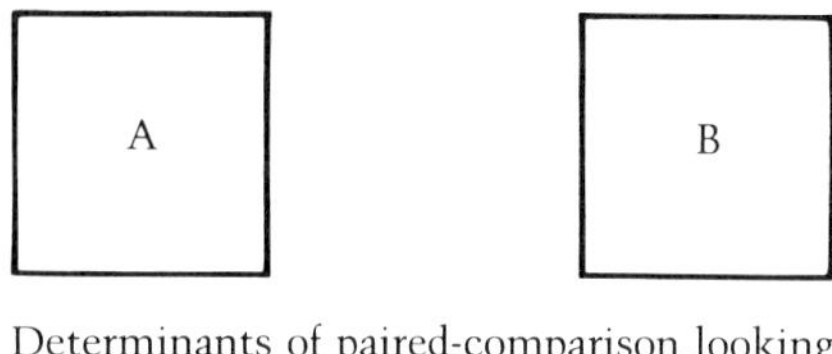

Determinants of paired-comparison looking

Discriminability
Interstimulus contrast
Codability

Preference
Perceptual features
Interpretation
Novelty familiarity

Response biases
Position habits
Criteria for shifting gaze
State

FIGURE 1–4 Determinants of looking on paired-comparison tests.

numbers see *A* and *B* as old stimuli in each condition of an experiment. By choosing stimuli that elicit comparable levels of looking prior to familiarization, the experimenter attempts to control the variance due to stimulus assignments interacting with nonmemory factors. As in the habituation paradigm, the counterbalancing insures that experimental effects averaged over stimulus assignments are memory effects.

To provide a concrete illustration of the design and results of a simple paired-comparison experiment, let us examine part of a study of long-term retention run in my laboratory. In one part of this experiment, thirty-four 8-month-old infants were tested for their ability to recognize colored photographs of faces. Three faces were used in a counterbalanced design, with both immediate and delayed tests. During familiarization, the to-be-remembered stimulus was presented to the infant until 60 seconds of total looking had been accumulated. At the end of this period, two 10-second paired-comparison trials were presented. These trials were timed from the onset of the infant's first look toward either picture, and unlike familiarization, lasted a fixed period of time. The second paired-comparison trial was identical to the first, except that the right-left position of the two pictures was reversed to control for any positional preferences infants might have.[4] The paired-comparison test was repeated 24 hours and 1 week later to provide measures of delayed recognition.

The data from the experiment, analyzed two ways, are shown in Table 2. One analysis compares the absolute amounts of looking

4 Many observers have noted that infants tend to look more toward the right side of such two-stimulus displays.

TABLE 1-2 Looking Data from a Typical Paired-Comparison Experiment

	Test delay		
Measure	Immediate	24-hour	1-week
Looking to novel stimulus			
Mean	9.69*	10.10*	8.70
SD	3.11	2.70	2.54
Looking to familiar stimulus			
Mean	7.17	6.89	8.29
SD	2.53	2.49	2.45
Percent looking to novel			
Mean	57.2*	60.0*	51.0
SD	13.1	12.2	11.3

*$p < .01$, two-tailed

Note: For each test delay, mean Looking to Novel Stimulus was compared to mean Looking to Familiar Stimulus, while Percent Looking to Novel was compared to 50 percent. $N = 30$ for each cell.

at the old and new stimuli; the other calculates a percent-looking-to-novel score and compares it to 50 percent. The percent-looking-to-novel scores are calculated by summing up for each infant the total time spent looking at both the old and new stimuli, and then calculating the following score:

$$\text{percent-looking to novel} = \frac{\text{total looking to new}}{(\text{total looking to new}) + (\text{total looking to old})} \times 100$$

If subjects were to look equally often to the two stimuli, this score would be 50 percent. Significant departures from 50 percent indicate recognition of the old stimulus. In this experiment, infants looked significantly longer at the novel stimulus in two of the three delay conditions, indicating both immediate and 24-hour recognition.

One advantage of the paired-comparison technique is that it can be used to test memory under conditions of very limited familiarization. Both Fagan (1974) and Olson (1979) have found significant novelty preferences in a paired-comparison task with as little as a few seconds of familiarization. This is briefer than most single trials in a habituation task.

Savings and Reinstatement in Habituation

Just as with the conditioning paradigm, savings phenomena can be examined using habituation or paired-comparison tasks. In the logic of the habituation paradigm, where learning is measured by its effects on visual attention, savings phenomena ought to be shown by appropriate shifts in attention following a retention interval.

The most direct way of showing savings would be to find that on a subsequent habituation experience, either following an earlier one or some other kind of familiarization, there was less looking at the outset or that a criterion of habituation was achieved in fewer trials relative to an appropriate control. A study from our laboratory shows how this demonstration of savings might work (Olson, Zimmerman, & Sherman, in preparation). A group of premature infants was given an infant control visual habituation task on two occasions separated by 24 hours. The same old stimulus and the same novel stimuli were used on each day. Further, the entire habituation sequence was preceded by single presentations of four different warm-up stimuli; the same warm-up stimuli were used on both days. A variety of measures of habituation showed savings: the length of the first fixation to the habituation stimulus was 3.6 seconds shorter, criterion was achieved in 3.9 fewer trials, and the total time needed to reach criterion was 52.3 seconds less on the second day. Furthermore, neither the total looking to the stimuli on the prehabituation warm-up trials nor the total looking to the stimuli on the recovery trials during the posthabituation sequence showed any significant change across days, indicating that the savings effect was specific to the repeating stimulus and was not due to general shifts in attention across the two days.

A closely related phenomenon is reinstatement. Several investigators have found that a brief reshowing of the to-be-remembered stimulus prior to a delayed paired-comparison test can facilitate recognition (Cornell, 1979; Fagan, 1978). Cornell's study illustrates the logic of the reinstatement effect. He found that when the test was immediate, 5- to 6-month-old infants could recognize certain visual patterns in a paired-comparison experiment after only 10 or 20 seconds of familiarization, but following a retention interval they showed no significant novelty preferences. However, if infants were shown the to-be-remembered stimuli for 5 seconds prior to the delayed recognition test—an exposure insufficient on its own to produce reliable recognition effects—they *did* show significant novelty preferences even after such a delay.

Summary

The habituation phenomena open the door to the study of a number of important cognitive and perceptual processes. The earliest uses of the paradigm were designed to ask basic questions about learning and memory abilities in infants (see, e.g., Cohen & Gelber, 1975; Kessen et al., 1970; Olson, 1976). The amount, type, and spacing of the familiarization experiences and the delay between familiarization and novelty testing have obvious translations into basic questions about memory. But by clever design of the familiarization sequences and novelty tests, one can ask a broad range of questions about perceptual discrimination, encoding processes, abstraction and classification, and indeed any psychological process that can be defined operationally in terms of differential patterns of discrimination and generalization.

All of these manipulations are available with other paradigms, such as the conditioning methods described in the first section. One might ask why these other methods have not been as widely or as successfully used with infants as the habituation method. One reason is that the habituation method exploits basic attentional phenomena that are a natural part of the infant's behavior. Even the most casual observer of infants notices the extent to which they attend to stimuli in their environment. Thus, the behaviors that are central to the method are not contrived to fit the logic of a paradigm but are just the kinds of activities an infant engages in spontaneously when exposed to stimuli. Successful uses of conditioning paradigms are also probably due in part to the exploitation of natural infant behaviors. But in general, trying to teach the infant to respond to stimuli in an experimenter-designated way is much more difficult than to present stimuli and monitor how the infant attends.

Other Methods

Conditioning and habituation have been the primary methods for studying learning and memory in infants. However, they are not the only kinds of tasks available for examining infant memory. As described in more detail in Olson and Sherman (1983), the following behaviors are all potential indicators of significant learning and memory skills: imitation, object search tasks based on Piaget's work, play, and many forms of social interaction. Conditioning and habituation have been used most extensively to study infants during the first year. The other tasks just mentioned are especially useful for studying infants from midway through the first year on into the second year. This later period of infancy has been much less studied than the earlier months, but recent work is beginning to redress this shortcoming (e.g., Mandler, 1983; Nelson, in press; Sophian, 1980).

PERCEPTUAL CLASSIFICATION

In this section I have selected one important area of recent infant research for special consideration. My purpose in doing so is to show how the basic paradigms of habituation and conditioning can be used to ask significant questions about the infant's general information processing abilities, and also to show that infant research can be relevant to the considerations of general cognitive psychology. The specific example I have chosen is the infant's ability to classify, or categorize, its perceptual experiences. There is a growing body of recent literature that clearly documents the infant's ability by at least the second half of the first year to group its experience into classes or categories.

Studies of learning and memory using shifts of attention typically focus on memory for specific items. Thus, in a classic infant habituation experiment, a single stimulus is presented repeatedly, and recovery from habituation is examined by presenting another specific stimulus. The same is true of a classic paired-comparison experiment. To show successful habituation-dishabituation and paired-comparison behavior the infant has to recognize some commonality across a series of separate trials and thus abstract some information from the varying temporal and contextual particulars of individual trials. But the core experience—the to-be-remembered stimulus—is nominally the same. Therefore, these studies focus on recognition of *recurrence,* that is, on recognition that this specific pattern is one that was experienced before.

A new type of study emerged during the 1970s—studies that focus on recognition of *class membership.* In these studies infants are presented with a variety of stimuli, typically drawn from some class or category of stimuli specified by the experimenter. The recognition test is a test for generalization: test trials consist of presenting novel instances from the class or category used during familiarization and novel instances from some different category. Assuming that appropriate controls have been used, discriminative behavior on such test trials indicates that the infants noticed the abstract property shared by the category members during familiarization. Upon noticing this same property in the novel within-category item on the test, this item is regarded as less novel than the comparison test item from another category. This should result in preferential looking toward the outside-category stimulus.

There are important conceptual and methodological issues that pertain to experiments of this type. To facilitate our discussion, we will present an example of such a study so we can tie our points into a concrete case. In the subsequent discussion I will take up issues of design, control, and interpretation of such an experiment. A study by Strauss and Curtis (1981) on the infant's concept of number will serve as our example.

The question Strauss and Curtis addressed was whether or not 10- to 12-month-old infants are able to discriminate between stimuli which differ only in their numerosity. They presented infants with a series of familiarization trials in which each trial contained the same number of items. In one group, the infants saw different items (e.g., dogs, houses) in different sizes and positions on each trial (Heterogeneous Condition). In a second group, the same type of item (e.g., dogs) was presented on each trial, with the size and position varied (Homogeneous Condition). But in both conditions, the *number* of items presented on each trial was constant. Different infants were familiarized with 2, 3, 4, or 5 items per trial. An infant-control procedure with a criterion of habituation was employed. Following habituation, four test trials were presented, two with the same numerosity as familiarization and two with either $N + 1$ or $N - 1$ items. Different groups were tested on the 2 vs. 3, 3 vs. 4, and 4 vs. 5 discriminations.

For the 2 vs. 3 discrimination, all infants were able to make the discrimination regardless of the familiarization condition (Homogeneous vs. Heterogeneous). In the 4 vs. 5 discrimination, no infants showed differential attention on the test trials. An interaction of familiarization and sex occurred for the 3 vs. 4 discrimination. Females in the Homogeneous Condition and males in the Heterogeneous Condition discriminated 3 from 4. Strauss and Curtis (1981) concluded from these data that preverbal infants possess the ability to apprehend the numerosity of perceptual displays, at least for small numbers. A study by Starkey and Cooper (1980) reported similar results for younger infants (4 to 6 months).

What are such studies of perceptual classification all about? The first issue is the definition of a class or a category. A class or category is a mental representation of the common elements of a set of distinct experiences that are recognized as distinct by the infant. Distinct events whose differences are not noticed because of sensory or perceptual limitations or incomplete encoding do not produce category knowledge. The differences among the items in a class or category must be *noticed but ignored* by the infant within the context of the experiment.

Second, does the typical categorization experiment teach the infants the category or provide an opportunity for the infants to manifest category knowledge they already possess? It seems improbable that Strauss and Curtis (1981) and Starkey and Cooper (1980) taught anything about numbers to the infants in their studies.

More likely, the infants came to the experiments with the concept of numerosity and then exhibited it under the conditions of the experimental tasks. Category learning of this type is probably an extended process, based on long-term learning. A small number of trials in the laboratory cannot teach an infant the concept of numerosity. But nothing in these experiments or any others that have been done contain evidence to support this supposition. The distinction between category learning and category recognition is an important one, and it would be useful to see experiments performed that attempt to differentiate between the two.

Third, the perceptual knowledge displayed in a typical categorization experiment should not be thought of as concept knowledge. Concepts embody many types of knowledge, of which perceptual knowledge is only one. For instance, the concept of a face, a person, or a number is not exhausted by the perceptual knowledge that underlies the abilities infants have to notice categorizations built into experimental designs. Perceptual knowledge is an important constituent of *some* concepts, so such work should properly be thought of as studies on the *use* of knowledge about perceptual categories. Misleading claims about infant abilities can result when terms like "concept" are thrown around too loosely.

Let us examine several implications of these conceptual issues for categorization experiments. First, the precise nature of the category being investigated must be clearly explicated so that the types of controls to be run are also clear. In particular, the relevant and irrelevant perceptual features for any particular category must be defined explicitly. In both the Strauss and Curtis (1981) and Starkey and Cooper (1980) studies, the investigators attempted to examine the infant's conception of numerosity. They wanted to have the numerosity of their displays constant across familiarization trials, but irrelevant features which might also attract the infant's attention had to be controlled. The identity, size, orientation, and configuration of items in the display were all irrelevant features that had to be varied from trial to trial in order that the infants' test behavior not be based on these features. These issues are very tricky to resolve. Certainly there will be continuing debate among investigators interested in perceptual categorization about whether irrelevant and relevant features have been properly defined and controlled in particular experiments.

Second, there must be evidence that the infants can tell the different exemplars of the category apart. Few existing studies have coped with this issue in a satisfactory way. Some of the earliest studies that suggested infants were capable of displaying categorical knowledge in attentional experiments (McGurk, 1972; Cornell, 1974) did not address this issue at all. More recent studies (e.g.,

Fagan, 1976; Cohen & Strauss, 1979) showed that infants could discriminate the stimuli used in the categorization experiment, but they did not assess whether the infants could do so under the conditions of presentation used in the experiment itself. A recent study by Sherman (1980) directly addressed this issue. She used a subset of the face stimuli that Strauss (1979) had used, but employed a familiarization procedure that required the infant to demonstrate discrimination between category exemplars as they were presented during familiarization. Thus, Sherman's procedure guaranteed that the infants could discriminate all the category exemplars under the conditions used in her study. She still found evidence of categorization at 10 months of age, but the pattern of results regarding the infant's representation of the central tendency of the category was different from that reported by Strauss (1979). Although there were some other differences in the details of these two studies, Sherman's work at least raises the possibility that the kinds of categorization behavior one finds in infants may be strongly influenced by the extent to which the experimenter has guaranteed that the infants have discriminated the category exemplars within the experiment itself.

The criterion used in the Sherman study was quite stringent. In adult experiments, it is often the case that the subjects know that the stimuli are different from trial to trial, but cannot discriminate those they have seen from novel members of the same category (Posner & Keele, 1968, 1970). Knowing that the items are different is a more appropriate prerequisite for categorization in the sense I mean than remembering the specific instances. Testing for memory of specific instances is the most direct way of testing that infants can tell the items apart. However, requiring memory for specific instances may affect the way in which categorization occurs.

Let us now briefly examine the categorization literature for the 6- to 12-month period, within which most of the recent research has been done. The infant's ability to recognize categories of perceptual stimuli has been investigated in a wide variety of domains: shape independent of specific orientation (McGurk, 1972), gender of pictures of faces (Cohen & Strauss, 1979; Cornell, 1974; Fagan, 1976), same face independent of pose (Cohen & Strauss, 1979; Fagan, 1976), the form of objects independent of size, color, and orientation (Ruff, 1978), faces generated from a common pool of features versus faces having totally novel features (Sherman, 1980; Strauss, 1979), types of motion (Gibson, Owsley, & Johnston, 1978), toys representing letters, men, animals, foods, vehicles, and furniture (Revelle, 1982; Ross, 1980), and numerosity (Starkey & Cooper, 1980; Strauss & Curtis, 1981). Strauss (1979) investigated not just whether categorization occurs but also the nature of the *representation* of categories, focusing on the question of prototypes or the representation of the central tendency of a category. This experimental paradigm represents an important conceptual advance that is at the heart of the more general issue of the nature of categorization (Smith & Medin, 1981). All of these studies used the habituation logic.

At present the safest conclusion one can draw from all this work is that perceptual categorization emerges during the period extending from 6 to 12 months of age. There are many results which support this conclusion, including those that used the most stringent tests (Sherman, 1980). So far the question of whether categorization occurs earlier than 6 months of age remains unsettled. Studies conducted with younger infants have not examined whether the familiarization stimuli could be discriminated (Cornell, 1974; Gibson et al., 1978). It seems *probable* that some form of categorization skill is present prior to 6 months, but so far it has not been identified in appropriately controlled experiments.

What kinds of categories are recognized during the 6-12 month period? Most studies have examined categories from the real world, such as faces and various two- and three-dimensional objects. The evidence that real-world categories, such as furniture, animals, vehicles and foods, emerge toward the end of this period (Revelle, 1982; Ross, 1980) is important. These are the kinds of categories that will be labeled by the words the child acquires in its native language. Indeed, there have been several interesting recent experiments that have studied this link between perceptual classification and language development. Oviatt (1980) and Thomas, Campos, Shucard, Ramsey, and Shucard (1981) found that infants turned toward and looked longer at pictures of objects that are named, providing evidence of the emerging link between perceptual categories and the early stages of language acquisition.

Although the methods for studying perceptual classification are still relatively new, they promise to provide significant information about the development of categorization skills during the prelinguistic period. The ability to classify or categorize experiences is basic to intelligence. The fact that the recent literature on categorization in infants has focused on the second half of the first year is probably a temporary symptom of present research methods. Categorization skills may be very basic, and thus may be part of the infant's cognitive repertoire long before 6 months. What's clear during the 6- to 12-month period is that these skills are well-developed. Now that researchers have begun to ask questions about the nature of these skills and the knowledge they in turn construct in memory, we would expect rapid progress in our understanding of the ontogeny of the process of perceptual categorization.

CONCLUSIONS

A decade-and-a-half of extensive experimental investigation of the learning and memory abilities of infants has begun to clarify how these skills emerge at the beginning of life. This chapter has scarcely skimmed the surface. The interested reader can consult a number of review articles for the details that have only been hinted at here (Cohen, 1976; Cohen & Gelber, 1975; Fagan, 1975, in press; Fitzgerald & Brackbill, 1976; Kessen et al., 1970; Mandler, 1983, in press; Olson, 1976; Olson & Sherman, 1983, in press; Olson & Strauss, in press; Rovee-Collier & Gekoski, 1979; Rovee-Collier & Lipsitt, 1980; Ruff, in press; Sameroff, 1972; Sameroff & Cavanagh, 1979; Watson, 1980; Werner & Perlmutter, 1979). Though there is still much that needs to be learned about the infant's abilities, this research provides an important first step toward understanding the ontogeny of those basic information processing skills that are at the heart of all intelligent behavior.

REFERENCES

Brackbill, Y., Fitzgerald, H. E., & Lintz, L. M. A developmental study of classical conditioning. *Monographs of the Society for Research in Child Development*, 1967, *32* (8, Whole No. 116).

Brown, A. L., Bransford, J. D., Ferrara, R. A., & Campione, J. C. Learning, remembering, and understanding. In J. H. Flavell & E. M. Markman (Eds.), *Handbook of child psychology* (Vol. 3). *Cognitive development*. New York: Wiley, 1983.

Cohen, L. B. Habituation of infant visual attention. In T. J. Tighe & R. N. Leaton (Eds.), *Habituation: Perspectives from child development, animal behavior and neurophysiology*. Hillsdale, N.J.: Lawrence Erlbaum Associates, 1976.

Cohen, L. B., & Gelber, E. R. Infant visual memory. In L. B. Cohen & P. Salapatek (Eds.), *Infant perception: From sensation to cognition* (Vol. 1). New York: Academic Press, 1975.

Cohen, L. B., & Strauss, M. S. Concept acquisition in the human infant. *Child Development*, 1979, *50*, 419–24.

Cornell, E. H. Infants' discrimination of photographs of faces following redundant presentations. *Journal of Experimental Child Psychology*, 1974, *18*, 98–106.

Cornell, E. H. Infants' recognition memory, forgetting, and savings. *Journal of Experimental Child Psychology*, 1979, *28*, 359–74.

Fagan, J. F., III. Memory in the infant. *Journal of Experimental Child Psychology*, 1970, *9*, 217–26.

Fagan, J. F., III. Infant recognition memory: The effects of length of familiarization and type of discrimination task. *Child Development*, 1974, *45*, 351–56.

Fagan, J. F., III. Infant recognition memory as a present and future index of cognitive abilities. In N. R. Ellis (Ed.), *Aberrant development in infancy: Human and animal studies.* Hillsdale, N.J.: Lawrence Erlbaum Associates, 1975.

Fagan, J. F., III. Infants' recognition of invariant features of faces. *Child Development*, 1976, *47*, 627–38.

Fagan, J. F., III. Facilitation of infants' recognition memory. *Child Development*, 1978, *49*, 1066–75.

Fagan, J. F., III. Infant memory: History, current trends, relations to cognitive psychology. In M. Moscovitch (Ed.), *Infant memory*. New York: Plenum, in press.

Fagen, J. W. Interproblem learning in ten-month-old infants. *Child Development*, 1977, *48*, 786–96.

Fagen, J. W., & Rovee, C. K. Effects of quantitative shifts in a visual reinforcer on the instrumental response of infants. *Journal of Experimental Child Psychology*, 1976, *21*, 349–60.

Fantz, R. L. Visual experience in infants: Decreased attention to familiar patterns relative to novel ones. *Science*, 1964, *146*, 668–70.

Fitzgerald, H. E., & Brackbill, Y. Classical conditioning in infancy: Development and constraints. *Psychological Bulletin*, 1976, *83*, 353–76.

Gibson, E., Owsley, C., & Johnson, J. Perception of invariants by five-month-old infants: Differentiation of two types of motion. *Developmental Psychology*, 1978, *14*, 407–15.

Hinde, R. A., & Stevenson-Hinde, J. (Eds.). *Constraints on learning*. New York: Academic Press, 1973.

Horowitz, F., Paden, L., Bhana, K., & Self, P. An infant-control procedure for studying infant visual fixations. *Developmental Psychology*, 1972, *7*, 90.

Jeffrey, W. E., & Cohen, L. B. Habituation in the human infant. In H. W. Reese (Ed.), *Advances in child development and behavior* (Vol. 6). New York: Academic Press, 1971.

Kessen, W., Haith, M. M., & Salapatek, P. Human infancy: A bibliography and guide. In P. Mussen (Ed.), *Carmichael's manual of child psychology*. New York: Wiley, 1970.

Mandler, J. M. Representation. In J. H. Flavell & E. M. Markman (Eds.), *Handbook of child psychology* (Vol. 3): *Cognitive development*. New York: Wiley, 1983.

Mandler, J. M. Representation and retrieval in infancy. In M. Moscovitch (Ed.), *Infant memory*. New York: Plenum, in press.

Marquis, D. P. Can conditioned responses be established in the newborn infant? *Journal of Genetic Psychology*, 1931, *39*, 479–92.

McGurk, H. Infant discrimination of orientation. *Journal of Experimental Child Psychology*, 1972, *14*, 151–64.

Nelson, K. The transition from infant to child memory. In M. Moscovitch (Ed.), *Infant memory*. New York: Plenum, in press.

Nelson, T. O. Savings and forgetting from long-term memory. *Journal of Verbal Learning and Verbal Behavior*, 1971, *10*, 568–76.

Olson, G. M. An information-processing analysis of visual memory and habituation in infants. In T. J. Tighe & R. N. Leaton (Eds.), *Habituation: Perspectives from child development, animal behavior, and neurophysiology*. Hillsdale, N.J.: Lawrence Erlbaum Associates, 1976.

Olson, G. M. Infant recognition memory for briefly presented visual stimuli. *Infant Behavior and Development*, 1979, *2*, 123–34.

Olson, G. M. The recognition of specific persons. In M. E. Lamb & L. R. Sherrod (Eds.), *Infant social cognition: Empirical and theoretical considerations*. Hillsdale, N.J.: Lawrence Erlbaum Associates, 1981.

Olson, G. M., & Sherman, T. Attention, learning, and memory in infants. In M. Haith & J. Campos (Eds.), *Handbook of child psychology*, (Vol. 2): *Infancy and developmental psychobiology*. New York: Wiley, 1983.

Olson, G. M., & Sherman, T. Individual differences in infant visual attention and habituation. In L. P. Lipsitt (Ed.) *Advances in infancy* (Vol. 4). Norwood, N.J.: Ablex, in press.

Olson, G. M., & Strauss, M. S. The development of infant memory. In M. Moscovitch (Ed.), *Infant memory*. New York: Plenum, in press.

Olson, G. M., Zimmerman, B. L., & Sherman, T. Visual attention and risk status in premature infants. Manuscript in preparation.

Oviatt, S. L. The emerging ability to comprehend language: An experimental approach. *Child Development*, 1980, *51*, 97–106.

Papousek, H. A method of studying conditioned food reflexes in young children up to the age of 6 months. *Pavlov Journal of Higher Nervous Activities*, 1959, *9*, 136–40.

Papousek, H. Conditioned head rotation reflexes in infants in the first months of life. *Acta Pediatrica*, 1961, *50*, 565–76.

Papousek, H. Experimental studies of appetitional behavior in human newborns and infants. In H. W. Stevenson, E. H. Hess, & H. L. Rheingold (Eds.), *Early behavior*. New York: Wiley, 1967.

Posner, M. I., & Keele, S. W. On the genesis of abstract ideas. *Journal of Experimental Psychology*, 1968, *77*, 353–63.

Posner, M. I., & Keele, S. W. Retention of abstract ideas. *Journal of Experimental Psychology*, 1970, *83*, 304–8.

Rescorla, R. A. Pavlovian conditioning and its proper control procedures. *Psychological Review*, 1967, *74*, 71–80.

Rescorla, R. A. Informational variables in Pavlovian conditioning. In G. H. Bower (Ed.), *The psychology of learning and motivation* (Vol. 6). New York: Academic Press, 1972.

Rescorla, R. A., & Wagner, A. R. A theory of Pavlovian conditioning: Variations in the effectiveness of reinforcement and nonreinforcement. In A. H. Black & W. F. Prokasy (Eds.), *Classical conditioning II*. New York: Appleton-Century-Crofts, 1972.

Revelle, G. L. *Categorization abilities in preverbal infants*. Unpublished doctoral dissertation, University of Michigan, 1982.

Rheingold, H. L., Gewirtz, J. L., & Ross, H. W. Social conditioning of vocalization in the infant. *Journal of Comparative and Physiological Psychology*, 1959, *52*, 68–73.

Ross, G. S. Categorization in 1- to 2-year-olds. *Developmental Psychology*, 1980, *16*, 391–96.
Rovee, C. K., & Fagen, J. W. Extended conditioning and 24-hour retention in infants. *Journal of Experimental Child Psychology*, 1976, *21*, 1–11.
Rovee, C. K., & Rovee, D. T. Conjugate reinforcement of infant exploratory behavior. *Journal of Experimental Child Psychology*, 1969, *8*, 33–39.
Rovee-Collier, C. K., & Gekoski, M. J. The economics of infancy: A review of conjugate reinforcement. In H. W. Reese & L. P. Lipsitt (Eds.), *Advances in child development and behavior* (Vol. 13). New York: Academic Press, 1979.
Rovee-Collier, C. K., & Lipsitt, L. P. Learning, adaptation, and memory. In P. M. Stratton (Ed.), *Psychobiology of the human newborn*. New York: Wiley, 1980.
Rovee-Collier, C. K., Sullivan, M. W., Enright, M., Lucas, D., & Fagen, J. W. Reactivation of infant memory. *Science*, 1980, *208*, 1159–61.
Ruff, H. A. Infant recognition of the invariant form of objects. *Child Development*, 1978, *49*, 293–306.
Ruff, H. A. Infant memory from a Gibsonian point of view. In M. Moscovitch (Ed.), *Infant memory*. New York: Plenum, in press.
Sameroff, A. J. The components of sucking in the human newborn. *Journal of Experimental Child Psychology*, 1968, *6*, 607--23.
Sameroff, A. J. Learning and adaptation in infancy: A comparison of models. In H. W. Reese (Ed.), *Advances in child development and behavior* (Vol. 7). New York: Academic Press, 1972.
Sameroff, A. J., & Cavanagh, P. J. Learning in infancy: A developmental perspective. In J. D. Osofsky (Ed.), *Handbook of infant development*. New York: Wiley, 1979.
Seligman, M.E.P. On the generality of the laws of learning. *Psychological Review*, 1970, *77*, 406–18.
Sherman, T. L. *Categorization skills in infants*. Unpublished doctoral dissertation, University of Michigan, 1980.
Siqueland, E. R., & DeLucia, C. A. Visual reinforcement of nonnutritive sucking in human infants. *Science*, 1969, *165*, 1144–46.
Smith, E. E., & Medin, D. L. *Categories and concepts*. Cambridge, Mass.: Harvard University Press, 1981.
Sokolov, E. N. *Perception and the conditioned reflex*. New York: Macmillan, 1963.
Sophian, C. Habituation is not enough: Novelty preferences, search, and memory in infancy. *Merrill-Palmer Quarterly*, 1980, *26*, 239–57.
Spear, N. E., & Campbell, B. A. (Eds.). *Ontogeny of learning and memory*. Hillsdale, N.J.: Lawrence Erlbaum Associates, 1979.
Starkey, P., & Cooper, R. G. Numerosity perception in human infants. *Science*, 1980, *210*, 1033–35.
Strauss, M. S. Abstraction of prototypical information by adults and 10-month-old infants. *Journal of Experimental Psychology: Human Learning and Memory*. 1979, *5*, 618–32.
Strauss, M. S., & Curtis, L. E. Infant perception of numerosity. *Child Development*, 1981, *52*, 1146–52.

Sullivan, M. W., Rovee-Collier, C. K., & Tynes, D. M. A conditioning analysis of infant long-term memory. *Child Development,* 1979, *50,* 152–62.

Thomas, D. G., Campos, J. J., Shucard, D. W., Ramsay, D. S., & Shucard, J. Semantic comprehension in infancy: A signal detection analysis. *Child Development,* 1981, *52,* 798–803.

Thomas, H. Unfolding the baby's mind: The infant's selection of visual stimuli. *Psychological Review,* 1973, *80,* 468–88.

Tighe, T. J., & Leaton, R. N. (Eds.). *Habituation: Perspectives from child development, animal behavior, and neurophysiology.* Hillsdale, N.J.: Lawrence Erlbaum Associates, 1976.

Wagner, A. R., & Rescorla, R. A. Inhibition in Pavlovian conditioning: Application of a theory. In R. A. Boakes & M. S. Halliday (Eds.), *Inhibition and learning.* New York: Academic Press, 1972.

Watson, J. S. Memory in infancy. In J. Piaget, J. P. Bronkart, & P. Mounoud (Eds.), *Encyclopedie de la pleiade: La psychologie.* Paris: Gallimard, 1980.

Wenger, M. A. An investigation of conditioned responses in human infants. *University of Iowa Studies in Child Welfare,* 1936, *12* (1), 7–90.

Werner, J. S., & Perlmutter, M. Development of visual memory in infants. In H. W. Reese & L. P. Lipsitt (Eds.), *Advances in child development and behavior* (Vol. 14). New York: Academic Press, 1979.

Wickens, D. D., & Wickens, D. A study of conditioning in the neonate. *Journal of Experimental Psychology,* 1940, *26,* 94–102.

2

ACQUIRING EXPERTISE

Alan M. Lesgold
University of Pittsburgh

Many human activities require substantial training if they are to be performed with facility and accuracy. My concern in this chapter is with activities that are sufficiently complex to require thousands of hours of practice—the ability to do the arithmetic required by a home budget, the ability to diagnose disease from chest x rays, the ability to predict what the Soviet government will do in the face of crisis, the ability to find efficient routes in a large city (as taxi drivers do), even the ability to read best-sellers well enough to make interesting cocktail party conversation. As can be seen from these examples, some forms of expertise are part of common roles, whereas others are to be found only in the role of the specialist. This chapter considers psychological issues that span both forms of expertise.

The folk view of expertise may be a good starting point. I suppose that the average person thinks that expertise requires a combination of practice, special knowledge, and innate ability. This chapter is concerned with practice and with the effects of existing knowledge on both performance and further learning, but does not consider genetic factors in expertise. The latter are probably important in some extreme performances, but research on instruction

This chapter benefited from comments by Dale Klopfer, Harriet Rubinson, James Voss, and Carol White. Its preparation was supported by a contract from the Office of Naval Research (Personnel and Training Programs, Psychological Sciences Division, NR 667–430) and by grants from the National Institute of Education to the Learning Research and Development Center of the University of Pittsburgh. Neither agency has approved or endorsed the views presented herein.

seems more useful than research aimed at using selection to avoid the need for instruction. Issues of strategy are not covered either. Although strategy is an important aspect of expert performance, it is outside my own expertise.

Consider two specific examples of expertise: the long-distance runner and the chess master. The athlete prepares for his or her performances largely by practicing. He runs every day, building his endurance, cutting his running times. But, his efforts are relatively nonspecific. Perhaps world-class runners give greater attention to the specific types of practice, but one can hardly compose a list of the 100 things a runner must learn in order to be successful. In contrast, the chess master seems to know just how to respond to each of thousands of moves made by his or her opponents. Such expertise is extremely knowledge specific. If he played the same kind of chess game every day, never exposing himself to new opposition, learning would proceed rather slowly. A chess master needs to know about the problems he will face in each of hundreds of situations. In the sections that follow, I will be concerned with both aspects of learning: knowledge that comes from a variety of experiences and knowledge that comes from repetition (practice). Then, I will examine the ability to build mental representations of problem situations, a central capability that involves both variation and repetition. I conclude with a few recommendations for the training of cognitive skills.

THE ROLE OF KNOWLEDGE IN EXPERTISE

Chess

Comparing experts to novices allows us to discover what changes take place as expertise is acquired. Many forms of expertise were studied by early psychologists. For example, Bryan and Harter (1897) observed railroad telegraphers at various points in their development of Morse code skills. However, it will be more convenient to begin our discussion with the recent studies of chess experts by de Groot (1966) and Chase and Simon (1973a, 1973b). This work extended the quantitative expert-novice paradigm by shifting emphasis to qualitative comparisons as well. Some of the results were rather surprising.

Prior to de Groot's work, it was generally thought that the expert chess player can think many moves ahead in a game, following up on the implications of every possible move, whereas the novice is tripped up by an inability to think far enough ahead, something that presumably comes with practice. However, de Groot found that neither experts nor novices think more than a few moves ahead; if anything, it was the intermediate level player who did more thinking ahead, following up on the consequences of bad moves as well as good ones. Nor were there any differences in the number of moves considered or in the heuristics used to consider the consequences of those moves. What the experts could do better was to temporarily remember board positions. Chess masters could remember any real game board after seeing it for 5 seconds, although they did no better than weaker players in remembering random arrangements of chess pieces on the board.

William Chase and Herbert Simon were inspired by de Groot's work to conduct an extensive series of studies on chess experts (Chase & Simon, 1973a, 1973b; Simon & Barenfeld, 1969; Simon & Gilmartin, 1973). The outgrowth of this work was a picture of the chess master as an individual who can recognize and make the optimal response to 10,000 to 100,000 meaningful board positions. As Newell (1973) has pointed out, this description suggests a theory of expertise—the expert can recognize each situation that he might encounter and that he has a specific response associated with each such situation. Such a theory of knowledge-specific expertise might seem to offer a rather dismal future for cognitive psychologists—we become mere cataloguers of the thousands of microskills that constitute expertise. What has kept us going is the belief that there are elements of common structure in the expert's memory for different situations and in the mappings of those situations onto appropriate responses. Nonetheless, research on the game of chess suggests that a wide variety of specific knowledge must be learned in order to become an expert.

Reading

The general skill of reading also depends on specific knowledge. Voss and his research group have studied the role of domain-relevant knowledge in reading and other literate performances (Chiesi, Spilich, & Voss, 1979; Spilich, Vesonder, Chiesi, & Voss, 1979; Voss, Vesonder, & Spilich, 1980). In some respects, the picture they have built is similar to that of the chess master. People who know a lot about a particular subject are better recalling stories relevant to their expert knowledge than are those who are less expert. Voss and his co-workers also found that high-knowledge people use their expertise in at least three ways: to anticipate what a text will say, as an anchor for information that must temporarily be held in memory, and as a framework that permits recall of more elaborate story details. Again, as was found in the case of chess, these effects are knowledge-specific; the exceptional ability is found only when the text deals with a person's areas of expertise.

The evidence for these assertions comes from experiments in which Voss and his colleagues (1980) tested people for their knowledge of the intricacies of baseball. They identified a high-knowledge group of subjects, who knew quite a bit about the strategies of the game, and a low-knowledge group, who knew the basic rules of the game, a bit about how the professional teams were currently doing, but little about the game's finer points. Each group of subjects was asked to produce a narrative account of a half inning of a fictitious baseball game. Both groups produced about the same amount of text, with the same types of basic plots. However, the high-knowledge group devoted more text to elaboration of specific game activities, while the low-knowledge group produced more statements about irrelevant, nongame activities. Two weeks later, the subjects were asked to recall what they had written. The low-knowledge subjects were able to correctly recall less about what happened to each batter, were able to reproduce less of the basic action sequence, and remembered less game-relevant detail than the high-knowledge group.

Other work in Voss's laboratory deals more specifically with reading. For example, Spilich et al. (1979) attempted to apply a quantitative model of the short-term memory dynamics of reading to the task of specifying how the abilities of high-knowledge people differ from those of people with less knowledge. Using a variant of the Kintsch and van Dijk (1978) model of text comprehension, they showed that the short-term memory dynamics for the main points of a passage differed from those for details and that high-knowledge individuals could hold more main-point information in mind while reading a text relevant to their expertise.

Another study showed a more anticipatory, or top-down, capability in the baseball experts. Chiesi et al. (1979) asked subjects to write down all of the possible outcomes they could think of for a specific baseball situation. They found that high-knowledge individuals knew more possible outcomes and could better specify which ones were likely to occur. They were, at any point in reading a passage, more likely to be expecting what would come next in the text.

This series of studies leads to the following basic account of the effects of knowledge on expertise. Experts can use their knowledge to keep track of the information they are being given when they read. Their effective short-term memory is greater, especially for main-plot information. Their knowledge of the kinds of events that can occur in their domains of expertise allows them to remember complicated events more easily. Their ability to anticipate what is likely to happen decreases the effort they must invest. While we know quite a bit about expert knowledge and its role in reading facility, we do not yet understand much about how one learns or what one learns to become facile.

Knowledge and Problem Solving

Knowledge is also a component of problem solving expertise. For example, Voss, Tyler, and Yengo (in press) asked political scientists who were specialists in the Soviet political system to solve the following problem (and others like it) while thinking out loud:

> Assume you are the head of the Soviet Ministry of Agriculture, and assume crop productivity has been low over the past several years. You now have the responsibility to increase crop production. How would you go about doing this?

To control for the contributions of nonspecific political science reasoning, as well as for general scientific reasoning, Voss and his colleagues also included subjects who were political scientists from other specialties, scientists in a totally different field (chemistry), and undergraduate political science majors, who presumably knew many relevant facts but had not yet developed complete expertise.

In their analysis, Tyler and Yengo first considered the effort invested in building an initial representation of the problem situation. The statements of their subjects can be represented by a graph in which modes are assertions and links are causal and other relationships. Such graphs allow quantified characterizations of a thinking-out-loud protocol. For the problem stated above, for example, the initial representation would include the current agriculture scene in the Soviet Union, relevant political constraints, peculiar aspects of Soviet agricultural activity, and similar data, while the nonspecialist political scientists devoted more of their thinking aloud (16 percent of the nodes in their protocol graphs) to this initial representation information than did the chemists (1 percent) or the students (0 percent), the Soviet specialists devoted the most effort of all (24 percent) to initial representation of the problem. This suggests that specific knowledge is an important factor in the creation of such representations and that little expertise rests on general strategies (otherwise, the chemists would have appeared to be more expert).

Soviet-area experts tended to offer a small number of solutions that were stated in rather abstract form, developed in some depth, and backed by detailed support. (By *depth,* Voss and his co-workers meant the size of the chain of causes that backed up an assertion.) Expert arguments had three times as deep a structure of detailed support than did those of novices. Also, much more of the expert argument was an analysis of an abstracted representation of the problem rather than of the specifics of the problem statement.

This two-stage approach (representation, then solution) usually pays off by decreasing the amount of thinking needed to produce a good solution. An abstracted problem representation will adequately capture the constraints that are relevant to a solution, whereas working directly from the specific problem statements leaves the resolution of these constraints as a separate task to be done after a potential unwieldy set of possible solutions is generated. One analysis will serve to illustrate this important aspect of expertise. At the beginning of his discussion of the agriculture problem, this expert pointed out that the problem involved several ministries, plus the entire agriculture system, from its raw materials (fertilizer, seed), labor, and so on, to its ability to distribute the final product. By thinking this way, he was able to keep in mind from the outset that any changes requiring more fertilizer, for instance, might fail because substantial amounts of Soviet fertilizer are lost due to inadequate packaging. Thus, information about the ministry that controlled bag making was considered from the outset.

Voss, Greene, Post, and Penner (in press) have suggested some of the changes that take place in the course of acquiring expertise in a particular domain in which problems are wide ranging and solutions not easily verified, such as political science. They noticed that graduate students in this area showed three differences from undergraduates in their protocols: (1) They had some knowledge of subproblem interactions, that is, ways in which solving one subproblem might interfere with a solution that otherwise makes sense for another subproblem; (2) their descriptions of the problem situation were more abstract; and (3) their reasoning in support and evaluation of their plans was more extensive. These differences led Voss and his colleagues to conclude that the graduate students have more complete knowledge networks, containing more explicit causal knowledge that was organized more hierarchically.

Experts, they concluded, presented even more knowledge development, as well as refined discipline-specific and domain-specific strategies for using such knowledge. Some of the expert strategies were general across all of political science, whereas other strategies, such as extensive use of historical analysis, were more specific to the Soviet situation. Finally, Voss and his co-workers noted the importance of *flexibility* in the expert's use of knowledge, suggesting that this is the result of experience with a wide variety of problems. In certain other domains, such as engineering or physics, where problem solutions are more clearly defined, the amount of experience with problems of a single type might be more important; in political science, experience with problem variety seemed especially crucial.

Vocabulary

The work in Voss's laboratory has concentrated on the effects of knowing a lot about a specific subject on understanding discourses or solving problems involving that subject. It is also possible to consider the contribution of knowledge at a less specific level, namely, general vocabulary. Virtually every intelligence or verbal aptitude test includes a vocabulary component because vocabulary is so predictive of verbal competence. Beck, Perfetti, and McKeown (in press) and Curtis and Glaser (1983) have been attempting to discover why extensive and readily accessible word knowledge is important in the overall acquisition of reading skill and in other areas of verbal competence. Curtis and Glaser undertook the task of determining the specific vocabulary capabilities that distinguish the highly verbal person from the less skilled. Their basic findings are that the highly verbal person not only knows the definitions of more words, but also has more knowledge that relates to each known word. Thinking of human knowledge as a network of conceptual relationships, we can describe their results as showing that the highly verbal person has more words tied into his or her network and also has more links, on the average, from any given word's encoding to other concepts. Much of our power to understand complex or ambiguous text rests in word-specific knowledge (Small, 1980).

Classroom research by Beck et al. (in press) strongly suggests that reading ability can be improved by a vocabulary training program that emphasizes the speed of access for word knowledge as well as the richness of that knowledge. Fourth-grade children were taught approximately 100 words over a 5-month period. Following this instruction, the children performed tasks designed to require semantic processes ranging from single word semantic decisions to simple sentence verification and memory for connected text. On all these tasks, instructed subjects performed at a significantly higher level than control subjects matched on measures of vocabulary and comprehension prior to instruction. Furthermore, words for which more instruction was provided were processed more quickly by the subjects than words for which they had received less special intervention. Instructed subjects learned the word meanings taught by the program and used instructed words more efficiently in tasks involving comprehension. Indeed, they even improved faster on standardized reading comprehension tests than their matched control classmates.

This work leaves unresolved the relative importance of breadth of vocabulary knowledge and level of efficiency or facility that is needed. One possibility consistent with these results is that knowing all sorts of things about the words one is likely to encounter is the key to successful reading. On the other hand, the critical factor may be the extent to which the words one does know have been practiced sufficiently to produce recognition procedures that can be executed without substantial conscious planning. Quite probably, both of these effects are involved in reading.

Physics

Quite a bit of the work on differences between novices and experts has been done in the domain of physics (Chi, Glaser, & Rees, in press; Larkin, McDermott, Simon, & Simon, 1980; McCloskey, Caramazza, & Green, 1980). A central finding, stated more or less explicitly in different studies, is that representing the problem is a central part of problem solving for experts. Novices tend to invoke equations quickly, selecting those that include both what is given and what is to be found. In contrast, experts concentrate first on understanding the problem. Experts are more likely to draw diagrams, for example, and more problem solving time elapses before they write down any equations. Once the representation is built, the solution methods also differ. Simon and Simon (1978) found that novices are more likely to use a "working backwards" strategy when solving physics problems, while experts are more likely to use a "working forward" strategy.

One might initially be tempted to say that the novice merely needs to be taught the strategy of working forward. This is not likely to be sufficient. The problem is that a working-forward strategy requires (a) a sufficient representation of the problem from which straightforward inferences can lead to solution and (b) enough knowledge of the course such inferences will take to permit focusing attention on those partial solutions that are most promising. A working-backwards strategy, in contrast, requires little goal-related knowledge. At each step along the way, there is a list of unknowns that, if discovered, would result in solution. Less specific knowledge is required to use such a strategy, but more partial results must be kept in short-term memory.

The importance of knowledge is also illustrated by repeated findings that even those individuals who have taken a course in physics, maintain very naïve views about the effects of forces on objects (McCloskey et al., 1980). Even after they have spent a term solving mechanics problems, students' beliefs about the world are inconsistent with Newton's laws. For example, they believe that a body in motion will change speed even when no force is applied to it. Their qualitative predictions about physical events are often incorrect despite the fact that they are able to solve equations and quantitative problems about force, mass, acceleration, velocity, and displacement.

If we look at how physics is taught, we get some sense of why this disparity occurs. Much of an introductory physics course consists of solving numerical problems about masses, movements, and energy. Thus, there is emphasis on fundamental relationships, as captured by equations. Sufficient richness and facility in mentally representing physical events takes longer to develop; it involves not only knowing the principles in declarative form but also developing procedures for mapping those principles onto concrete situations. And, there are no final exams in mental representation, while there are tests requiring the knowledge of formulas and the use of such formulas to solve problems.

Radiological Diagnosis

To further illustrate the importance of organized knowledge, I will now discuss some work that Paul Feltovich, Robert Glaser, Yen Wang, Harriet Rubinson, and I have been doing on radiological expertise. (Lesgold, Feltovich, Glaser, and Wang, 1981, describes the earlier aspects of these studies.) Part of this work deals with the way in which physicians acquire the organized bodies of knowledge (schemas) that constitute radiological anatomy, the science of relationships between variations in anatomical structure and patterns seen in x-ray plates. To provide a richer sense of the development of such expert knowledge, as well as the data with which one deals in this area, this work is presented in some detail. This is necessary in order to show how the meaning of individual perceptual features can depend upon a complex decision-making context.

When a radiology resident in a teaching hospital learns a complex diagnostic schema for a disease, he or she is initially in a very precarious position. He knows about more possibilities for misdiagnosis than he can deal with. He must either ignore certain less likely possibilities or risk getting too confused to proceed to a final decision. This dilemma is illustrated by data from subjects who were asked to diagnose a film showing a collapsed lung lobe (atelectasis). The most obvious cue for collapsed lung tissue is the presence of a localized increase in tissue density (a white region on the film, as shown in Figures 2–1 and 2–2). Certain properties of the area of changed density (e.g., "triangular," "sharp borders") make it more likely to reflect atelectasis. But even a density with those special features is insufficient for a certain diagnosis, since other diseases could produce the same sign. Listed below are seven general indicators for atelectasis, including both the density indicator and indirect

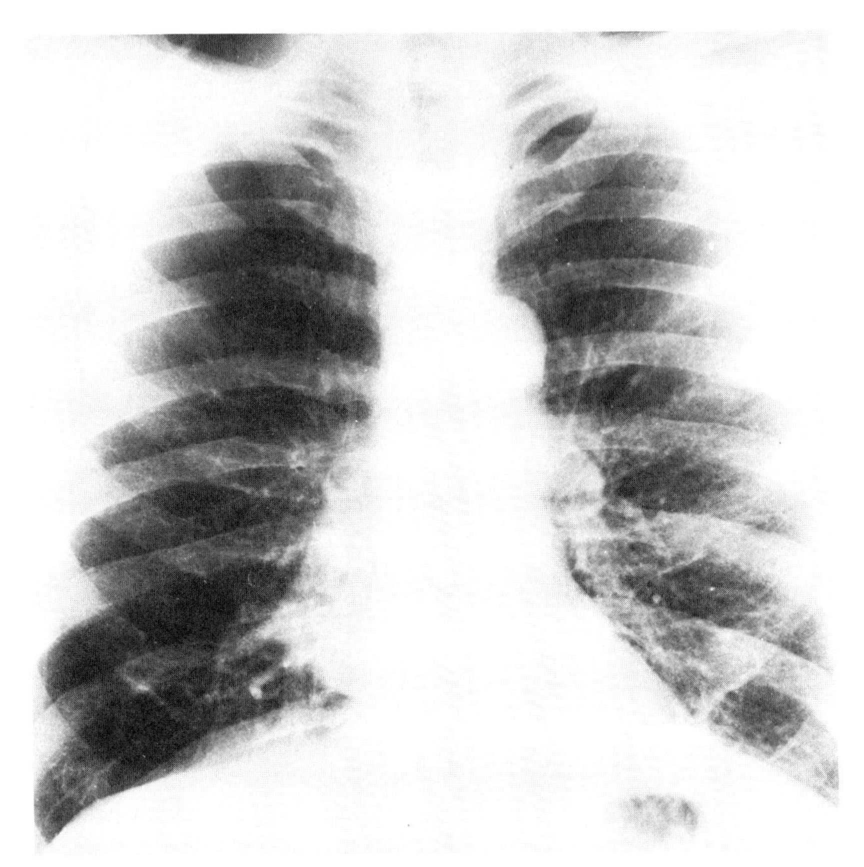

FIGURE 2–1 Frontal x-ray film of the chest of a patient with a collapsed right middle lung lobe. Patient faces forward (his right is on your left).

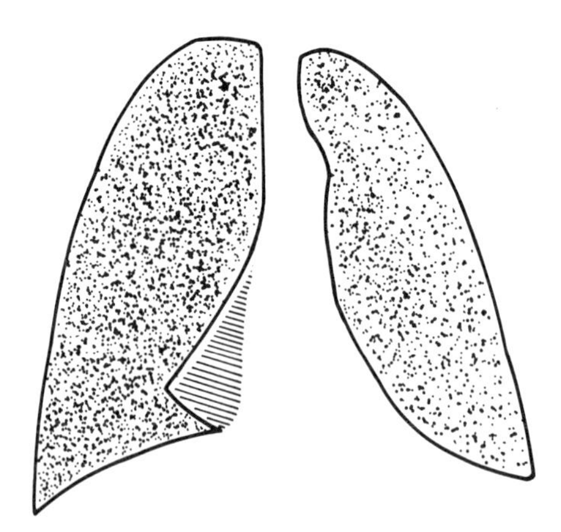

FIGURE 2–2 Illustration of the location of the collapsed lung tissue in Figure 2–1.

signs of the changes that occur throughout the chest when the space taken up by a previously inflated lung tissue becomes unoccupied.

1 *Increase in tissue density*: the collapsed lung tissue blocks more of the x-ray beam than air-filled tissue.

2 *Mediastinal shift*: the anatomy contained between the lungs is pushed to one side or the other.

3 *Displaced fissure*: the boundaries between lung lobes are not in their normal locations.

4 *Elevation of the diaphragm*: the diaphragm is pressed higher into the chest than is usual.

5 *Narrowing of the rib cage*: lung deflation means less support for the ribs.

6 *Compensatory hyperinflation*: the noncollapsed lung balloons because of decreased external pressure.

7 *Hilar displacement*: the major vascular structures feeding the lungs are not in their normal places.

We assume that the atelectasis schema is triggered by the presence of a subset of the seven features and further, that all seven are conditional criteria supporting the diagnosis over some alternative one. However, the indirect features vary with the location, severity, and recency of the collapse. A radiologist must develop a well-tuned understanding of dynamic changes that occur when the lung loses volume and be able to use that understanding in constructing the representation of a chest from an x ray. The presence of one feature may increase the importance of another as a criterion, while decreasing the likelihood of a third sign. Verifying atelectasis thus requires a mental representation of the patient that takes into account all these complexities.

The predicament of the novice can be illustrated with the following simplified account of a series of simulations that we conducted. In these studies, there were rules that represented the triggering conditions for schemata. For example, a general rule for atelectasis states that

RULE 1

IF you have seen local increase in density,

THEN assume a diagnosis of atelectasis

IF ANY OF THE FOLLOWING has been seen:

mediastinal shift
displaced fissure
elevated diaphragm
narrowed rib cage
compensatory hyperinflation
hilar displacement

Furthermore, it seems likely that once such a rule has triggered the atelectasis schema, one would expect to see the other features. The next rule provides for such conditional expectation.

RULE 2

IF the diagnosis is atelectasis,

THEN expect to see ALL of the following:
local increase in density
mediastinal shift
displaced fissure
elevated diaphragm
narrowed rib cage
compensatory hyperinflation
hilar displacement

Finally, it seems reasonable to raise a flag of caution whenever one cannot see something one expected, so we have a third rule:

RULE 3

IF you expect to see X but don't,

THEN declare a contradiction

This rule, though, sets the stage for the physician to talk himself out of the atelectasis diagnosis after first talking himself into it, at least in some cases. This occurs through a process of truth maintenance, in which an individual attempts to maintain the consistency of his or her beliefs as new assumptions are being "tried out" (see, e.g., de Kleer et al., 1977).

Consider the simulation in which there is local increase in density and hilar displacement but no visible displacement of the appropriate fissure. Experienced experts and radiology residents at several levels of training were asked to diagnose this case. Some residents reacted to the contradiction between the inference of atelectasis and the failure to see the displaced fissure by dismissing the atelectasis hypothesis. One of our subjects, a second-year resident, said this very directly:

> I am also indicating, drawing a line, over what I think is the minor fissure because the other differential to be considered is right middle lobe collapse, and there's no depression of the minor fissure or loss of volume in the right lung lobe to support right middle lobe collapse. I'm also showing that the right hemidiaphragm is in proper position and not elevated as you would see in right middle lobe collapse.

This subject needed each of several signs to be present to be sure of his diagnosis. He missed some features that were present but more subtle and attenuated than usual.

There is some complexity to what a successful subject should have done to arrive at a diagnosis on the basis of the film in question. An expert would have known that when the specific kind of atelectasis shown in Figure 2–1 occurs, the fissure is hard to see in a frontal view; his recognition capability would be tuned to expect the fissure to be hidden. We can specify this condition by changing Rule 2, which sets our expectations for atelectasis, to include the fact that we really only expect a fissure displacement to show in a lateral view.

Some of our more expert subjects had more elaborated knowledge. Specifically, they had learned special indications for different atelectasis forms. There is a feature in the film shown in Figure 2–1 that strongly signals the possibility of atelectasis, even in the absence of some of the usual signs. The sharply pointed, sail-shaped area of changed density located near the right heart border is the shadow of the deflated right middle lobe itself, which is sandwiched between the upper and lower lobes.[1] The location and unique characteristics of areas of density change are an important additional cue, which can be incorporated into a specialized schema for right middle lobe collapse.

In both the simulations and the experts' protocols, the diagnosis of atelectasis raised by the *general* atelectasis schema is *rejected* because of a contradiction of expectation with observation, as in our first simulation, but the diagnosis of right-middle-lobe *chronic* atelectasis made by a more specific schema-triggering rule is *retained*.

What can we learn from this type of data analysis and modeling? Basically, two points are apparent. First, the use of schemata is an important means by which knowledge can be organized. A *schema*, for our purposes, is a set of assumptions and rules for interpreting new information that is triggered when certain conditions are satisfied. A likely trigger is the presence of information that confirms a threshold number of the schema's assumptions, but more refined trigger mechanisms are probably learned with practice.

The second conclusion drawn from our studies of experienced experts and residents in training is that there have to be ways in which a schema can spawn an offspring that is a more specific and detailed version of the original. In this "clone-and-refine" process, the initial atelectasis schema is retained, but a specialized schema also develops as an expansion of the initial one. This specialized

[1]The right lung is divided into three connected lobes; the left lung has two.

schema is not merely a general reweighting of the diagnostic value of different perceptual features. Rather, the importance of some features is contingent on whether certain other features have been noticed.

Specialized, derivative schemata operate at the perceptual level in domains like radiology. In a domain like chess, they may operate at a slightly higher level. A rook in a particular space will not be misinterpreted as a pawn; the contingent meaning lies in how the locations of other pieces and the movement restrictions they have bias the meaning of the rook's location.

Much work remains to be done in the development and testing of a detailed model of the schema specialization process. Two principles might guide further theorizing. First, while many aspects of expertise are best understood when studied at the level of schemata, some aspects of learning may be easier to understand at a more detailed level. Second, new learning must, in some way, operate on a trace of the recent course of thinking. That is, the episodic memory trace of recent schema activity, recent actions (mental or physical), and the immediate consequences of those actions must be the foundation for new learning. I will next consider a number of learning mechanisms that are consistent with these principles.

Learning and Refining Cognitive Skills

John Anderson (1982) has recently developed a theory of skill acquisition that is a good starting point for understanding the acquisition of specific knowledge and the effects of practice. Taking the work of Fitts (1964) as a starting point, his theory divides the course of learning into three parts: the declarative stage, the knowledge-compilation stage, and the procedural stage. Anderson's theory allows a clearer understanding of the types of knowledge that are involved in skilled behavior and how each of those types is acquired.

Anderson proposes that initial performance in a novel situation involves the operation of general strategies that use *declarative knowledge* to guide performance. In our case, for example, we can imagine some very general strategies for diagnosis that a physician might acquire in medical school. The basic process might go something like this:

1. Make a list of all abnormalities or patient complaints you can notice.
2. Is there a disease that you know to be associated with all of these complaints? If there is exactly one, then it is the appropriate diagnosis, so stop. If there are more than one, then go on to Step 3. If no disease matches perfectly, go to Step 4.

3 Search your memory for information on data that might separate the disease candidates. Collect some of that data and start again at Step 1.

4 Make a list of the diseases that are consistent with the symptoms. Look for data that are needed to confirm one or more of the candidates on the list and then continue at Step 2. If you hit a dead end, then use other procedures to decide which of the potential candidates to pick. (Use of other procedures might depend upon the cost of treatment and the consequences of nontreatment.)

By reading textbooks, receiving advice from attending physicians, and monitoring one's success in patient management, a variety of bits of declarative knowledge (facts about how to perform rather than procedures for performance) can be acquired. However, these bits of knowledge must be accessed as needed by the general diagnosis procedure, a slow process subject to capacity limits. Much of the training time that is invested by radiologists, for instance, involves the conversion of slow declarative-knowledge interpretation into faster compiled procedures.

Anderson suggests that we think of the second stage, *knowledge compilation*, as being somewhat analogous to the operation of a compiler for a computer language. Languages such as BASIC and LISP permit programs to be specified in two forms—interpreted and compiled. Stated simply, compiled knowledge, like compiled computer programs, runs faster, but at the cost of greater difficulty of modification.

Actually, the situation is a bit more complex, according to Anderson. Newly acquired knowledge should not be trusted as much as that resulting from well-practiced procedures. Hence, it is useful for such new knowledge to have effect only as a result of conscious processing. Compiled procedures, according to Anderson, are relatively automatic, taking the form of *productions*, or condition-action pairs. When a production's conditions are satisfied, its corresponding action can be performed, within the constraints of an execution discipline that may limit how many productions can act at once.

The only conscious control over a production tends to lie in the fact that some of the conditions for productions are likely to be goal states that can be consciously set. Nonetheless, a production may well fire accidentally even if the goal states do not match perfectly (Norman, 1981). Consequently, there is probably adaptive significance to the Anderson formulation, in which new knowledge is slowly, but consciously, processed.

Anderson proposes two processes for knowledge compilation. The first is called *proceduralization*, in which "snapshots" are made of a successful, just-completed activity. The scenario proceeds as follows:

> 1 A compiled general strategy procedure finds a potentially useful piece of declarative knowledge and sets up a task of checking conditions of the knowledge and then performing the relevant actions.
>
> 2 The task is successful in achieving a conscious goal.
>
> 3 A *record* of the conditions at the time of the successful action is combined with a *record* of the action itself and is stored in memory as a production.

Anderson's second compilation process is known as *composition,* the process whereby two productions that are executed successfully and in immediate sequence can be combined into a single production. The conditions for the composed production are the same as those for the original first production plus those of the second production that are not created by the first. The composed action is the sequence of the two original actions. Composition, then, is essentially an abbreviation process, while proceduralization is an automation process.

In Anderson's third stage, the *procedural* stage, newly acquired productions are refined, or tuned. The snapshot process, based upon recording specific successful applications of declarative knowledge, is likely to result in productions that are too specific. Also, there are bound to be occasions when a piece of declarative knowledge is successful for accidental reasons. For example, if you had a production that diagnoses atelectasis every time you see a sail-shaped area of increased density, you would have a skill that is correct part of the time but not enough to be useful, since some other diseases you may not know about can mimic these conditions.

Tuning is accomplished by three mechanisms that look a lot like those of behavioral learning theory, except that they operate on bonds between mental events and mental actions rather than between physical events and behaviors. The first mechanism, *strengthening,* involves the execution discipline imposed on productions. Limits on human thinking capacity result in a limit on the number of productions with matched conditions that can be executed at once. The probability of a matched production being selected is a function of strength values assigned to each production. New productions start out weak and thus tend to be executed mainly when their conditions match the current mental state more closely than other productions. Each time they are followed by success, they become stronger and dominate alternatives with a poorer track record.

The other two methods of tuning are *generalization* and *discrimination*. Generalization applies to two productions whose conditions have identical structure but slightly different content. The result of generalization is a production that has the same structure but with a variable at the point of difference. Discrimination involves adding new conditions to productions whose execution was followed by failure.

PRACTICE

Anderson's work helps to integrate knowledge acquisition and practice, two central components of learning. This section considers the issue of practice, attending to classical studies of the effects of overlearning trials in simple learning paradigms and to the effects of cognitive practice which might be accounted for by such theories as Anderson's. We start by considering relevant work on the effects of practice in simple perceptual search tasks.

Automatic And Controlled Processes

Schneider and Shiffrin (1977; Shiffrin & Schneider, 1977) proposed a theory of information processing that dealt with practice in which the mappings of inputs onto necessary responses is consistent over the course of the practice trials. Such consistent practice, they asserted, leads to the development of automated processes, in which the input triggers a response sequence that operates independently of the subject's control. Such automated responses *require no attention* or conscious processing, but they can attract such resources in some cases. In contrast, controlled responses are not yet adequately practiced or are not consistently mapped onto possible inputs. These controlled processes *require attention*, use limited short-term capacity, and tend to be more serial in nature. One can think of this distinction between automated and controlled processing as being similar to Anderson's distinction between declarative and proceduralized knowledge.

Schneider and Shiffrin supported their theory with data from experiments in which subjects had to search a tachistoscopically presented display for target letters. In some conditions, the targets were from a set that were always targets. In other cases, the same symbol could be a target on one trial and a distractor on a later trial. Consistency of mapping led to better search performance. Both the number of items in the memory set and the number of items in the display were varied. Ordinarily, as the size of the memory set (Sternberg, 1975) or the display set (Atkinson, Holmgren, & Juola, 1969) is increased, a linear increase in response time is observed. However, after consistent practice, the functions became almost flat, suggesting that processing was not only rapid but also parallel rather than serial. That is, response times were consistent with a model in which each target letter had a production "watching for it." For inconsistent mappings, where items were targets on some trials and distractors on others, this did not happen, even after substantial practice. These results support Anderson's theory and suggest the importance of defining the meaningful units of a task in ways that preserve consistent mappings over the course of practice.

Training Effects On Negative Transfer

While a consistent relationship between mental events and the mental acts these events should trigger can help induce efficient learning, such consistency is not always possible. It is of great adaptive importance that a person be able to learn new responses to the same apparent conditions. Fortunately, there is some indication that the interference produced by inconsistencies can be overcome with sufficient practice. Muensterberg (1889, as cited in Siipola & Israel, 1933) claimed to have conducted relevant experiments on himself. Every so often, he would switch his watch from his right pocket to his left or back again. Each switch meant that habits of reaching for his watch on one side would have to be changed. He claimed that after maintaining this inconsistent practice regimen for long enough, the temporary interference effect of each switch attenuated and eventually disappeared.

Muensterberg's assertion was directly tested by Siipola and Israel (1933) in an experiment on telegraphy. After varying amounts of practice (up to an average of 308 trials for the most-practiced condition), the code was changed so that each symbol represented a different letter, clearly an interference condition. The new telegraphy scheme was then practiced to a high level of proficiency. The results were expressed in terms of percentage of positive or negative transfer, defined by

$$\frac{F_1 - F_2}{F_1}$$

where $F1$ is the amount of training time needed to reach a given performance criterion on the first task and $F2$ is the time needed to reach the same criterion on the second. The general pattern, in line with earlier results, was that as the level of learning of the first task increased, negative transfer increased up to a certain point, after which the transfer effects became more positive as the level of first-task training rose further. Substantial positive transfer was found if the first-task training lasted long enough. The relationship between transfer and amount of original training, then, was U-shaped. However, as the criterion for learning was increased, the negative transfer effect extended to greater amounts of initial training, suggesting that negative transfer is an increasing problem as the target level of ultimate skill is increased.

How can these findings be explained? Mandler (1954) examined the U-shaped functions reported by Siipola and Israel and by other workers and theorized that they arose because of a combination of response learning and association learning at both the response level and at a cognitive level. Several aspects of Morse code task performance should transfer positively when the codes are reassigned. First, the motor program to send each code will still be used. Second, each letter of the alphabet will have to be quickly recognized in the experimental context. Third, a cognitive representation of each code may have to be formed. The negative factors will involve the ties between letter and code, both direct and symbolic. Presumably, the positive effects of practice on the code sequences eventually outweigh the negative effects of incorrect pairings.

A high final-task criterion may require learning to the procedural level. Here, the interfering effects of proceduralized interference should play a role. In contrast, a low criterion for final task performance primarily will involve use of declarative knowledge about the letter-to-code mapping. Automation of the code-sending response will facilitate final performance even if competing declarative knowledge from the initial learning poses some problems. In the high criterion case, interference will be present at both the declarative and procedural levels, making it unlikely that automation of the code-sending response alone will overcome the negative factors.

Extra Practice Improves Speed Of Response

There are several other types of findings that help in clarifying the role of practice. One implication of multistage skill acquisition theories, such as that proposed by Anderson, is that one can expect to find nonlinearities in curves that map measures of performance onto amount of training. This result arises from the different processes that are involved at each stage. Judd and Glaser (1969) reported one such finding. They examined accuracy and latency in a paired-associate learning task and found that for any individual item, response latency was constant until the trial of last error. After that, additional trials produced a drop in response time. Presumably, the trial of last error is a reasonable indicator of a point at (or before) which proceduralized performance becomes dominant over performance driven by declarative knowledge.

Different performance measures, then, are sensitive to different stages of learning. Also, it seems likely that complex tasks involve multidirectional flows of control between procedural and declaratively driven components. Because of the cognitive processing limits faced by processes that use declarative knowledge interpretively, it should often be the case that some of the declarative learning cannot take place until other subprocesses have been proceduralized. Thus, not only will there be procedural capabilities that depend upon earlier declarative learning, but there will also be declarative learning goals that cannot be realized until some subprocesses have been compiled.

Complex Performances Require Component Proceduralization

Perfetti and Lesgold (1978) applied a variation of this notion to the problem of explaining why some children cannot read well. Building on theoretical accounts of the use of schemas in comprehension of discourse (LaBerge & Samuels, 1974; Rumelhart & Ortony, 1977; Schank & Abelson, 1977; and many others), they suggested the following theoretical assertion:

> The reading process is too complex to operate completely at the declarative processing level. It can only work well when every component that can be automated is practiced enough to be compiled into an automatic form.

There are two kinds of data that support this assertion. First, there are numerous studies (e.g., Frederiksen, 1978; Perfetti & Hogaboam, 1975) that show specific speed-of-processing differences between children who do or do not read at normal levels for their age. In longitudinal studies of reading acquisition (Lesgold & Curtis, 1981; Lesgold & Resnick, 1982), there are strong suggestions that overall reading achievement (measured by standardized comprehension tests) has accurate and rapid word recognition as a prerequisite. Along with other researchers, we have also noticed in our laboratory that both text structure manipulations and global reading ability differences seem to affect learning of the main points of a discourse less than the learning of details.

These results are consistent with a model of reading skill in which students have a good plan in mind for reading but can carry out their plan adequately only if many aspects of it are automated. Consider, for example, the following small passage:

> Howard went to the bank. He wanted to buy the house he had seen yesterday. The owner had said that the bank gave the best interest rates in town.

After reading the first sentence, the only main point is that Howard went to the bank. However, given adequately automated understanding of *bank* (i.e., an adequately automated bank schema), certain facts ought to be activated from long-term memory (e.g., that banks give mortgage loans). If the bank schema is less automated, the activation will not occur until the second or third sentence is read. If the recognition capability for the words of the first sentence are not automated, short-term memory will be swamped with the episodic trace of the word decoding process. This overloading will decrease the effectiveness of automated domain-relevant knowledge, as well as the likelihood that a house-buying schema could be activated enough to make the expectation of going to the bank to get a mortgage salient. Reading between the lines (in this case, not very far between the lines) depends heavily on the ability to automatically activate knowledge that is relevant to what is being read and to make use of that knowledge in elaborating text meaning. Issues that have not yet come up directly need to be anticipated. The success of this expectation process will depend on the extent to which components of the reading process are proceduralized (automated).

Because of capacity limitations, reverting to the declarative level of processing may hurt more than it helps. Characteristically, effective strategies call for putting off decisions as long as possible while making a mental note about information that imposes a constraint or that may eventually require a decision. In almost every human endeavor, trying to make decisions as soon as new constraints arise diverts attention from systematic planning. This leads to the hypothesis that while elaborated, active understanding activity is essential to adequate comprehension of a complex text, uncontrolled elaboration can be counterproductive.

Radiology

I return now to the diagnostic reading of x-ray films, a learning phenomenon that demonstrates the role of practice and proceduralization in acquisition of skill. In our continuing analyses of the statements made by radiologists while diagnosing x-ray pictures, my colleagues and I have found a nonlinear, U-shaped relationship among beginning, intermediate, and expert radiologists; beginning residents and experts were better than intermediates (Lesgold et al.,

1981). This does not happen in every case, but it is a recurrent result in our studies.[2]

What follows is a shortened description of our analyses of the radiologists' verbal protocol (the transcripts of their statements). For new residents, film analysis is tightly bound to physical features captured in the image on the x-ray (e.g., densities of various textures, sizes, and shapes). These features are perceived independent of context. Thus, for example, a rather well-defined, dense abnormality might be interpreted as a collapsed lung, without consideration of either the context in which it appears or the physiological condition of the patient. In fact, though, the actual shadow cast on the x-ray film by certain lung collapses is no different from the shadow cast by certain tumors. Only context can distinguish between the two.

Diagnosis that is insensitive to context, that only maps shapes on the film to perceptual prototypes, will often lead the diagnostician to error, since many alternative structural forms can produce the same feature in an x-ray. Correct diagnosis, when it occurs, will be highly dependent on a fortuitous relationship between true pathology and the novice's primary interpretations of chest features.

Trainees functioning at an intermediate level are in the process of compiling and tuning their ability to perceive complex anatomical details. They are also learning to take into account interactions or constraints imposed by film context and variations in film quality. Finally, they are developing their ability to construct a global model of the patient's medical condition and the conditions of film production. However, their performance suffers in those cases where their new, more complete, schemas assert partial control but are insufficiently automated to finish the job; that is, they no longer have the simplistic recognition abilities of the new trainee, but they have not yet automated the refinements they have acquired.

This period of short-term loss, however, is a necessary developmental phase that ends in the automated, refined, flexible schemata of the expert. Expert interpretations are, once again, relatively direct, but in the process of their construction, they come to incorporate appropriate contextual factors. For example, the expert might develop a set of "chest forms" (e.g., the emphysematous chest, the underinflated chest, the under- or over-exposed chest), along with distinct and specially tailored recognition, interpretation, and evaluation rules applicable to each of these forms.

2All of our films involve situations in which several alternative possibilities must be considered. As John Anderson pointed out in comments on an earlier draft, it is unlikely that the learning curve averaged over the mix of films on which radiologists are trained is nonmonotone.

REPRESENTATION CONSTRUCTION

While much of what seems important about expertise can be lumped under the categories knowledge and practice, there is one more aspect that deserves special mention. This is representational skill. Again, the case of radiology helps us make the point. Radiologists need to see a *patient* when they look at a film, not just a complex visual stimulus. All of their medical knowledge is organized around the human body; it would be counterproductive to reorganize it around blips on a film. Also, the meaning of any given film feature is determined in part by surrounding context. The same blob will appear to be a tumor in one set of surrounding features and just an engorged blood vessel in a different context. Again, the best way to organize this contextual knowledge is around principles of human physiology and learned variations (both benign and pathological).

Our analyses of expert and resident radiologists showed that subjects differed in the precision with which they "zeroed in on" the target feature within the film. In those analyses, we found that not all subjects thought primarily about a mental representation of the patient. Some thought aloud more in terms of film properties.

To examine this difference in precision more systematically, we looked at statements about locations of abnormalities from all of our subjects' discussions of one film. These statements were classified into four categories in order of increasing anatomic specificity:

1 *Spatial* statements referred to two-dimensional surface areas of the film itself and were, in a sense, nonanatomical.

2 *Gross* anatomical location statements referred to components of anatomy as a conglomerate, without indication of which specific components were involved (e.g., "hilar vasculature").

3 *Nominal* anatomical location statements mentioned anatomical components by name (e.g., the "pulmonary artery").

4 *Target* anatomical localization statements explicitly restricted the abnormality to an appropriate part of an anatomical structure.

Examples of these four kinds of location statements are given in Table 2–1.

Table 2–2 shows the number of subjects within each group who achieved the increasingly specific levels of anatomical localization within their analyses of the target abnormality. Spatial location statements were all that some of our subjects generated. For example, one subject spoke of a *prominent right hilum or mediastinum.*

TABLE 2-1 Examples of Different Levels of Localization (Film 9)

Localization level	Examples
Spatial	. . . Prominent right hilum or mediastinum
Anatomical: Gross	. . . hilar prominence . . . may be due to right hilar vasculature . . .
Anatomical: Nominal	. . . could be pulmonary arterial hypertension . . . enlarged pulmonary arteries from chronic obstructive pulmonary disease . . .
Anatomical: Target	. . . slight density above right hilum; I think it's the azygos vein . . . Pulmonary hila themselves not enlarged . . . fullness in the right mediastinum . . . a little above the hilum . . . not part of the aorta . . . definitely separate from the aorta . . .

None of these terms refers to specific, systemic anatomy. In contrast, 17 out of 19 subjects who correctly detected abnormality used anatomic location statements. However, these localizations ranged from gross anatomy to components of specific anatomy within the target area of the film. Table 2–2 shows that this anatomical specificity was tied closely to expertise—all experts mentioned specific components of anatomy within the target region, whereas hardly any first- or second-year residents did (1 out of 7).

Our studies suggest that experts rely on a mental representation of specific anatomic structures to separate abnormalities from other structures in the area. Third- and fourth-year residents, perhaps more knowledgeable of the structure of anatomy within the target region than new residents, were nonetheless largely unsuccessful in appropriately referring x-ray shadows to this anatomy. This failure could be due to imprecision in their knowledge of the anatomical structures themselves, to limitation in knowledge of how these structures vary normally and under perturbation, or, more directly, to deficiency in mapping this anatomy onto the mark-

TABLE 2-2 Most Detailed Level of Anatomical Localization for Each Subject (Film 9)

Level of* localization	Residents† 1st/2nd year	Residents 3rd/4th year	Experts
Spatial	1	1	0
Anatomical			
Gross	2	1	0
Nominal	3	1	0
Target	1	4	5

*See text for description of levels of anatomic localization.

†Excludes four 1st/2nd year residents who failed to even detect an abnormality.

ings in an x ray. First- and second-year residents were perhaps more limited to recognizing gross visual properties of the film and were equally likely to respond with interpretations of tumor or vascularity.

One of the most striking findings from these data was that many diagnostic errors resulted from a combination of misperception of anatomy and the inability to differentiate between two structures projected onto the same region of a film. The phenomenon is seen clearly in the atelectasis film discussed previously (Figures 2–1 and 2–2). Recall that the triangular (sail-shaped) area of increased density in the right lung is a critical feature. This feature is also pretty obvious, even to nonphysicians. However, some of our subjects simply did not see it. The reason is that they attributed part of the whitened area to the pulmonary artery, leaving a much smaller abnormality, which they then thought was a tumor. This can be seen in Figure 2–3a, which shows the entire sail-shaped region and the portion that some residents marked off as being artery.

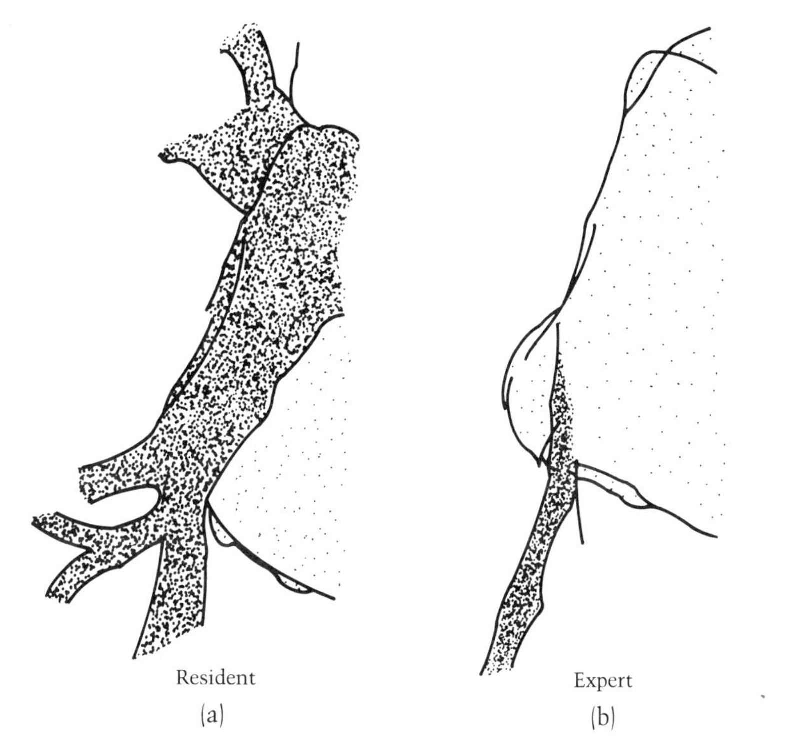

FIGURE 2–3 Anatomical sketches of structures seen by subjects in the triangular region of higher density shown in Figure 2–1. (a) Residents often "used up" the region by filling it with pulmonary artery. (b) Experts correctly drew only a small collateral of the pulmonary artery in the critical region.

In outlining critical regions on the film, half of our residents showed the pulmonary artery taking up part of the sail-shaped region. All then reported a smaller abnormality instead of the sail-shaped hallmark of middle lobe collapse. The only others to draw any pulmonary artery in the sail-shaped region were two experts who correctly drew a collateral branch of the artery that occupied 5 to 10 percent of the region, overlapping the sail abnormality, as shown in Figure 2–3b. (The contours in Figure 2–3 are actual lines drawn by subjects in an anatomy sketching task.)

We can summarize this result, which was obtained in at least one other film as well, by recasting it a bit. To our residents, reading an x-ray picture is like doing an embedded figures test. At any instant, each local feature in the film can only be assigned to a single anatomical structure. For our experts, though, there is a greater ability to recognize overlapping anatomical structures. Their mental representation of the patient can be decoupled from film features. We speculate that this automated capability is a part of the apparently greater ability of the expert to envision the patient's internal anatomy.

IMPLICATIONS FOR INSTRUCTION

Consider the stereotypic Socratic dialogue that goes on when a resident is questioned during grand rounds. He or she proposes a diagnosis, which turns out to be wrong. Then the senior attending physician asks a series of rhetorical questions that lead the student to a correct diagnosis. The student realizes that he knew the rules for making the right diagnosis but did not use them at the right time. He thinks that he was negligent or inattentive, but the kind of model proposed by Anderson (1982) suggests otherwise. Perhaps the knowledge of the resident student is not sufficiently proceduralized, something that happens only with practice. Or, it may not be able to take account of the ways in which x-ray features must be interpreted relative to all that is known about a patient. This ability to use context might be improved through appropriate variation in the cases the resident experiences.

A more serious research issue also arises when we think about the status of complex procedures that can only be executed when many of their components have been automated (proceduralized). We have assumed in this chapter that expert performance involves the neatly sequential execution of complex procedures. However, the mechanisms of automation that we have discussed apply to individual productions; that is, snapshots of small pieces of a complex procedure, each of which must become automated. Should those automated pieces execute in a fixed sequence a number of times, they can then be composed into longer sequences. Nonetheless, there is a likely state of affairs in the midst of learning when the components of a procedure are each automated but their sequence is not fully constrained.

In this state of affairs, thinking is not well described by sequential procedure descriptions. It is more like Selfridge's (1959), "pandemonium" model, in which many fragments of the target activity occur in parallel. Indeed, some researchers (e.g., McClelland & Rumelhart, 1982; Rumelhart & McClelland, 1981, 1982) have proposed models for mature performance which remain parallel and fragmented. Nonetheless, it seems likely that linear plans do drive problem solving in experts, at least to some extent. An open research question is: Where do these linear plans come from? One obvious source is the composition mechanism, which will tend to form recurrent, successful sequences of processing into unified procedures. A second source is declarative knowledge. Specifically, I suggest that a verbal plan, that is, a list of steps toward solution, can help in the composition process. Such a plan, taught only to the declarative level, can act by introducing a useful oscillation between self-conscious attempts to achieve successive subgoals of the plan and the pandemonium-like activity of automated fragments. The verbal plan components can act to entrain the parallel processing activity of automated fragments that are not quite reliable enough to assure an efficient processing sequence without such intervention.

If this is the case, then we need to consider whether the plans that we teach the student should be a caricature of the master's activities or whether there are other alternatives that are more effective in shaping efficient and reliable performance. Glaser (1982) has spoken of pedagogical theories—theories for a phenomenon that are used as temporary teaching tools and then discarded as more sophistication develops. My suggestion is a specific instance of this idea. Just as we teach physics students Newton's laws first and then show why they aren't quite adequate given the special theory of relativity, we might teach simple verbal rules to guide problem solving and then replace them as bigger components of the overall target performance are automated.

If one examines the training exercises used by ballet instructors, gymnastics coaches, and many other teachers, we see hints that teachers' practical wisdom includes this concept. Certain drills are repeated regularly even though they are not, themselves, target performances. However, they may have the effect of building the right procedural subsequences. Sometimes this training involves a separate activity, like a ballet exercise; sometimes it involves a mnemonic, as when a mother helps a child put on mittens by saying "thumb in the thumb place, fingers all together"; sometimes it involves verbal coaching, as when a teacher "talks" a student through the proof of a geometry theorem. In any case, devising a theory of the principles for guiding the development of systematic procedures from incompletely organized pandemonia of fragmentary productions is a major task for cognitive psychologists who wish to improve instruction aimed at high levels of skill.

REFERENCES

Anderson, J. R. Acquisition of cognitive skill. *Psychological Review*, 1982, *89*, 369–406.

Atkinson, R. C., Holmgren, J. E., & Juola, J. F. Processing time as a function of the number of elements in a visual display. *Perception and Psychophysics*, 1969, *6*, 321–26.

Beck, I. L., Perfetti, C. A., & McKeown, M. G. The effects of long-term vocabulary instruction on lexical access and reading comprehension. *Journal of Educational Psychology*, 1982, *74*, 506–521.

Bryan, W. L., & Harter, N. Studies in the physiology and psychology of the telegraphic language. *Psychological Review*, 1897, *4*, 27–53.

Chase, W. G., & Simon, H. A. The mind's eye in chess. In W. G. Chase (Ed.), *Visual information processing*. New York: Academic Press, 1973. (a)

Chase, W. G., & Simon, H. A. Perception in chess. *Cognitive Psychology*, 1973, *4*, 55–81. (b)

Chi, M. T. H., Glaser, R., & Rees, E. Expertise in problem solving. In R. Sternberg (Ed.), *Advances in the psychology of human intelligence*. Hillsdale, N.J.: Lawrence Erlbaum Associates, 1983.

Chiesi, H. L., Spilich, G. J., & Voss, J. F. Acquisition of domain-related information in relation to high and low domain knowledge. *Journal of Verbal Learning and Verbal Behavior*, 1979, *18*, 257–74.

Curtis, M. E., & Glaser, R. Reading theory and the assessment of reading achievement. *Journal of Educational Measurement*, 1983, 20, 133–147.

de Groot, A. Perception and memory versus thought: Some old ideas and recent findings. In B. Kleinmuntz (Ed.), *Problem solving*. New York: Wiley, 1966.

de Kleer, J., Doyle, J., Steele, G. L., Jr., & Sussman, G. J. *Explicit control of reasoning* (MIT AI Lab Memo 427). Cambridge, Mass.: Massachusetts Institute of Technology, 1977.

Fitts, P. M. Perceptual-motor skill learning. In A. W. Melton (Ed.), *Categories of human learning*. New York: Academic Press, 1964.

Frederiksen, J. R. Assessment of perceptual decoding and lexical skills and their relation to reading proficiency. In A. M. Lesgold, J. W. Pellegrino, S. D. Fokkema, & R. Glaser (Eds.), *Cognitive psychology and instruction*. New York: Plenum, 1978.

Glaser, R. *Education and thinking*. Thorndike Award Address to the annual meeting of the American Psychological Association, Washington, D.C., August, 1982.

Judd, W. A., & Glaser, R. Response latency as a function of training method, information level, acquisition, and overlearning. *Journal of Educational Psychology Monograph*, 1969, *60* (4, Pt. 2).

Kintsch, W., & van Dijk, T. A. Toward a model of text comprehension and production. *Psychological Review*, 1978, *85*, 363–94.

Laberge, P., & Samuels, S. J. Toward a theory of automatic information processing in reading. *Cognitive Psychology*, 1974, *6*, 293–323.

Larkin, J., McDermott, J., Simon, D. P., & Simon, H. A. Expert and novice performance in solving physics problems. *Science*, 1980, *208*, 1335–42.

Lesgold, A. M., & Curtis, M. E. Learning to read words efficiently. In A. M. Lesgold & C. A. Perfetti (Eds.), *Interactive processes in reading*. Hillsdale, N.J.: Lawrence Erlbaum Associates, 1981.

Lesgold, A. M., Feltovich, P. J., Glaser, R., & Wang, Y. *The acquisition of perceptual diagnostic skill in radiology* (Technical report no. PDS-1). Learning Research and Development Center, University of Pittsburgh, September, 1981.

Lesgold, A. M., & Resnick, L. B. How reading difficulties develop: Perspectives from a longitudinal study. In J. P. Das, R. F. Mulcahy, & A. E. Wall (Eds.), *Theory and research in reading disabilities*. New York: Plenum, 1982.

Mandler, G. Response factors in human learning. *Psychological Review*, 1954, *61*, 235–44.

McClelland, J. L., & Rumelhart, D. E. An interactive activation model of context effects in letter perception: Part 1. An account of basic findings. *Psychological Review*, 1981, *88*, 375–407.

McCloskey, M., Caramazza, A., & Green, B. Curvilinear motion in the absence of external forces: Naïve beliefs about the motion of objects. *Science*, 1980, *210*, 1139–41.

Newell, A. You can't play twenty questions with nature and win: Projective comments on the papers of this symposium. In W. G. Chase (Ed.), *Visual information processing*. New York: Academic Press, 1973.

Norman, D. A. Categorization of action slips. *Psychological Review*, 1981, *88*, 1–15.

Perfetti, C. A., & Hogaboam, T. Relationship between single word decoding and reading comprehension skill. *Journal of Educational Psychology*, 1975, *67*, 461–69.

Perfetti, C. A., & Lesgold, A. M. Discourse comprehension and sources of individual differences. In M. Just and P. Carpenter (Eds.), *Cognitive processes in comprehension*. Hillsdale, N.J.: Lawrence Erlbaum Associates, 1978.

Rumelhart, D. E., & McClelland, J. L. Interactive processing through spreading activation. In A. M. Lesgold & C. A. Perfetti (Eds.), *Interactive processes in reading*. Hillsdale, N.J.: Lawrence Erlbaum Associates, 1981.

Rumelhart, D. E., & McClelland, J. L. An interactive activation model of context effects in letter perception: Part 2. The contextual enhancement effect and some tests and extensions of the model. *Psychological Review*, 1982, *89*, 60–94.

Rumelhart, D. E., & Ortony, A. The representation of knowledge in memory. In R. C. Anderson, R. J. Spiro, and W. E. Montague (Eds.), *Schooling and the acquisition of knowledge*. Hillsdale, N.J.: Lawrence Erlbaum Associates, 1977.

Schank, R. C., & Abelson, R. P. *Scripts, plans, goals and understanding: An inquiry into human knowledge structures*. Hillsdale, N.J.: Lawrence Erlbaum Associates, 1977.

Schneider, W., & Shiffrin, R. M. Controlled and automatic human information processing: I. Detection, search, and attention. *Psychological Review*, 1977, *84*, 1–66.

Selfridge, O. G. Pandemonium: A paradigm for learning. In *The mechanisation of thought processes*. London: H. M. Stationery Office, 1959.

Shiffrin, R. M., & Schneider, W. Controlled and automatic human information processing: II. Perceptual learning, automatic attending, and a general theory. *Psychological Review*, 1977, *84*, 127–90.

Siipola, E. M., & Israel, H. E. Habit-interference as dependent upon stage of training. *American Journal of Psychology*, 1933, *45*, 205–27.

Simon, H. A., & Barenfeld, M. Information processing analysis of perceptual processes in problem solving. *Psychological Review*, 1969, *76*, 473–83.

Simon, H. A., & Gilmartin, K. A simulation of memory for chess positions. *Cognitive Psychology*, 1973, *5*, 29–46.

Simon, D. P., & Simon, H. A. Individual differences in solving physics problems. In R. Siegler (Ed.), *Children's thinking: What develops?* Hillsdale, N.J.: Lawrence Erlbaum Associates, 1978.

Small, S. *Word expert parsing: A theory of distributed word-based natural language understanding*. Technical Report TR-954 (NSG-7253). College Park, Md: Department of Computer Science, University of Maryland, September, 1980.

Spilich, G. J., Vesonder, G. T., Chiesi, H. L., & Voss, J. F. Text processing of domain-related information for individuals with high and low domain knowledge. *Journal of Verbal Learning and Verbal Behavior*, 1979, *18*, 275–90.

Sternberg, S. Memory Scanning: New findings and current controversies. *Quarterly Journal of Experimental Psychology*, 1975, *27*, 1–32.

Voss, J. F., Greene, T. R., Post, T. A., & Penner, B. C. Problem solving skill in the social sciences. In G. H. Bower (Ed.), *The psychology of learning and motivation* (Vol. 18). New York: Academic Press, 1984.

Voss, J. F., Tyler, S. W., & Yengo, L. A. Individual differences in the solving of social science problems. In R. F. Dillon & R. R. Schmeck (Eds.), *Individual differences in cognition*. New York: Academic Press, in press.

Voss, J. F., Vesonder, G. T., & Spilich, G. J. Generation and recall by high-knowledge and low-knowledge individuals. *Journal of Verbal Learning and Verbal Behavior*, 1980, *19*, 651–67.

3

SPREADING ACTIVATION

John R. Anderson
Carnegie-Mellon University

INTRODUCTION

Over the last 15 years, cognitive psychologists have been slowly developing the concept of spreading activation. There are three basic premises behind the spreading activation construct:

1 *The Representational Premise* Human knowledge can be represented as a network of nodes, where nodes correspond to concepts, and links to associations among these concepts.

2 *The State Premise* The nodes in this network can be in various states that correspond to their levels of activation. More active nodes are processed "better."

3 *The Process Premise* Activation can spread along these network paths by a mechanism whereby nodes can cause their neighboring nodes to become active.

As we will see these three premises hardly constitute a complete theory of the spreading activation process. There are, in fact, different theories that ascribe to these three premises. Even given a complete theory of spreading activation, it is not a trivial matter to

Preparation of this manuscript was supported by NSF grant 82–08189. I wish to thank Peter Pirolli for his comments on the manuscript.

determine how it will relate to cognitive phenomena. Much work in cognitive psychology has been devoted to developing theories of spreading activation and to testing their empirical consequences. This chapter will describe the experimental paradigms which have been used to test theories of spreading activation and discuss four different theories—Quillian (1969), Anderson (1976), McClelland & Rumelhart (1981), and Anderson (1983).

Experimental Paradigms

Premise 2 contains the assertion that more active information is processed better—where "better" usually means more rapidly as measured in a reaction-time paradigm. There have been two principal types of reaction-time paradigms—priming and fact retrieval. In one of the early examples of the *priming* paradigm, Meyer & Schvaneveldt (1971) showed that subjects could more rapidly judge that *butter* was a word if they had just judged that the associated *bread* was a word. In terms of spreading activation, this effect occurs because activation spread from *bread* to *butter* and made information about the word *butter* more active (see Figure 3–1).

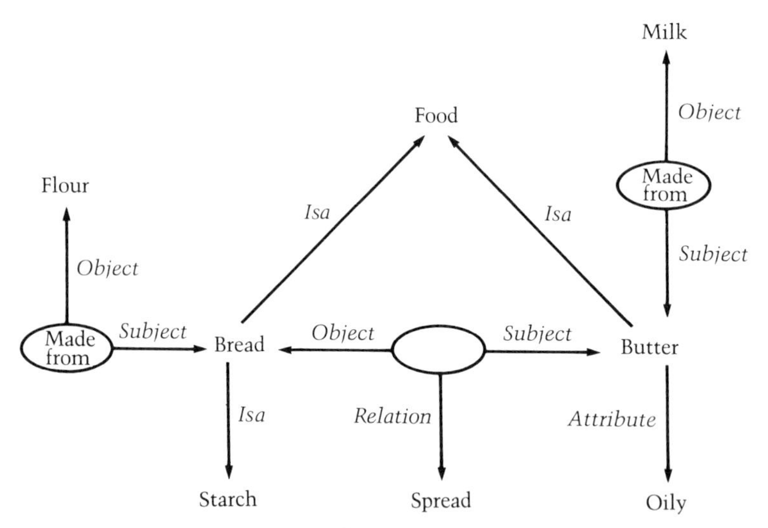

FIGURE 3–1 A representation of the hypothetical network structure for the Meyer and Schvaneveldt (1971) experiment. The network encodes some of the facts known about the words BREAD and BUTTER—both are foods, butter is spread on bread, bread is a starch, butter is oily, bread is made from flour, and butter is made from milk. The oval nodes stand for propositions about the concepts.

An early example of the second reaction-time paradigm—the *fact retrieval paradigm*—can be found in an experiment conducted by Collins and Quillian (1969). They observed that subjects could more rapidly judge statements like "A fish can swim" than those like "A salmon can swim." They argued that this finding arose because there was a direct connection between *fish* and *swim* but not between *salmon* and *swim*. Rather there was only an indirect association from *salmon* to *fish* to *swim* (see Figure 3–2). It took activation more time to spread over this longer, indirect path. Therefore, it took longer for the processing of the second sentence to benefit from activation.

It will be useful to identify the principal features of the priming paradigm and the fact-retrieval paradigm. In the priming paradigm, information from an earlier or concurrent task (e.g., judging

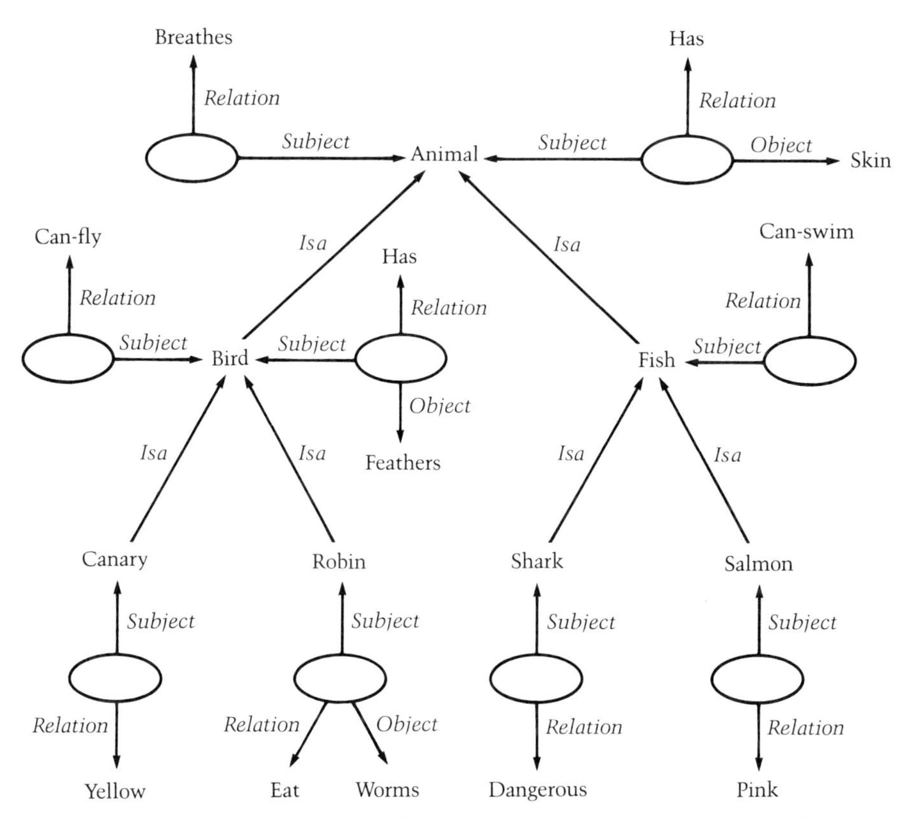

FIGURE 3–2 A representation of the hypothetical network structure for the Collins and Quillian (1969) experiment. This encodes the hierarchical structure of various animals and facts about animals at various levels in the hierarchy.

whether an item is a word) affects information in the current task (e.g., again judging whether another item is a word). Thus, the manipulated source of activation and the judged material are distinct. In the fact-retrieval paradigm, subjects are asked to recognize an association (fact) between a set of items. In this case the manipulated sources of activation (the items) are part of the judged material. It should be said that the interpretation of the results from these paradigms has evolved over time, and few people accept the original interpretations. Nonetheless, spreading activation of some form has remained a frequent construct in the recent as well as the original theoretical interpretations. An important question concerns how to formulate the construct of spreading activation so as to cover both of these paradigms.

Background to the Spreading Activation Concept

There are numerous reasons for believing in a spreading activation mechanism. For example, it seems to correspond well with our understandings of the mechanisms of neurophysiology. The neurons and their connections can be thought of as a network, and the rate of firing a neuron can be thought of as level of activation. It is believed (Hinton & Anderson, 1981) that neurons encode information by changes in their rate of firing. However, there are many ways to make a correspondence between neural constructs and the cognitive constructs of a spreading activation model, and there is no compelling basis for deciding among them. For instance, rather than a node-to-neuron correspondence, it may be more reasonable to have nodes correspond to sets of neurons (Hinton & Anderson, 1981). Nonetheless, the general set of neurophysiological "hunches" that we possess are probably an important consideration in much of the current acceptance of the spreading activation construct.

It is hard to pinpoint the intellectual origins of the idea of spreading activation. Some of it is anticipated in associationist models of thought that go back to Aristotle (see Anderson & Bower, 1973, for a discussion of the history of associative models). The process of tracing out chains of connections can be found in early experimental psychology programs, in Freud's psychodynamics, and in Pavlov's ideas. These models were largely serial, with one thought leading to just one other. On the other hand, the neural-net models of the 1940's and 1950's (e.g., Hebb, 1949) stressed parallel interactions among many elements.

The work of Quillian (1969) was important to the current resurgence of work on spreading activation. He is probably responsible for the use of the term *spreading activation*. His major contribution was to relate this construct to the growing understanding of symbolic computation and to suggest how the concept might be used to facilitate search of semantic networks. The work of Collins and Quillian (1969, 1972) popularized an application of this construct to retrieval of categorical facts (e.g., "A canary is a bird)" and led to a technique once called the *semantic memory paradigm*. This paradigm has been expanded to the current *fact-retrieval paradigm*. Many experiments in the fact-retrieval paradigm now use material that the subject learns in the experiment rather than pre-experimental facts.

The Fan Effect

There is one particular phenomenon in the fact-retrieval literature that has been particularly important to my understanding of spreading activation. This is the fan effect, which was discovered while I was a graduate student with Gordon Bower. The basic phenomenon is that subjects are slower to recognize a fact about a concept, the more other facts they have already learned about the concept. The first experiments were reported in Anderson and Bower (1973). We had subjects study facts such as "a lawyer is in the bank." Subjects studied one, two, or three facts about the person and one, two, or three facts about the location. They were trained on this material until they could recall it all to probes such as "where are the lawyers?" and "who is in the park?"

Subjects were then transferred to a fact recognition paradigm where they were presented with various person–location facts and had to recognize whether these facts had been studied. Foils were created by pairing studied people and locations in combinations that had not been studied. Both target sentences and foil sentences could be classified by the number of facts studied about the person and about the location. Targets and foils were created that realized all combinations possible by crossing one to three facts about the person with one to three facts about the location.

Table 3–1 presents the results of that experiment in terms of mean time to accept targets and reject foils. There is a systematic increase in the time to recognize a target or reject a foil as more facts are studied about the person and location. This is the fan effect, and it has been replicated in numerous experiments (e.g., Anderson, 1976; Hayes-Roth, 1977; King & Anderson, 1976; Lewis & Anderson, 1976; Thorndyke & Bower, 1974).

The original theoretical explanation that Gordon and I offered for the fan effect proved to be wrong. However, it and current explanations rested on a propositional network representation. Figure

TABLE 3-1 Mean Verification Times and Error Rates for Targets and Foils from Anderson (1974)

		Targets				Foils			
		Number of propositions per person							
		1	2	3	Mean	1	2	3	Mean
Number of propositions per locations	1	1.111 (.051)	1.174 (.042)	1.222 (.046)	1.169 (.046)	1.197 (.019)	1.221 (.042)	1.264 (.030)	1.227 (.030)
	2	1.167 (.065)	1.198 (.056)	1.222 (.060)	1.196 (.060)	1.250 (.014)	1.356 (.037)	1.291 (.044)	1.299 (.032)
	3	1.153 (.063)	1.233 (.044)	1.357 (.054)	1.248 (.054)	1.262 (.042)	1.471 (.079)	1.465 (.051)	1.399 (.057)
	Mean	1.144 (.059)	1.202 (.048)	1.267 (.054)	1.204 (.053)	1.236 (.025)	1.349 (.053)	1.340 (.042)	1.308 (.040)

3–3 illustrates a representation of some of the experimental material. Each oval node represents a proposition and it is connected by labelled network links to the concepts which are its arguments. Note that as the number of facts associated with a concept increases, the "fan" of network paths out of that concept increases.

Current explanations of the fan effect relate it to spreading activation. The basic idea is that when the subject is presented with a probe like "the lawyer is in the bank," the network nodes corresponding to the concepts, *lawyer, in,* and *bank* become active and activation spreads from these nodes out through the network. Vari-

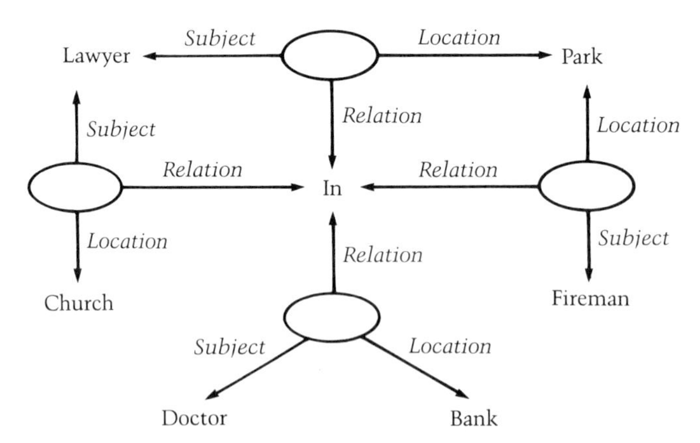

FIGURE 3–3 A representation of the hypothetical network structure for the Anderson and Bower (1973) experiment.

ous associated nodes are activated, including the proposition node that encodes the memory of having studied that the lawyer was in the park. The basic assumption is that rate of response will be a function of the level of activation of that particular proposition node. This level of activation will depend on the amount of activation it receives from the concept nodes. A concept node is assumed to be limited in terms of the amount of activation it can emit. Therefore, if it is associated to more propositions less activation will be spread to any particular proposition. Thus, propositions with high-fan concepts will be responded to more slowly.

One deficit of this explanation as stated is that it does not address the issue of how subjects reject foils or, more generally, how they decide they do not know something. Note that the fan manipulation has the same effect on foil rejection as it does on target acceptance. If this spreading activation analysis of target acceptance is correct, one would think it should extend somehow to foils. This is an issue that I will return to later in the chapter.

THE QUILLIAN-COLLINS-LOFTUS MODEL

One theory of spreading activation started with the work of Quillian (1969), evolved further in the work of Collins & Quillian (1969, 1972), and evolved still further in Collins & Loftus (1975). The spreading activation process was developed by Quillian to account for comprehension of linguistic material. He was also concerned with how to get computers to understand language and developed a computer implementation of his spreading activation process. He was interested in how the relevant information could be identified in long-term memory to enable the disambiguation of words and phrases. So, for instance, how do we know the right meaning of *bank* when we hear *river bank*, or how do we decide that a *seed box* is a box that contains *seed*, but a *glass box* is a box made from glass. Quillian proposed to solve these problems by spreading activation from the terms in the phrase and looking for paths by which activation intersected. Thus, given *seed box*, activation would intersect between *seed* and *box* by way of the facts *seeds are found in containers* and *boxes are containers*.

Another example for language comprehension is illustrated in Figure 3–4. If presented with *the collie ate the hamburger*, one might find an intersection among the concepts involving the facts *collies are dogs*, *dogs eat meat*, and *hamburger is meat*. The facts retrieved along the path of intersection could be used to understand

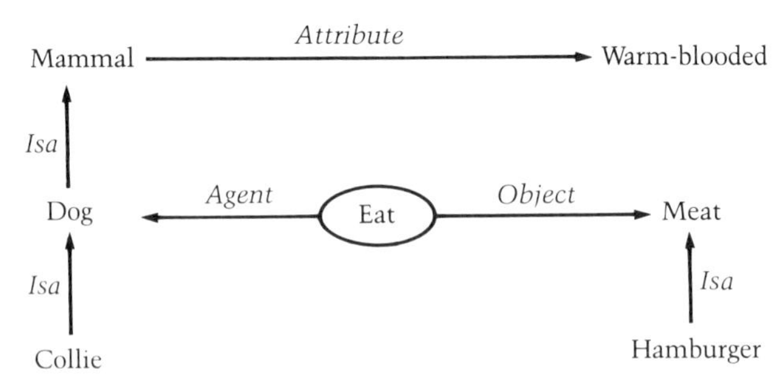

FIGURE 3–4 The network structure relevant to comprehension of *The collie ate the hamburger.* Also represented is information about *mammal,* a superset of *dog.*

the sentence presented. Spreading activation was Quillian's method for implementing this search for intersections. As search moved from a node, Quillian's computer system left activation tags at each node it touched. When activation tags from two sources were deposited at the same node, Quillian's system knew there was an intersection.

Quillian's spreading activation theory led to a natural experimental prediction that Collins and Quillian set out to test. Contrast *collies are warm blooded, dogs are warm blooded, mammals are warm blooded* in Figure 3–4. It should take subjects longest to verify *collies are warm blooded* in that figure because the path of intersection is longest. This is based on the belief that time for activation to spread should be a significant factor. Their initial experiments confirmed this prediction.

Difficulties with the Theory

The empirical picture rapidly became muddied. First, it was shown that there was an important effect of frequency of association (Conrad, 1972; Glass, Holyoak, & O'Dell, 1974). Subjects were faster to verify *dogs have hair* than *mammals have hair* even though one might argue that hair is more closely associated with mammals. A very good predictor of recognition times was production frequency—the frequency with which the subject will generate a particular property (*hair*) given a particular stimulus (*dog*).[1] Quillian's notion of spreading activation had been one of all-or-none tags asso-

[1]This particular fact has been given a number of theoretical interpretations including some that exclude the network representation. The most popular alternate interpretation is that the critical factor is how typical a feature like hair is of a concept like dog. (Rosch, 1972; Smith, Shoben, & Rips, 1974).

ciated with nodes in the network. It was beginning to look like activation was better conceived as a continuously varying property.

In response to the first difficulty concerning effects of frequency of association, Collins and Loftus proposed a continuous version of the spreading activation theory. They proposed that links in the network had strengths and that the amount of activation to go down a link was proportional to its strength. They continued to emphasize intersections of activation but proposed that an intersection would only be available when enough activation had accumulated so that the activation exceeded a threshold.

A second problem had to do with rejection of foils like *dogs can meow* versus *rocks can meow*. The network path between *dog* and *meow* is closer than the path between *rock* and *meow*. Therefore, on the obvious application of the Quillian theory it should take less time to retrieve adequate information to reject *dogs can meow* (cats and dogs are mutually exclusive, only cats meow). In fact, subjects took longer. This brings us once again to the issue of how one decides he does not know something (see the earlier discussion for foil rejection with respect to the fan effect). It appears that rejection cannot be based on the explicit retrieval of contradicting information.

The Quillian-Collins-Loftus theory is unique in stressing intersection discovery. This emphasis derives from its origins in natural language understanding, where important problems are to identify relevant knowledge and to disambiguate concepts. However, it seems unlikely that the full range of relevant phenomena attributed to spreading activation can be explained in terms of finding intersections. For instance, consider one version of the priming paradigm—subjects are faster to say a word after seeing an associatively related word (Warren, 1977). What possible role can the path of intersection between *bread* and *butter* have on saying *butter*? Now it may be that such priming phenomena are to be explained by different mechanisms than the fact-retrieval phenomena that Collins and Quillian addressed. However, it would clearly be more parsimonious if there were a single process underlying both findings. There are also now experiments showing that fact-retrieval judgments can be primed (Anderson, 1983, Fischler, Bryant, & Querns, submitted; McKoon & Ratcliff, 1979). For instance, I have shown that speed of recognizing a primed fact like *The lawyer is in the bank* is increased if this sentence is preceded by words associated with *lawyer* and *bank* (Anderson, 1982). A serious question is what activation controls if it does not control time for an intersection to reach threshold. Simply having a network in a state of activation leads to no behavior, let alone differences in response times. One must have some process that converts level of activation into behavior.

ACTE AND PRODUCTION SYSTEMS

The spreading activation concept was incorporated into the ACTE production system (Anderson, 1976) and has subsequently been incorporated into a large number of other production systems (e.g., Langley & Neches, 1981; Newell, 1980; Thibadeau, Just, & Carpenter, 1982). Production systems originated with the work of Newell (1972, 1973) and of Waterman (1970). Productions are condition-action pairs, where the condition specifies certain features that should be true of working memory, and the action specifies what to do in that case. Two possible productions are:

PRODUCTION 1

IF person 1 is the father of person 2
and person 2 is the father of person 3

THEN: person 1 is the grandfather of person 3.

PRODUCTION 2

IF I am asked who is in a location
and person 1 is in the location

THEN: say person 1.

The first production performs an inference and the second generates recall to a memory probe such as *Who is in the park?*

In the ACTE production system, there are two important distinctions. First, there is the distinction between *declarative memory* and *procedural memory*. Declarative memory contains facts, while procedural memory contains specifications of what to do. The two productions above are examples of the contents of procedural memory; while facts are the things that they would match in their conditions, like *Fred is the father of Bill* or *the doctor is in the bank*. Second, within declarative memory there is a distinction between a general *long-term memory*, which contains permanently stored knowledge, and a *working memory*, containing facts of which we are currently aware. Production conditions can only be matched to working memory.

An important factor controlling the rate of production execution is getting from long-term memory to working memory the information that will match the conditions of the production. Consider the second production above. For this production to match in a specific situation, the question *Who is in the park?* must be in working memory to match the first line of its condition. Second, we have to retrieve *The lawyer is in the park* from long-term memory and place it in working memory so that a match to the second line of the condition can be made.

In ACTE, the spreading activation process is conceived as controlling the rate that information is retrieved from long-term memory and placed in working memory. Working memory is thus equated with the active portion of long-term memory. When a probe like *Who is in the park?* is presented, a representation of the concepts (i.e., park) it contains is activated. Activation will then spread from such concepts to associated information in long-term memory. Suppose the subject had *The lawyer is in the park* encoded in a propositional structure in memory. Activation would spread from *park* to this propositional structure. When the propositional structure encoding the fact became active, it would enter working memory and a production like P2 would have its condition matched. Then P2 would fire and generate an answer to the question. Thus, the time for the production to fire would be a function of the time for activation to spread.

All links from a node in ACTE have a particular strength associated with them which reflects the strength of that link relative to the strength of other links leaving that node.[2] The time for activation to spread down a path from a node is a function of the strength of that path. Thus, ACTE could easily handle the data about frequency of association noted with respect to the Quillian theory. It could also easily handle the fan effect—the greater the number of paths emanating from a node the less the relative strength of any one path.

Also, because it did not require intersection from multiple sources, ACTE could handle the priming data that had been difficult for the Quillian-Collins-Loftus theory. For instance, consider the associative priming of the reading of a word. Word generation might be handled by a production of the form

IF a word is presented to be said
and CODE is the articulatory code for the word
THEN: generate CODE.

Presenting *dog* before *cat* might activate the articulatory code for *cat* and so deposit that code in working memory. Thus, when *cat* was presented the production could apply right away.

[2] To be precise if s is the strength of one link attached to a node, and S is the sum of the strength of all links, then s/S is the relative strength of that link.

Difficulties with ACTE

The ACTE theory was not without its own difficulties. One problem stemmed from the fact that, while network paths had continuously varying strengths, activation was required to be an all-or-none concept just as in the Quillian theory. One consequence (discussed in Anderson, Kline & Lewis, 1977) was that ACT could not perform disambiguation that Quillian's theory could. Thus, presented with *river bank*, the Quillian theory could use the intersection between *river* and *bank* to identify the correct sense of *bank*. In ACTE, presentation of *river* and *bank* would activate both the correct sense, as well as the monetary institution sense of *bank*, and would provide no basis for choosing. This ambiguity could be remedied if we made two assumptions. First, that activation would have to be a continuously varying quantity and activation arriving from multiple nodes would be allowed to sum. Second, if more than one structure could match a production, then the most active would be selected. Then the sum of activation from *river* and *bank* would favor selection of the correct sense.

A second problem arose from a more fundamental flaw in the ACTE conception of spreading activation. This had to do with the fact that the rate-limiting factor was retrieval of information into working memory (or the active state). Once in working memory, activation had no effect on the rate at which the production was matched or executed. However, consider an experiment by Anderson (1976). First, I had subjects learn facts like:

1 People who hated Nixon were smart.

Later they were asked to use this knowledge in one of two reaction-time tests—either to verify whether they had studied sentences like:

2 People who hated Nixon were smart.

or to verify the correctness of inferences like:

3 Fred hates Nixon.
Therefore, Fred is smart.

The first kind of judgment we can call a *recognition judgment*, the second an *inference judgment*.

The fan of these facts was also manipulated. In one condition subjects learned one fact (like fact 1) about the person (e.g., Nixon), verb (e.g., kick), and adjective (e.g., tall). This defined a unique condition. In the fan condition subjects learned two facts about each concept. Table 3–2 presents the data classified according to the crossing of these two factors—type of judgment and fan.

TABLE 3-2 Mean Verification Times from Anderson (1976)

Type of judgment	Type of material		
	Unique	Fan	Fan effect
Recognition	1791 msec	2129 msec	338 msec
Inference	2077 msec	2543 msec	466 msec

Once again subjects are slower in the fan condition. They are also slower to make the inference judgments. This is not surprising because the inference judgments involve a more complex computation. The interesting result from the point of view of ACTE, however, is that the fan effect is larger for the inference judgments. This is surprising because subjects have to retrieve the same information into memory for both judgments. Fan controls relative strengths of paths that in turn control the rate at which this information is retrieved. It is only after the information is in working memory that the complexity of computation should have an effect. But after it is in working memory, there should be no effect of activation. Thus, it appears that ACTE is wrong in the clean separation it made between retrieval of information and the processing of the information. This interaction between complexity and activation has been found numerous times (Anderson 1976, 1983).

McCLELLAND AND RUMELHART THEORY

The activation-based model of McClelland and Rumelhart (1981; McClelland & Rumelhart, 1982) is much more like current understandings of neural processing. In addition, their theory does not distinguish between the retrieval of information and the processing of the information. Unfortunately, its application has been largely confined to pattern-matching tasks, like letter perception, and it is unclear exactly how it would extend to the priming and fact-retrieval studies that are the focus of this chapter. Still, it introduces some very important concepts, so its review is worthwhile. In particular, the formulation of McClelland and Rumelhart is an example of a precise development of how activation arises, decays, and sums in a continuous manner over time, something that prior theories of spreading activation were unable to do.

Mathematical Formulation

Each node in the networks in this activation-based model is conceived as receiving input from associated nodes. This input can be positive or negative (inhibitory), and its absolute magnitude will depend on the strength of connection. This is summarized by the following equation:

$$n_i(t) = \sum_j a_{ij} a_j(t) - \sum_k v_{ik} a_k(t) \tag{1}$$

where $n_i(t)$ is the net activation input to node i at time t, the first summation is over all positively associated nodes, the second summation is over negatively associated nodes, a_{ij} is the strength of positive connections, v_{ik} is the strength of negative connections, and $a_j(t)$ and $a_k(t)$ are activations of nodes j and k at time t. Thus, there is simply a linearly weighted combination of all input at time t.

Each node is conceived as having a maximum M and a minimum m level of activation. If the net input to the node is positive, its level of activation will move toward the maximum; if negative, the level will move toward the minimum. This movement is expressed as a net effect $e_i(t)$ on node i at time t:

$$e_i(t) = n_i(t)\,[M - a_i(t)] \tag{2}$$

$$e_i(t) = n_i(t)\,[a_i(t) - m] \tag{3}$$

where (2) holds if $n_i(t)$ is positive and (3) holds if it is negative.

This net effect has to be integrated with a tendency of the node to decay toward a resting level r_i. Thus, the rate of change in level of activation can be described by the following differential equation:

$$\frac{da_i(t)}{d(t)} = e_i(t) - \Theta[a_i(t) - r_i] \tag{4}$$

where Θ gives rate of decay. McClelland and Rumelhart use a discrete simulation in which case the differential equation becomes

$$a_i(t + \Delta t) = a_i(t) - \Theta\,[a_i(t) - r_i] + e_i(t) \tag{4'}$$

This equation allows them to update the pattern of activation at $t + \Delta t$ according to the pattern at the previous time t. Given a large, interconnected network of nodes, the activation interactions implied by these equations can be quite complex. There is no choice but to simply use the discrete update equation (4′) over and over again to calculate the state of each node at each time slice.

Behavior of the System

McClelland and Rumelhart assumed that there are some source nodes that enter activation into the network. For instance, in their work on reading they assumed that primitive letter-stroke features function as source nodes. Given a stable set of source nodes, all the nodes in the network tend to be driven to their maximum or minimum values.

Figure 3–5 illustrates a fragment of their network for letter and word recognition. They define a probabilistic process by which a node will lead to perceptual recognition when the node has had enough activation for long enough. Thus, the nodes in their network are actually associated with behavior.

This association also holds for the similar model of typing proposed by Rumelhart and Norman (1982). In that model, if certain nodes in that network accumulate enough activation they lead to the execution of a typing stroke. Thus, the activation computations

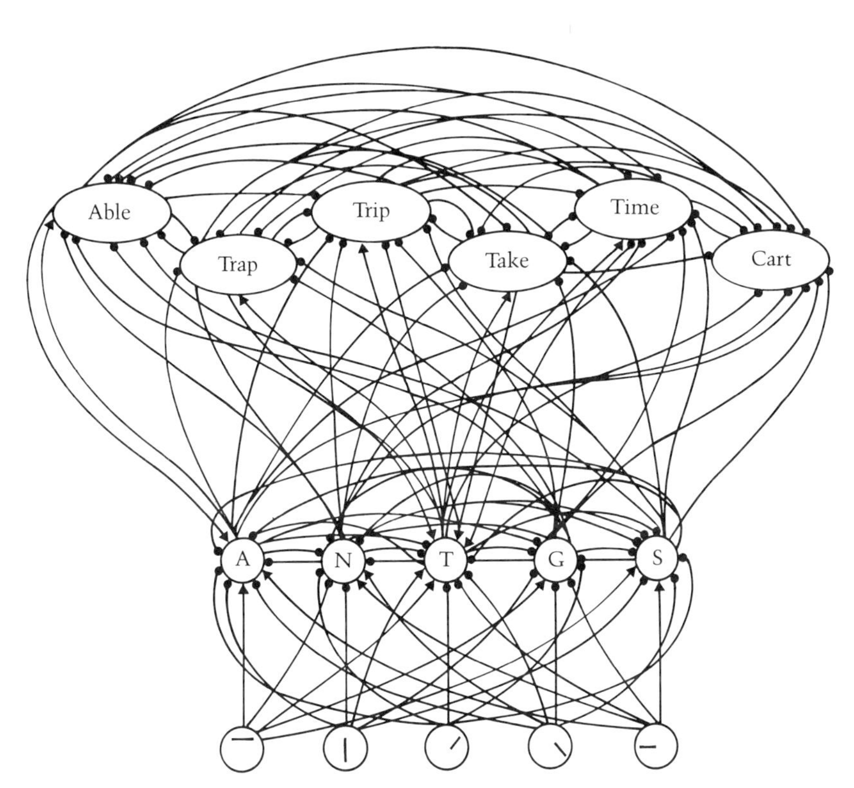

FIGURE 3–5 The McClelland and Rumelhart network for recognition of letters and words. The primitive letter strokes at the bottom combine to form letters which combine to form words.

described in equations (1)–(4′) directly result in the behavior. This is to be distinguished from the ACTE model, where activation made data available for other processes that resulted in behavior.

The McClelland and Rumelhart theory is developed basically as a model of pattern matching. Its strengths and weaknesses as a pattern-matching model have been discussed elsewhere (Anderson, 1983). Here I want to comment on how well it would fare if interpreted without modification as a model of the activation processes underlying priming and fact retrieval.

Potential Problems

One potential problem with this activation-based model is the assumption that activation levels of all nodes tend to go to the maximum or minimum levels. These extreme states make sense in a situation where one wants all-or-none decisions about whether patterns match or not. It makes less sense when we talk about the activation of facts that are more or less relevant to the current processing, where we would like the nodes to exhibit some gradation of activation levels.

A major difficulty with applying this model to fact retrieval is that the nodes in the network have specific behaviors associated with them. One node corresponds to recognizing a letter, another to pressing a key, and so on. However, the declarative knowledge involved in fact retrieval is not committed to use. Depending on the task, the same proposition can be used for recall, recognition, inference, and so on. Both the overt responses and the type of computations can vary greatly. This was the advantage of the ACT production system, where different productions could apply to the same knowledge. That model separated the factual knowledge from the processes that operate on it. The McClelland and Rumelhart model fails to make this needed separation.

The McClelland and Rumelhart model differs from many spreading-activation models in that it allows for the possibility of inhibitory links among nodes. Inhibitory effects are sometimes observed in the priming paradigms, where they appear to depend on whether the subject is aware of the priming relationship and thus consciously expects a word or class of words to be presented. An experiment by Neely (1977) is a fairly clear demonstration of this phenomenon. Subjects were presented with a stimulus for a word–nonword judgment. Subjects were told when they saw the prime *body* they should expect a building part (e.g., *window*). One-third of the time, however, they were presented with something other than a building part. One-sixth of the time they saw a body part, like *arm*, and one-sixth of the time a bird, like *robin*. Times to judge building parts, body parts, and birds were compared to control judgment times when the prime had been a neutral "XXX."

It is interesting to compare Neely's results for the conditions when the interval from prime to stimulus was 250 msec. and when it was 700 msec. At 250 msec., there was no significant difference between the times to judge building parts or birds when preceded by either the body prime or the control prime. However, subjects were significantly faster to judge a body part, like *arm*. Thus, at a short interval, subjects' expectations that they would see a building part had no facilitating effect, while prior semantic associations did. Neely's results were quite different when he tested at a 700 msec. delay. Subjects then responded significantly faster to building parts in the presence of the *body* prime than the control prime. They were significantly slower to body parts and birds in the presence of the experimental prime than the control prime. Now there was facilitation for the expected word and inhibition for everything else.

Neely related this difference to Posner's distinction between automatic activation and conscious attention (see also, Posner, 1978; Posner & Snyder, 1975). According to Posner, automatic activation produces only facilitation but cannot be affected by expectation, whereas conscious activation produces facilitation for whatever is expected but at an inhibitory cost to what is not expected. It was Neely's assumption that it took 700 msec. for a subject to set up conscious expectations about what he would see. This basic distinction between activation and attention has been confirmed in other studies (e.g., Stanovich & West, 1979).

The McClelland and Rumelhart model would not have any difficulty with the inhibitory effects per se. However, it does seem more problematic that the inhibition depends on a conscious set. The links in the McClelland and Rumelhart model are not dynamic and are not subject to momentary change depending on expectation.

Another interesting implication of the Neely study is that the effects of automatic activation are so rapid, an observation that has been confirmed elsewhere. Ratcliff & McKoon (1981) found full priming effects when the prime precedes the target by only 150 msec., but they failed to show any effect of associative distance on priming. Schustack (1981) actually found full priming effects when the prime (presented aurally) followed the word to be judged (presented visually). This superficially anomalous result can be understood when we consider that the processing of the target may take place over an interval that overlaps with the presentation of the prime. Thus, priming effects are felt very rapidly.

Also, there has not been any good evidence for a gradual buildup of priming effects. Rather, they seem to appear almost immediately in full force. This is a problem for the McClelland and

Rumelhart model, which identifies temporal effects with time for activation to accumulate to threshold. If priming has its full impact instantaneously, it does not appear there are the gradual changes in activation level as envisioned by McClelland and Rumelhart.

ACT★

From the review of past results and theoretical interpretations we can now identify a list of desiderata for an adequate theory of spreading activation.

1 It should allow for continuous levels of activation.

2 It should explain how level of activation in the network maps onto improved performance.

3 It should integrate results from both the priming and the fact-retrieval paradigms.

4 It should predict that less activation goes from a concept to an associated target structure as the frequency of the association decreases, as the fan of competing associations increases, and as the distance of association increases.

5 It should account for the rejection of foils in a fact-retrieval paradigm, including why the time to reject foils increases with fan and with similarity of the foils to a target.

6 It should predict the interaction (superadditivility) that occurs between level of activation and complexity of the computation being performed on the information.

7 It should have a precise, neurally plausible model of the calculus of spreading activation.

8 It should address the issue of when inhibition occurs and when it is not obtained in priming paradigms.

9 It should deal with the fact that priming effects are very rapidly felt throughout the network.

The ACT★ (pronounced "act star") model was developed out of ACTE to provide a better model of spreading activation (among other things). It preserves the distinction in ACTE between a declarative network of factual knowledge and a production system of procedural knowledge. As we will see, this distinction is important in the ability of the model to account for certain observed interactions. There is a spreading activation process defined on the declarative network of this model that, unlike ACTE, has differing levels of activation. Level of activation of information in the declarative network determines how rapidly it is processed by the productions. As we will see, this feature is a key to understanding many of the subtle interactions involving spreading activation.

Mathematical Development

The calculus of spreading activation in ACT★ is somewhat similar to that proposed by McClelland and Rumelhart. Like McClelland and Rumelhart's Equation (1), the activation input to a node *i* at time *t* is a linear combination of activation from associated nodes:

$$n_i(t) = \sum_j r_{ji}\, a_j(t) \tag{5}$$

where the summation is over the nodes *j* associated to *i*. The r_{ji} are the strengths of association. Unlike McClelland and Rumelhart, all connections are positive; there are no inhibitory effects. The values of the strengths of association are defined in the terms of the relative strengths of the nodes:

$$r_{ji} = s_i \,/\, \sum_k s_k \tag{6}$$

where s_i is the strength of *i* and the summation is over all nodes connected to *j*. The strength of a node is a function of its frequency of exposure. Equations (5) and (6) describe a process by which the activation from a node is divided among its associated nodes according to their relative strengths of connection. Equation (6) immediately produces two effects we want from our spreading activation model—that of frequency of association and that of fan. The effect of fan occurs because relative strength will be lower in the face of more competing associations.

The following differential equation describes the relationship between input and level of activation of a node.

$$\frac{da(t)}{d(t)} = Bn_i(t) - p^{\star}a_i(t) \tag{7}$$

Thus, as in McClelland and Rumelhart, activation increases in proportion (B is the proportionality) to the input and decays at an exponential rate ($p^{\star}$ is the rate). Unlike the McClelland and Rumelhart model, however, there is no explicit upper bound (M in their model) on the level of activation. All nodes in this model have a lower bound of zero. Provided that $p^{\star} > \mathrm{B}$ in equation (7), activation levels will not go to infinity. The net result is a distribution of activation over the network, with level of activation of a node reflecting distance and strength of association to source nodes.

Certain nodes are sources of activation in the network. These can receive activation from external stimulation or from internal foci of activation. If a node is a source node, it not only receives activation from its associated nodes but also a source activation c_i. In this case, the input activation, Equation (5), must be modified to include the source activation.

$$n_i(t) = c_i + \sum_j r_{ji} a_j(t) \tag{5'}$$

These equations can all be cast more generally in term of vectors and matrices. Let $C(t)$ be an n-element vector giving the source activations for all n nodes in the element at time t. Now, most of the entries in $C(t)$ will be zero. Similarly, let $A(t)$ be a vector giving the levels of activation of all n nodes. Let R be $n \times n$ matrix giving the strengths of association between each pair of nodes. In a large network most entries in R will be zero, since most nodes will not be directly connected. Then, we can rewrite Equation (7) as:

$$\frac{dA(t)}{dt} = BC(t) + BRA(t) - p^* A(t) \tag{8}$$

If the source activations stay constant, $p^* > B$, and $\sum_j r_{ij} = 1$, then the network will converge on a stable activation pattern (i.e., the value of the differential above approaches 0). We can determine this asymptotic activation pattern A by solving the following set of linear equations:

$$A = \frac{B}{p^*} C + \frac{B}{p^*} RA \tag{9}$$

The important assumption of the ACT★ theory is that p^* is large—on the order of 10 where time is measured in milliseconds. In this case, 90 percent of the asymptotic pattern will be achieved in the first 100 msec. Thus, we can predict the very rapid priming effects that are observed. Of course, one consequence is that we cannot explain the reaction-time observed in these experiments in terms of time for activation to spread through the network: It simply spreads too rapidly.

It is assumed that the level of activation of information in memory determines the rate at which the condition of a production is matched against that information. In this assumption, ACT★ predicts the superadditivility that is observed between level of activation and complexity of mental computation (as in Table 3–2). In a production system, the mental computation is performed in production pattern matching. Let C be a measure of that complexity.

Let *A* be the level of activation of the structure being processed. Then the time for processing to complete will be *C/A*, since activation determines rate of processing. Thus, we predict a multiplicative relationship between these factors.

Production Implementation

Productions P1 through P4 in Table 3–3 model recognition and rejection of probes in the fact-retrieval experiment described by Anderson (1976, p. 258). In this experiment, subjects studied location–subject–verb sentences of the form "In the bank the lawyer laughed." After committing the sentences to memory, subjects went into a recognition phase where they saw four types of probes:

1 3-element targets: these were identical to the sentences studied.

2 3-element foils: these consisted of a location, subject, and verb that were all studied but not in the same combination.

3 2-element targets: although there were other examples of this condition, I will consider here the 2-element case where subject and verb came from the target sentence.

4 2-element foils: subject and verb combinations where each element came from a different sentence.

TABLE 3-3 Productions for Performance in a Fact Retrieval Task

P1:	IF	the goal is to recognize the sentence and the probe is "In the L V location the L V person L V action" and (L V action L V person L V location) has been studied
	THEN	say YES
P2:	IF	the goal is to recognize the sentence and the probe is "In the L V location the L V person L V action" and (L V action L V person L V location) has not been studied
	THEN	say NO
P3:	IF	the goal is to recognize the sentence and the probe is "The L V person L V action" and (L V action L V person L V location) has been studied
	THEN	say YES
P4:	IF	the goal is to recognize the sentence "The L V person L V action" and (L V action L V person L V location) has not been studied
	THEN	say NO

Response to these four types of probes are handled by productions P1 through P4, respectively, in Table 3–3.

Production P1 recognizes that the current probe matches a proposition previously stored in memory. The elements in quotes refer to the probe and the elements in parentheses refer to the proposition in memory. Production P1 determines whether the probe and proposition match by checking whether the variables, prefixed by LV (L V location, L V person, L V action), bind to the same elements in the probe and proposition. Production P2 will fire if the variables do not match in a 3-element probe. Productions P3 and P4 are like P1 and P2 except that they respond to 2-element probes.

Pattern-Matching Structure

Figure 3–6 illustrates schematically the structure of production memory for P1 through P4 and their connection to declarative memory. Here each of these productions is represented as consisting

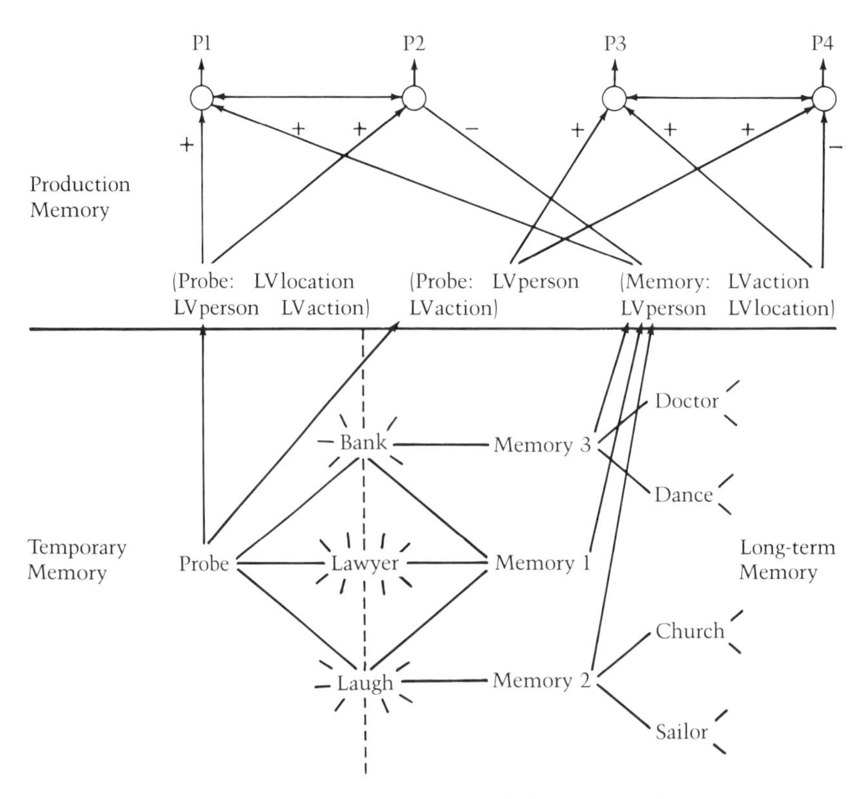

FIGURE 3–6 The pattern matching network for the conditions of the productions in Table 3–3.

of two clauses,[3] represented as separate elements at the bottom of the "Production Memory" portion of the figure. These elements (called terminal nodes) perform tests to find clauses in declarative memory that match. These clauses are combined at higher nodes. So, for instance, P1 combines a clause representing a 3-element probe with a clause representing the memory proposition. The higher nodes with two positive lines (indicated by plus signs) perform tests of the variable identity between the two clauses. So P1 checks that L V location, L V person, and L V action are the same in the probe as in memory structure. A negative two-input node like P2 will fire if there is input on its positive line and there is not a compatible input on its negative line.

In Figure 6 declarative memory is partitioned into a temporary memory representing the probe and long-term memory encoding the studied facts. The main sources of activation are the individual elements (bank, lawyer, and laugh) which are encodings of the external probe. From these elements activation spreads to the probe and throughout long-term memory. The probe is connected to two terminal nodes in production memory that test for the two probe patterns (i.e., the 2-element probe and the 3-element probe.) The rate at which they perform their tests is determined by the level of activation of the probe structure. Similarly, the propositions in declarative memory are connected to the proposition terminal node in production memory. Again, the rate at which any proposition is processed by this pattern node is a function of the level of activation of that proposition. Activation also spreads through this pattern network, although the principles of activation spread are somewhat different from the ones discussed for the declarative network (see Anderson, 1983). The activation of a higher two-input node like the one for P1 will be a function of the level of activation of the nodes below it. In the case of the positive P1 and P3, this will be the sum of the activation of both the probe and the memory elements. In the case of the negative P2 and P4 this will be only affected by the probe activation.

Activation of higher positive nodes (P1 and P3) determines the rate at which they perform tests for the compatibility of their two inputs. When the tests are completed and if the tests are found compatible, the production represented by the node can fire.

Negative higher nodes (like P2 and P4) do not have such compatibility tests to perform. Rather, they use activation directly to determine whether they are matched. The absence test in P2 is implemented by setting up an inhibitory relation between P1 and

[3] For purposes of simplification the first goal clause is ignored, since it is constant across the productions.

P2. Similarly, the absence test in P4 is handled by an inhibitory relation between P3 and P4. If there is strong evidence for P1 it will repress P2 and prevent it from firing. If there is not sufficient evidence for P1, P2 will build up evidence for itself and eventually fire. P2 in this model is set to accumulate activation from the proposition twice as fast as P1. Thus, if there is not a good match to P1, P2 will repress P1 and will accumulate sufficient activation to fire. The effect of this inhibitory relationship is to make P2 wait for P1 to see if it will match.

There are three important features to note about how the pattern matcher treats P1 through P4:

1 Pattern matching will take longer with high-fan probes, that is, probes whose elements appear in more than one study sentence. The fan out of an element reduces the amount of activation that can go to any propositional trace or to the probe encoding. Pattern matching for targets is a function of the activation of the propositional trace and the probe.

2 It should take longer to recognize larger probes (those containing more elements) because more tests have to be performed. In particular, 3-element probes took longer than 2-element probes. For ample evidence in support of this prediction, see Anderson (1976).

3 Foils that are more similar to studied sentences should be harder to reject. In this experiment "overlap" foils were used which had two out of three elements in common with a studied sentence. Subjects found these harder to reject than non-overlapping foils. The reason ACT★ predicts this result is that there will be a partial match of the positive production pattern (P1) which will inhibit growth of evidence at the negative production pattern (P2). More generally, ACT★ predicts a difficulty in rejecting partial matches. For many other confirmations of this prediction, see Anderson (1976).

Rejection of Foils

An interesting question concerns how one decides that one does not know something.[4] In fact-retrieval experiments, the most obvious model for foil rejection—that subjects exhaustively search their memories about a concept—is also obviously incorrect. The times to reject foils, typically only slightly longer than the times to accept targets, are much too short for this. Anderson (1976) and King and Anderson (1976) proposed a waiting model, in which subjects waited some amount of time for the probe to be recognized. If the probe was

[4]I thank Robert Frederking for pointing out to me the analysis of foil judgments reported in this subsection.

not recognized within that time, they would reject it. The assumption was that subjects would adjust their waiting time to reflect factors (like fan) that determined time to recognize targets.

Implementation of the Waiting Model

The ACT★ theory provides a mechanism that realizes the waiting model. As indicated in Figure 3–6, the productions that reject foils (P2 and P4) are in an inhibitory relation with the productions that accept targets (P1 and P3). These foil productions are looking for the presence of a subpattern S1 (the encoding of the probe) and the *absence* of a second subpattern S2 (the matching memory proposition). We will refer to this combination as S1 & ~S2. The competing target productions are looking for S1 & S2—that is S1 and the *presence* of S2. An inhibitory relation is established between the positive S1 & S2 and the negative S1 & ~S2. Both positive and negative patterns receive activation from S1 but only the positive pattern receives activation from S2. The S1 & ~S2 pattern builds up activation either until its total activation reaches a threshold or until it is repressed by accruing evidence for the positive S1 & S2 pattern.

A long-standing question in the ACT theory has concerned how subjects adjust their waiting time to reflect the fan of the elements in a foil. It makes sense that they should make such an adjustment. If they did not wait long enough for high-fan targets, they would be in danger of spuriously rejecting them. For a long time, however, there was a lack of plausible mechanism for adjusting the waiting time. The obvious idea of counting links out of a node and setting the waiting time according to the counted fan is implausible. A mechanism for adjusting the waiting time can be derived with no added assumptions from the current pattern-matching system. Note in Figure 3–6 that the fan of the elements will affect not only the activation of the memory elements but also that of the probe encoding. The probe activation will determine the amount of activation that arrives at the S1 & ~S2 conjunctions in P2 and P4. Thus, in presence of high-fan probes activation will build more slowly to threshold for the foil-detecting productions, which will produce the desired fan effect for foils and will give high-fan targets more time to complete pattern matching.

Tests of the Waiting Model

To the extent that they share features with memory propositions (and so lead to activation of S2 in the above analysis), foils are predicted to be harder to reject. So, as Anderson (1976) reported, overlap foils that involved a number of words from one studied sentence took longer to reject than nonoverlapping foils. The experiment by King and Anderson (1976) illustrates another kind of similarity that can also slow down foil rejection. We had subjects study sets, or pairs, of sentences such as

The doctor hated the lawyer.
The doctor ignored the model.

Such pairs were called a *connected* set because the two sentences shared the same agent. *Unconnected* sets were created in the same mold except that they did not share the agent. For example

The soldier hated the lawyer.
The baker ignored the model.

The task was to recognize whether verb-object pairs came from the same sentence. So *hated the lawyer* would be a positive probe and *hated the model* a negative probe. Negative probes or foils were always constructed by pairing verb and object from different sentences in a set (either connected or unconnected).

Subjects showed no difference in recognition of positive probes from connected versus unconnected sentence sets. On the other hand, subjects were slower and made more errors in rejecting foils from connected than from unconnected sets. There was a spurious relationship in the connected foils from verb to object through the shared agent, which caused a partial match to the positive conjunction (S1 & S2) and so was inhibiting the production that detected the absence (S1 & ~S2).

Anderson and Ross (1980) have employed an extension of this logic to study what is nominally called semantic memory. Subjects studied sentences like *The cat attacked the snake* in the first phase of the experiment. Then subjects judged the truth of categorical probes like *A cat is a snake* in the second phase. Subjects were slower and made more errors in these categorical judgments when they had learned an irrelevant sentence linking the two categories in the first phase.

Anderson and Ross suggested the similarity effects in semantic memory are to be understood in terms of spurious intersections. These similarity effects in semantic memory are the findings that it is harder to reject a pair of the form "*An A is a B*" the more similar *A* and *B* are. So, a "*dog is a bird*" is correctly predicted to be harder by this principle than "*a dog is a rock*." One can understand this in terms of the number of prior connections between the subject and predicate of the sentence. Thinking of the similarity effect in these terms makes it possible to understand instances (Collins & Quillian, 1972) where subjects are slow to reject foils if the relationship between subject and predicate is not one of similarity but rather some other associative relation, such as *"an almond has a fortune"* and *"Madrid is Mexican."*

Automatic Activation versus Conscious Attention

As discussed in Anderson (1983), ACT★ also can predict some of the differences between the patterns of priming results obtained with automatic activation and those obtained with conscious attention. This explanation depends critically on the distinction between declarative memory and procedural memory. Automatic activation is associated with the spread of activation through declarative memory of ACT. In typical priming paradigms, such activation can only have beneficial influence in making needed information more available. There are no inhibitory effects in the spreading activation process.

To consciously expect a word or set of words it is necessary to create a production to recognize the word specifically. If the anticipated word comes up, a rapid response will occur. However, if expectation is violated, the subject will take time to decide that this special production cannot match and to enable the normal automatic recognition productions to apply. So there will be a cost in the case of conscious attention. (See Anderson, 1983, for a discussion of some of the effects that can be explained by these two constructs.)

CONCLUSIONS

Although the ACT★ model satisfies all the desiderata of a spreading activation model, if the past is any predictor, it will prove to have difficulties just as did the models that came before. This review of four theories considerably underrepresents the frequency of the spreading activation construct in distinct cognitive theories. Only for lack of space have some of the many other theories (e.g., Bower & Cohen, 1983; Levin, 1976; Thibadeau et al., 1982; Wickelgren, 1976) not been covered here. The prevalence of the spreading activation construct reflects the fact that it captures some fundamental aspects of human cognition; it is truly remarkable how often theorists keep returning to this basic concept.

REFERENCES

Anderson, J. R. Retrieval of propositional information from long-term memory, *Cognitive Psychology*, 1974, *5*, 451–74.

Anderson, J. R. *Language, memory and thought*. Hillsdale, N.J.: Lawrence Erlbaum Associates, 1976.

Anderson, J. R. Spreading activation: An integration of two paradigms. Paper presented at the 23rd Annual Psychonomics Meetings, Minneapolis, November 1982.

Anderson, J. R. *The architecture of cognition*. Cambridge, Mass.: Harvard University Press, 1983.

Anderson, J. R., & Bower, G. H. *Human associative memory*. Washington, D.C.: Hemisphere Press, 1973.

Anderson, J. R., Kline, P., & Lewis, C. A production system model for language processing. In P. Carpenter & M. Just (Eds.), *Cognitive processes in comprehension*. Hillsdale, N.J.: Lawrence Erlbaum Associates, 1977.

Anderson, J. R., & Ross, B. H. Evidence against a semantic-episodic distinction. *Journal of Experimental Psychology: Human Learning and Memory*, 1980, *6*, 441–478.

Bower, G. H., & Cohen, P. R. Emotional influences in memory and thinking: Data and theory. In M. S. Clark & S. T. Fiske (Eds.), *Affect and Cognition*. Hillsdale, N.J.: Lawrence Erlbaum Associates, 1983.

Collins, A. M., & Loftus, E. F. A spreading activation theory of semantic processing. *Psychological Review*, 1975, *85*, 407–28.

Collins, A. M., & Quillian, M. R. Retrieval time from semantic memory. *Journal of Verbal Learning and Verbal Behavior*, 1969, *8*, 240–47.

Collins, A. M., & Quillian, M. R. Experiments on semantic memory and language comprehension. In L. Gregg (Ed.), *Cognition and learning*. New York: Wiley, 1972.

Conrad, C. Cognitive economy in semantic memory. *Journal of Experimental Psychology*, 1972, *92*, 149–54.

Fischler, I., Bryant, K., & Querns, E. Rapid priming of episodic and semantic word recognition, submitted.

Glass, A. L., Holyoak, K. J., & O'Dell, C. Production frequency and the verification of quantified statements. *Journal of Verbal Learning and Verbal Behavior*, 1974, *13*, 237–54.

Hayes-Roth, B. Evolution of cognitive structures and processes. *Psychological Review*, 1977, *84*, 260–78.

Hebb, D. O. *The organization of behavior*. New York: Wiley, 1949.

Hinton, G. E., & Anderson, J. A. *Parallel models of associative memory*. Hillsdale, N.J.: Lawrence Erlbaum Associates, 1981.

King, D. R. W., & Anderson, J. R. Long-term memory search: An intersecting activation process. *Journal of Verbal Learning and Verbal Behavior*, *15*, 587–606.

Langley, P., & Neches, R. PRISM User's Manual, Unpublished manuscript, Carnegie-Mellon University, Pittsburgh, 1981.

Levin, J. A. Proteus: An activation framework for cognitive process models. Unpublished doctoral dissertation. University of California, San Diego, 1976.

Lewis, C. H., & Anderson, J. R. Interference with real world knowledge. *Cognitive Psychology*, 1976, *8*, 311–35.

McClelland, J. L., & Rumelhart, D. E. An interactive model of context effects in letter perception: Part I. An account of basic findings. *Psychological Review*, 1981, *88*, 375–407.

McKoon, G., & Ratcliff, R. Priming in episodic and semantic memory. *Journal of Verbal Learning and Verbal Behavior*, 1979, *18*, 463–80.

Meyer, D. E., & Schvaneveldt, R. W. Facilitation in recognizing pairs of words: Evidence of a dependence between retrieval operations. *Journal of Experimental Psychology*, 1971, *90*, 227–34.

Neely, J. H. Semantic priming and retrieval from lexical memory: Roles of inhibitionless spreading activation and limited-capacity attention. *Journal of Experimental Psychology: General*, 1977, *106*, 226–54.

Newell, A. A theoretical explanation of mechanisms for coding the stimulus. In A. W. Melton, & E. Martin (Eds.), *Coding processes in human memory*, Washington, D.C.: Winston, 1972.

Newell, A. Production systems: Models of control structures. In W. G. Chase (Ed.), *Visual information processing*. New York: Academic Press, 1973.

Newell, A. Harpy, production systems, and human cognition. In R. A. Cole (Ed.), *Perception and production of fluent speech*. Hillsdale, N.J.: Lawrence Erlbaum Associates, 1980.

Quillian, M. R. The teachable language comprehender. *Communications of the ACM*, 1969, *12*, 459–76.

Posner, M. I. *Chronomeiric explorations of mind*. Hillsdale, N.J.: Lawrence Erlbaum Associates, 1978.

Posner, M. I., & Snyder, C. R. R. Attention and cognitive control. In R. L. Solso (Ed.), *Information processing and cognition*. Hillsdale, N.J.: Lawrence Erlbaum Associates, 1975.

Ratcliff, R., & McKoon, G. Does activation really spread? *Psychological Review*, 1981, *88*, 454–62.

Rosch, E. H. On the internal structure of perceptual and semantic categories. In T. E. Moore (Ed.), *Cognitive development and the acquisition of language*. New York: Academic Press, 1973.

Rumelhart, D. E., & McClelland, J. L. An interactive activation model of context effects in letter perception: Part 2. The contextual enhancement effect and some tests and extensions of the model. *Psychological Review*, 1982, *89*, 60–94.

Rumelhart, D. E., & Norman, D. A. Simulating a skilled typist: A study of skilled cognitive-motor performance. *Cognitive Science*, 1982, *6*, 1–36.

Schustack, M. W. Word-meaning comprehension: Syntactic and associative effects of sentential context. Unpublished doctoral dissertation, Carnegie-Mellon University, Pittsburgh, 1981.

Smith, E. E., Shoben, E., & Rips, L. Comparison processes in semantic memory. In G. H. Bower (Ed.), *Psychology of learning and motivation*, New York: Academic Press, 1974.

Stanovich, K. E., & West, R. F. Mechanisms of sentence context effects in reading: Automatic activation and conscious attention. *Memory and cognition*, 1979, *7*, 77–85.

Thibadeau, R., Just, M. A., & Carpenter, P. A. A model of the time course and content of reading. *Cognitive Science*, 1982, *6*, 157–203.

Thorndyke, P. W., & Bower, G. H. Storage and retrieval processes in sentence memory. *Cognitive Psychology*, 1974, *5*, 515–43.

Warren, R. E. Time and the spread of activation in memory. *Journal of Experimental Psychology: Learning and Memory*, 1977, *3*, 458–66.

Waterman, D. A. Generalization learning techniques for automating the learning of heuristics. *Artificial Intelligence*, 1970, *1*, 121–170.

Wickelgren, W. A. Network strength theory of storage and retrieval dynamics. *Psychological Review*, 1976, *83*, 466–78.

4

MENTAL REPRESENTATION

Stephen Michael Kosslyn
Harvard University

The behaviorists tried to eliminate all discussion of the mind or mental events. They tried to explain behavior by positing that particular stimuli were directly associated with particular responses. However, this approach proved untenable. A stimulus cannot be defined in physical terms, but depends on what an organism attends to, encodes, and comprehends. Even something as simple as a flashing light offers numerous opportunities for interpretation; the functional stimulus could be the hue, frequency, intensity, size, location or shape of the light, or some combination thereof. Similarly, a learned response cannot be defined in physical terms, such as by specifying particular kinds of muscle actions. For example, rats that learn to run a maze can swim the correct path just as well, even though very different movements are used. A response must be understood in terms of the knowledge acquired by the organism. Furthermore, the rules relating stimuli and responses are not always or often, with humans, based on simple associations. For example, it is possible to prove that direct stimulus-response associations cannot explain how we arrange words into a sentence (see Chomsky, 1957, 1959).

The preparation of this manuscript was supported by NSF Grant BNS 82–40259 and NIMH RCDA award 1 K02MH00352–01A1 MHK. I wish to thank Alfonso Caramazza, Howard Egeth, Martha Farah, Duncan Luce, Michael McCloskey, Terry Sejnowski, Ed Smith, Eric Wanner, Bruce Wolpe, Edgar Zurif and especially, Gary Hatfield for useful comments made on an earlier version of this chapter.

If we are ever to understand behavior, then, we must invoke notions like "attention," "encoding" and "knowledge." All of these notions rest on the idea that the organism learns by storing some sort of internal representations, which can then be used to guide a variety of behavior. The study of "mental representation," how information is stored and used in the mind, has evolved rapidly in the past two decades; there is now an emerging consensus about what the problems are and what the solutions should look like. The overview presented in this chapter is derived from Anderson (1976, 1978), Anderson and Bower (1973), Block (1981), Chomsky (1957, 1965, 1980), Dennett (1978), Fodor (1968, 1975, 1980), Kolers and Smythe (1979), Kosslyn (1980), Marr (1982), Newell and Simon (1972), Palmer (1978), Putnam (1960, 1973), Pylyshyn (1980), Ullman (1979), and the commentators in the first issue of the 1980 volume of the *Behavioral and Brain Sciences*. Rather than review the details of each writer's ideas, I will strive to synthesize their various views into a coherent picture of the current status of the study of mental representation.

In what circumstances is it appropriate to ask questions about mental representations? Most researchers assume that mental representations are used in tasks in which one's knowledge or beliefs can affect performance. The workings of simple reflexes, the operation of the sensory receptors, and the like presumably do not involve mental representations. Questions about mental representation typically can be assigned to one of four broad areas:

1 *Language,* including questions about how information is stored and used in language learning, comprehension, and production;

2 *Reasoning,* including questions about the usefulness of different ways of storing information and strategies for solving different types of problems;

3 *Perception,* including questions of how information about stimuli is stored and how objects are recognized;

4 *Motor control,* including questions of how motor skills are stored, how the stored information changes with practice, and how one prepares to execute a series of actions.

In addition to studying these specific topics, questions are often asked about the interactions among them. The study of mental imagery, for example, involves interactions among stored information used in language, perception, and reasoning. Questions are also sometimes asked about capacities that are shared among different abilities. For example, questions about "memory" per se (as opposed to perceptual memories, linguistic memories, and so on) often challenge the assumption that the types of information used in different domains are different.

Although the emphasis in this chapter will be on the nature of representation, for reasons that will become clear shortly, we must of necessity also consider some aspects of how representations are used.

LEVELS OF ANALYSIS

Theories in cognitive psychology are not always theories of mental representations. Mental representations are entities that are taken to actually exist in the head, which not only must be labeled but must be characterized. Often cognitive psychologists supply the label but do not go on to present a theory of the entities themselves. For example, much of the work on "naive physics" (what people believe about physical law) ascribes particular beliefs to people, but does not indicate how such beliefs are internally represented (e.g., see McCloskey, 1983). These sorts of explanations are at the "intentional" level, which must be distinguished from explanations that rest on characterizations of properties of mental representations themselves. It will behoove us to consider intentional explanations before considering the nature of mental representations per se.

Intentional Explanations

Psychological explanations often arise in everyday discourse, as when we are gossiping about why so-and-so did such-and-such. Such explanations are called "intentional explanations" and hinge on attributions of *beliefs* and *desires*. For example, in explaining why John yelled at his dog, we may posit that he desired a change in the dog's behavior and that he believed that yelling would intimidate the animal and thus effect the desired change.

Intentional explanations rest on verbs such as "intend," "want," "expect," "like," and "desire" (preference terms) and on terms such as "know," "recognize," "think," "foresee," and "believe" (belief terms). (Philosophers have devised a number of criteria for identifying these "intentional" terms. The most common is to test whether a synonym can be substituted in the predicate; for intentional verbs, it cannot. For example, if "John knows that George Washington wore false teeth," this does not necessarily imply that "John knows that the first president of the United States wore false teeth.") Once you attribute a given set of beliefs and desires to a person, certain implications follow: saying that John *likes* reindeer, for example, implies that (all other things being equal) he will be nice to them, prevent them from being harmed when he can, try to be around them, and so on. The predictive power of an intentional explanation arises from the implications of the belief and preference terms; once you have classified someone as being in a specific "mental state," some kinds of behaviors are to be expected and other kinds are not.

An *intentional system* is one whose behavior can be understood by using intentional explanations. As Dennett (1978) has pointed out, complex computer programs often can be described using intentional vocabulary; if "wanting" to achieve a goal implies trying to reach it, trying alternative strategies when foiled, and so on, then "wanting" can usefully be applied to certain computer programs (particularly some of those being developed in the field of artificial intelligence). The danger here, of course, is that the terms have complex implicational structures, and not all implications that are appropriate for people will be appropriate for a computer program. Thus, use of an intentional vocabulary can mislead us into assuming that a program is more subtle or sophisticated than it is (cf. McDermott, 1981).

It is important to realize that intentional explanations need not implicate specific ways information is processed. For example, consider the belief term "recognize." Have you ever seen a "friend" and rushed up to him with a big smile, only to discover that it was a stranger? In the extreme case, where it was your friend's twin brother, the same internal events would have occurred if it had been your friend and you actually had recognized him. Exactly the same stimuli would have been encoded, made contact with the same stored memories, and so on. However, if it was not your friend, you did not *recognize* him—you just thought you did. "Recognition" depends in part on reality, on the state of the real world. Two different intentional explanations—recognition and mistaken recognition—correspond to the same internal events. This correspondence can occur with any of the intentional terms, such as "know," "perceive," "realize," and so on, that imply "success."

Even intentional explanations that do not involve "success verbs" may not correspond in a simple way to internal events. Many philosophers argue that the meanings of words in general depend on context and on a person's cultural background. Wittgenstein (1953) likened language to a game that has only vaguely defined rules; meanings, according to Wittgenstein, are determined by how words are used by a community of speakers (cf. Grice, 1968). If he is correct, then no intentional explanation, based on the meanings of belief and desire words, can correspond in a simple way to a single internal event occurring in one person's mind.

In short, intentional explanations clearly are not adequate as theories of mental representation; they ultimately rest on the "folk psychology" implicit in the language, and they are inherently imprecise. Intentional explanations are assigned purely on the basis of behaviors observed in context. Depending on what John does, you categorize him as being in a given "mental state." But the mental state itself is not characterized, it is just labeled. Because we want answers to questions about how information is stored and processed in the mind, we need some characterization of the mental states themselves, not merely their implications for behavior.

Functional Explanations

Organs of the body can be described not only in terms of their physical properties but in terms of their function. For example, consider stomachs: they can be described in terms of kinds of cells, acids, enzymes and so on; and they can be described in terms of what they do, namely in terms of their role in digestion. Brains can also be described at both levels. A description of the physical properties of the brain will characterize cells, their interconnections, and various chemical and electrical activities. Unlike stomachs, the primary function of brains is to store and process information. Thus, a description of the functional properties of brains will characterize the way information is stored and processed. Theories of mental representation, then, are in fact theories of brain activity cast as the functional level of analysis, and "mental events" are considered to be brain activity described at the functional level.

In order to distinguish between the intentional and functional levels of analysis, consider an analogy: the ways in which we can explain the operation of an automated bank teller (a "cash machine"). On the intentional level, we could say that the machine will give you money only after it is "convinced" (a belief term) that you are who you say you are; if you give it your card and the correct code number, we could say that it was "satisfied." But these attributions are made simply by observing the cash machine's behavior in context, and describe the machine as a single entity.

We could also provide an analysis of the internal events by which the machine produces the behavior in question. On this functional level of analysis, we attempt to describe the way information is processed by the machine. For example, we could say that the machine first reads in the ID number from your card and your personal code number; it then looks up the personal code number associated with the ID number stored in its memory and compares this number with the one you just punched in; if the two numbers match, the machine then prints out a request for a command, registers which button you push, and so on.

The functional level of analysis of internal events is the level we use when we describe a computer's operation in terms of its program. In contrast, on the physical level we would describe the operation of transistors, capacitors, circuits, how current flows depending on which inputs are active, and so on. (The physical level corresponds to that of neurophysiological explanation, which will be discussed later in this chapter.)

Note that intentional terms can be used to describe the separate steps going on inside, treating them as active entities; but this use of the terms is very different from using this vocabulary to describe the behavior of the machine—or the person—as an unanalyzed whole (cf. Dennett, 1978). However, if we do use an intentional vocabulary to describe information processing, we must ultimately give the terms more precise definitions than those found in common discourse, otherwise the theory will inherit the vagueness of the terms themselves.

To be more concrete, the best way to understand the idea of a functional level of analysis in terms of "information processing" is by examining how digital computers work. Let us start off with another analogy: Imagine that there is a row of tin cans in front of you. The cans are numbered in order, and each one contains a slip of paper. You pull out the slip of paper in the first can, and see a message in code; the code consists of a series of 0s (zeroes) and 1s (ones). You have an answer key in front of you, and along the left side are various sequences of 0s and 1s. You look up the sequence corresponding to the one written on the slip of paper and see the command "add together the numbers in the next two cans." So you pull out the slip from the next can and see "00000011," which you read as a binary representation of the number "3," and then you pull out the following slip and see "00000001," which you read as "1." You then add the numbers and pull out the next slip, which has written on it another sequence of 0s and 1s. You look up this numerical series on the key and see the command "write sum in the next can." So you pull out the next slip, write down the total, and then go on to the next can for a new command.

The computer design illustrated by this analogy was developed by John von Neumann, and it is often referred to as a "von Neumann architecture." Three important aspects of a von Neumann, or standard digital, computer's operation are illustrated in our analogy: First, in standard digital computers there is a distinction between the memory (the tin cans in our analogy) and the central processing unit (you armed with your answer key, in the analogy). Second, instructions and data are stored the same way, as series of 0s and 1s written on slips of paper in the analogy. The way a given message is interpreted depends on the state of the central processor: if the central processing unit "expects" numbers, it "reads" the 0s and 1s as binary digits; if it is set to "expect" commands, it reads the code as instructions. In the actual computer, of course, series of 0s and 1s (i.e., bits—from *b*inary dig*its*) can be "read" as representing digits, letters, and in fact a large number of different kinds of symbols. Third, the machine operates serially, one step at a time, just as you did in going from can to can in the analogy.[1]

The most important point about the analogy is that if one wants to understand what a computer will do when one types on a terminal, its behavior is best understood not by regarding the electronic equivalent of the 0s and 1s as patterns of electrical current, but rather as *symbols*, standing for something else—a digit, a letter, or whatever. If a series of 0s and 1s stands for a command to "multiply," very different things will happen than if it directs the central processor to treat another entry as standing for a letter of the alphabet. A description of the computer's operation in terms of the symbols being processed provides a description of information processing at the functional level of analysis.

The brain can also be described at the functional level of analysis using the vocabulary developed to describe the operation of computers (see Putnam, 1960, and various papers in the "functionalism" section of Block, 1981). We focus not on the physical nature of cells or patterns of neural activation, but rather on what those physical events serve to represent. Just given our analogy, it is clear that such a mechanistic system can be understood in terms of physical laws, which would be appropriate if one wanted to understand how to redesign a computer (e.g., so it would radiate less heat) or discover the antidote for a poison in the brain, or in terms of the interactions among "symbolic representations," which would be appropriate if one wanted to understand what information is stored and how it is processed.

Another concept that is clear in our analogy is that the properties of representations are embedded in the properties of a *representational system*, which consists of both data and the processes that operate on them. Depending on how data is "read," it can have a completely different status in the system (e.g., digit or instruction).

[1] There is one other important aspect of von Neumann architecture illustrated in the analogy: the contents of the cans can be changed by writing new code on the slips of paper. It is this property that makes these machines "general purpose." The code corresponding to instructions is called a "program," and the machine is "reprogrammable" because new instructions can always be entered. The analogy is not perfect, however: A better analogy for the way a computer works would have the slips be seen through little windows in the cans; the contents are not actually removed, but rather are "copied." Furthermore, we should specify that the central processing unit automatically goes to the memory location addressed by a number one larger than the memory location just accessed, unless it is specifically directed to go to some other numbered location. In addition, we would need to discuss special purpose "registers," places where particular operations, such as addition, take place very quickly, as well as a multitude of other special features. The actual design of modern computers is almost incomprehensibly complex.

Stored data constitute a "representation" only if processed appropriately. In fact, the contribution of properties of the processes that use representations is in principle unavoidable. If there were no processes, we would never use the representations; hence, for all intents and purposes, they would not exist. From a practical point of view, the properties of a representation in fact are *due* to the properties of the processes that access the data. For example, if a simple list were stored in a computer, the functional order of the items on the list is determined by the retrieval process that accesses the items. It is only by specifying the nature of the data access processes that one can discuss properties of the representation itself; once the order of access is fixed, variations in the order of items can be attributed to their "positions" on the list. In fact, the very status of a representation as a representation depends on processing: The proper processing can make anything a representation; for example, a coffee mug could be a representation if one had rules for deriving information from the shape of the handle, the thickness of the rim, and so on. And without proper processing, nothing is a representation—just as a painting conveys no information for a blind man. Thus, theories of mental representation, by necessity, require theorizing about the processing system in which the representation exists.

Levels of Functional Analysis

An information-processing analysis can be broken into three sublevels, differing in part in their degree of abstraction. The most abstract is the level of the *computation*; the next, the level of the *functional architecture*; and the last the level of the *algorithm* (see Marr, 1982; Newell & Simon, 1972; Pylyshyn, 1980).

It is worth discussing these levels in detail for three reasons. First, various fruitless disputes have arisen in the past because different researchers were working at different levels and did not realize it. For example, Winograd (1972) criticized Chomsky's (1965) theory because it did not specify how language is actually used—but this criticism is inappropriate given the level of abstraction of the theory. Second, how one tests a theory depends on its level; different sorts of data are relevant for evaluating the different sorts of theories. For example, claims about the nature of a computation do not necessarily lead to predictions about processing time, whereas claims about the nature of algorithms almost always do. Third, each of the different levels provides a slightly different perspective on mental events, and a comprehensive theory will require integrating insights from all three levels of abstraction. For example, a mathematical treatment of the computations that underlie learning can complement a theory of the mental machinery used in encoding, storing, and retrieving information from memory. Different kinds of theories illuminate different facets of the same phenomena, as should become clear from the examples provided below.

The Theory of the Computation The most abstract kind of theory at the functional level specifies the nature of a "computation," a transformation of information into new information. A theory of a computation specifies *what* is computed, without regard for *how* it is computed. Although in principle one could describe very complex computations carried out by the mind as a whole, in practice this is unmanageable. Thus, the mind is usually analyzed into a set of more-or-less independent *modules*, and then the computations carried out by these components are described. For example, returning to the automated bank teller analogy, we might describe two of its modules—a "bookkeeping" module that adds or subtracts money from an account, and an input/output module that accepts typed input and displays the appropriate messages on a screen. Modules themselves may have a complex internal structure. For example, the input/output module of a cash machine includes computations that determine what message should be displayed as well as computations that actually generate the display.

A good example of a theory of a computation in psychology is Ullman's (1979) theory of how shape is derived from motion, which specifies: 1) the purpose of the computation (to derive shape by observing changes on a surface as an object moves); 2) the input necessary for the computation to operate (at least three views of four noncoplanar points on a surface), with background assumptions about the input that must be met in order for the computation to operate correctly (the object giving rise to the input is rigid); and 3) the rules that characterize what is actually computed (expressed mathematically). The background assumption is critical because it limits the effectiveness of the computation; these limitations are empirically testable. Background assumptions need not be an actual part of the computation; they merely spell out limitations on the range of situations in which the computation will operate correctly.

Other examples of theories of computations can be found in the field of linguistics, particularly in the work of Chomsky (1965). Chomsky delineates a set of rules, a "grammar," that specifies what an idealized person learns about the structure of a language; namely, the rules that characterize well-formed strings. Again, the theory specifies the purpose of the computation (to derive the syntactic rules of a language), the information necessary (a string of words classified into "form classes," such as nouns, verbs, determiners and so on), and the rules characterizing what is actually computed (the grammar). And again, there are background assumptions about the nature of the input (it must be utterances from a natural human language); Chomsky assumes that the computation is innately determined and can only recover the structure from a restricted class of inputs (we can draw an analogy here to Ullman's "rigidity assumption"). The theory does not specify *how* descriptions of syntactic rules are produced, only *what* is done (in specific circumstances) by a processing module that produces them.

Chomsky defines an independent syntax module, which is concerned only with the formal rules that dictate which form classes (taken as givens) can be combined in which ways. "Semantics," the assignment of meanings to words and combinations of words, is presumed to be carried out by another module or modules.

Similarly, in vision, Marr (1982) defines modules that derive information about depth from stereo images produced by two eyes, other modules that match descriptions of shapes to descriptions stored in memory, and so on. In cognition, Tversky (1977) offers a theory of the computations that determine perceived similarity, and Shepard (1981) presents a theory of the computations involved in visual transformations.

Theories of a computation have three characteristics in common, and they vary with respect to three other characteristics. Let us begin with what they share. First, theories of a computation specify the purpose of a computation, what information it uses as input (plus any assumptions about the information that must be met for the computation to operate, such as Ullman's (1979) rigidity assumption), and a description of what is actually computed.

Second, the theory describes the operation of a module that is part of an information-processing system; it is *not* simply a description of systematic regularities in data. This distinction, between describing a computation and describing data, is sometimes a subtle one. For example, Stevens's (1975) "Power law" describes systematic regularities between the actual magnitude of a stimulus (measured in physical units, like inches and decibels) and reported magnitude of sensation (usually measured by ratings of subjective magnitude, but also by rate of responding in animals that have been appropriately conditioned). This formulation is not a theory of a computation; it does not include a specification of the purpose of the module in the context of a processing system. In contrast, Luce, Green and Weber (1976) offer a formula that describes the operation of "attention bands" moving in the auditory processing system. This is part of a theory of a computation. One hallmark of a theory of a computation is that one can usually describe, roughly, in English what the computation is supposed to do. And, not unrelated, if one has a theory of a computation it should be possible, at least in principle, to specify an algorithm to carry out the computation (as will be discussed shortly).

Some theories in mathematical psychology are theories of computations (especially in the literature on learning, e.g., the stimulus sampling theory of Estes, 1959), but many are not (such as Wickelgren's (1973) description of memory decay functions). Similarly, some theories of "competence" in linguistics are theories of a set of computations and some are descriptions of regularities in the data.

Third, theories of a computation need not provide information about the intermediate states produced when the computation is actually carried out by the brain. A theory of a computation posits *what* a computation does, not *how* it is accomplished (this is the job of the algorithm, which will be discussed shortly).

Now, consider the three ways in which theories of a computation can differ. First, the terms used in the theory may be taken more or less seriously as reflecting something actually represented in the head. For example, Chomsky (1965) sometimes seems to imply that the rules of grammar are actually stored as such (as opposed to merely describing the computation carried out by other things in the head). In contrast, the formulas used to express the theory of what is computed to derive structure from motion are not meant to be taken as actual representations in the mind, they merely characterize its operation.

Second, theories of a computation—as is true of theories in general—vary in their degree of *idealization*. They often specify a simplified computation, as would be appropriate in the absence of limiting factors that arise when the operation is actually performed. For example, Chomsky's (1965) theory of grammar excluded the operation of such "performance" factors as a limited memory span, burps, talking with one's mouth full, and the like.

Third, theories of a computation differ in terms of the importance of various a priori constraints. Marr (1982) emphasizes the importance of a well-defined purpose for the computation and a clear specification of what information is to be used to reach that end, pointing out that these constraints sometimes can be satisfied by only a single kind of computation. For example, knowing that the purpose of the bookkeeping module is to keep track of the total deposit, to come out with the same sum regardless of the order in which the amounts are entered, to subtract amounts and so on, the purpose can only be accomplished by a computation that performs arithmetic. Marr argues that something like this is also true in low-level vision, where the constraints imposed by the structure of the world itself feed directly into information processing. For example, the fact that the intensity of reflected light tends to change most rapidly at edges makes such intensity changes a useful cue for detecting edges. In order to use this cue, then, the visual system must perform a computation that discovers contiguous points where intensity changes rapidly (see Marr, 1982).

However, after even a few steps beyond the earliest stages of perceptual processing, the situation becomes much less well defined, in part because we must discover the basic abilities in need of explanation. For example, with the development of new methodologies for studying "mental rotation," our picture of the nature of mental imagery was enriched enormously (for reviews, see Kosslyn, 1980; Shepard & Cooper, 1982). Even for abilities we can describe, such as our ability to classify objects, we often cannot easily identify the input to the computation (which is information represented internally, not some easily observed property of the world), and we often cannot be certain about the output of the computation (e.g., does object classification conclude with a single name? with a description of classes and their interrelations? with activation and inhibition within a network of concepts?). Hence, for most theories of mental events, the available constraints do not shed much light on what must be computed. This is one reason why empirical studies of mental events are so important at this stage in the development of theories of mental representation.

The Functional Architecture The theory of a computation is essentially a theory of *what* a "black box" accomplishes, whereas the theory of the functional architecture puts constraints on *how* the processing is actually performed. The theory of the functional architecture tells us what structures and processes are available in the "box" for performing the computation. For example, for the bookkeeping module in our automated bank teller analogy, the functional architecture would specify how digits can be represented (e.g., in either decimal, binary, or log notation) and the processors available (e.g., a separate one for addition and for subtraction, or one that can perform both operations). For any theory of a computation, there are many different theories of the functional architecture that are compatible with it, and vice versa. Thus, the question as to what is the functional architecture of the mind is an empirical one.

A theory of a computation is often a theory of what is computed by a specific processor working on a specific representation, but not always. A given computation might be carried out by numerous processors (this is probably true of how we derive syntactic structures) or by any one of several available processors (as could occur if either binary or decimal notation were used to represent digits, with the choice depending on what subsequent computations were going to take place). Furthermore, the same processor could be used in carrying out numerous different computations (as might occur if multiplication were accomplished by adding the exponents of logs).

In describing the functional architecture, we will draw heavily on concepts from computer science. However, the *possible* functional architectures of the mind are more diverse than those found in von Neumann computers. In principle, any functional architecture can be simulated on a von Neumann computer. However, because it is very awkward to do so for many designs, only a limited number of different architectures are actually implemented on these machines. (As a personal aside, I have been impressed at how insidiously the machine design, particularly the idea that data simply "wait" inertly to be processed, has unjustifiably influenced my own thinking about the mind.)

All theories of the functional architecture make claims about the nature of the *structures* and *processes* used in the storage and manipulation of information. Structures are concerned with the storage of information, and it is often useful to distinguish between two kinds. A *medium* is a structure that conveys no information in its own right, but rather is a "place" where information is embedded. A *representation* is a structure that actually carries information. For example, in vision the shape of a surface (as seen from a particular point of view) could be represented by filling in points in a matrix; the matrix would be a medium, whereas the pattern of points would be the representation. The functional architecture includes different kinds of media. To return to our automated bank teller analogy, the machine might have a buffer for storing the symbols to be displayed on the screen, and another to hold information about what button had just been pressed, and another for storing the code numbers, and so on. These buffers are media for the storage of the representations. In the human mind, there is evidence that there are special structures for short-term visual memory and short-term verbal memory, as well as a long-term memory structure that stores descriptions (e.g., see Kosslyn, 1980; Posner, 1978).

Properties of the available media place constraints on information processing in two ways: First, they may limit how much information can be stored at once. Second, the kinds of representations that exist are to some degree dependent on the kinds of media; for example, if there were no array to put them in, patterns of points could not be used to depict information in a computer.

Representations can vary in their *format, content*, and *organization*. The format is the qualitative type of code, whereas the content is the specific information conveyed. Any given content can be represented using multiple formats, just as the information in this sentence could be conveyed by whistling Morse code or speaking English words. In addition, the individual units in a format can be organized in different ways (as will be discussed shortly). Much of the research on the functional architecture focuses on the nature of the format of different sorts of representations. For example, the long-standing controversy about mental imagery concerns the format of the representations that underlie the conscious experience of "seeing with the mind's eye," not the nature of the visual content stored in memory or the fact that people have such experiences (see Chapter 2 of Kosslyn, 1980). Thus, it is important to specify the nature of a given format clearly if we are to draw inferences about format from empirical findings.

The format of a representation is defined by a *syntax* and a *semantics*. The syntax is determined by the "primitive" symbols and the rules governing how they can be combined. A primitive symbol is one that cannot be further decomposed into other symbols in that symbol system. For example, in written English "a" is a primitive symbol, whereas "as" is not. Symbols usually belong to specific "form classes," and the rules of combination for a system are defined in terms of form classes. For example, words are nouns, verbs, determiners, and so on, and the rules of grammar are defined over these classes (which allows the rules to generalize over an open-ended number of specific words). The semantics is determined by how the symbols and their combinations convey meaning. For example, a sentence in English could be used by a CIA agent to carry an entirely different meaning if unusual rules were used to interpret it (e.g., substituting the opposite meanings for verbs). The rules of semantics pair a representation with a specific meaning, and two representations can be identical syntactically but be in different formats if the semantics is different. For example, the symbol "A" is in one format if taken to be an indefinite article, and another if taken to be a depiction of the flight pattern of a flock of geese.

To return again to our automated bank teller analogy, suppose that the Model Mark V will identify you by your thumbprint. You press against a plate and it encodes the pattern and compares it to your pattern stored in its memory. We have several different options of format, that is, how to represent your thumbprint in the machine's memory (or in human memory, for that matter). To get a better feel for the idea of format, let us consider the two most widely studied examples: propositional representations and depictions.

A *propositional representation* is a description, usually written using a notation like ON (BALL, BOX) for "A ball is on a box," or ABOVE(ARC1, ARC2) for the relation between two different types of arcs in a thumbprint. (This sort of notation makes it clear that the representation is not English, and is also close to both the logical formalisms originally developed to express propositions and the way such propositions can easily be represented in a computer.) Note that a "propositional representation" is equivalent to a *sentence* in logic; philosophers use the term "proposition" to refer to the idea itself, not to an expression of the idea in some language. Psychologists use the terms "proposition" and "propositional representation" interchangeably, and both refer to a representation with a particular format.

A propositional format can be defined as follows:

1 The syntax:

a. A number of types of symbols can occur, standing for relations (e.g., the marks "ON," "EATS"), a predicate or predicates (things about which the assertion is made) such as symbols for objects (e.g., ball, box) and properties (e.g., red, old), and logical conditions (e.g., if, all, not, and so on).

b. The rules of formation state that all representations must have at least one relation, and specific relations require specific numbers and types of *arguments* (symbols to which the relation applies). For example, ON(BALL) is an unacceptable fragment because ON requires two arguments.

2 The semantics:

a. The representation is defined to be unambiguous, unlike English or some other natural language. A different symbol, for instance, would be used to represent "ball" if it referred to a dance instead of a spherical toy.

b. The representation is abstract, in two senses of the word:
i. It can refer to classes (such as balls in general), not just individual instances.
ii. It is amodal, being a representation of input from the eyes, from a linguistic description, a tactile exploration, and so on.

c. In some theories, propositional representations are posited to be true or false (e.g., Anderson & Bower, 1973). However, this often depends on more than the meaning of the representation: it also depends on the existence of a specific state of affairs in the world. Thus, it is not clear if this should be treated as a property of the representation itself.

Another widely studied format of mental representation is the *depiction*, which could be approximated by a line drawing of a ball on a box or a template-like pattern of a thumbprint in a matrix in the automated bank teller. A mental depictive representation is very different from a propositional representation, not clearly sharing any of the foregoing properties. There is no symbol standing for the relation ("on" is implicit in the spatial arrangement of the ball and the box, there is no independent representation of "on" per se). The rules of formation are not defined over classes of symbols (any symbol can be placed in any spatial relation with another). And, the semantics is defined in terms of resemblance; unlike propositional representations, continuous variations in the size, orientation, and shape of the representation carry meaning for a depiction. This kind of semantics results in depictions often being ambiguous (the ball on the box could be an abstract bust of Beethoven), and in their not being abstract in either sense: a class cannot be depicted directly and depictions are inherently visual (not amodal).

One could argue that a depiction *can* be interpreted as representing a class, as when a picture of a tree is used to stand for "woods" on a map. However, this use of depictions involves a semantics that treats the picture as a propositional symbol (continuous variations, for instance, no longer carry meaning). Although the pairing of symbol and meaning is not arbitrary, the meaning itself is established by convention (the tree could have labeled a park, lumberyard, or juice stand; see Schwartz, 1981; Kolers and Smythe, 1979). Thus, although we recognize the symbol, it is not playing a role as a depiction; in such cases it is like a written word, requiring additional interpretation.

The syntax of depictions is simple:

1 The symbols are in one basic class—points—which can be so "dense" as to be continuous or so "differentiated" as to appear as distinct entities (such as the bulbs on the Times Square billboard; see Goodman, 1968, for a discussion of dense and differentiated symbol systems).

2 The rules of combination require only that points be placed in spatial juxtaposition. However, this notion of spatial juxtaposition requires that points be placed in a medium that functions as a coordinate space; it need not be an actual, physical space. For example, in a computer, an array is defined by the way the central processing unit (CPU) retrieves individual locations in memory (tin cans, in our previous analogy). The computer "pretends" that one location is at the upper left cell of an array, another is immediately to its right, and so on. By accessing the locations in the right way, the CPU organizes a functional space. An important part of this idea is that "empty space" is explicitly included in the representation. The syntax of the representation as a whole includes not only points, but the empty space between the points contributed by the medium.

The semantics of depiction can be characterized in terms of an "abstract isomorphism" between the parts of the depiction and the object being depicted. That is, each part of the depiction must correspond to a visible part of the object such that the distance among the points on the object are preserved by the corresponding "distances" (including empty locations) among their representations. (Depictions usually represent objects seen from a particular point of view; hence the relevant distances between points on the object are distances in the planar projection. However, statues are three-dimensional depictions, and such a shape can be depicted using a three dimensional array in a computer.) The reason this isomorphism is abstract is because it is defined at the functional level. A pattern in a computer's array can be a depiction, then, because the points in the array and empty cells correspond to points on an object and space between the points, and the functional distances between the points (corresponding to the number of intervening "cells" in the computer's array) preserve the actual distances between the points on the object. Thus, depictions convey meaning by resemblance, and variations in the distribution of the symbols in the medium carry meaning.

To summarize, a format defines a set of symbols and rules for making sense of them. A given format can be used to convey a wide range of information, but any given format will be better suited for conveying some kinds of information than others. For example, depictions are easier to use than propositions to store information about subtle variations in shape, but *vice versa* for information about ownership or monetary value.

In addition to media, then, the functional architecture provides the capacity to use different types of representations. A *representation type* is defined by a specification of a particular format, organization, and kind of permissible content. For example, Anderson and Bower (1973) claimed that all information is stored in memory using hierarchies of propositions. The format is propositional, and the organization is hierarchical (as opposed to heterarchies, general graphs, one-dimensional lists, etc.). Furthermore, they specified that each representation had to include two types of content—a fact and the context in which the fact applied (for example, its location, time, or associated event). Another example would be the "2½-D Sketch" Marr & Nishihara (1978) used to represent visible surfaces in visual processing. The 2½-D Sketch is an array with each cell indicating the orientation and depth of a segment of a surface. The format here is depictive; the organization corresponds to the organization of the objects in space; and the content is information about the location, orientation, and relative distances of segments of visible surfaces.

Different representation types make different information more explicit, make two pieces of information more or less confusable, and have a number of other characteristics (see, e.g., Marr, 1982; Palmer, 1978). The different characteristics of representations make them more or less appropriate for carrying out specific computations. For example, in our bookkeeping module, we would not use Roman numeral representations if multiplication were required, because such representations do not easily decompose into multiples of a base number, unlike decimal or binary representations. Marr (1982) goes so far as to suggest that the specification of what is computed (for a specific purpose, given specific input) will almost require use of a specific representation when the computation is carried out. Much of the study of mental representation is concerned with discovering the representation types that can be used in mental processing (Anderson, 1978, 1983; Anderson & Bower, 1973, Kosslyn, 1980; Palmer, 1978; Pylyshyn, 1980, 1981).

Although the functional architecture can be described at an abstract level in terms of the kinds of media and representation types the processing system can use, in practice there are of course no content-free representations. That is, mental representations are always representations of some particular information; a representation in Anderson and Bower's (1973) model conveys information about facts and events, such as "The hippy touched the debutante in the park," and Marr and Nishihara's (1978) "2½-D Sketch" is of a particular surface seen from a particular point of view. These representation *tokens* (particular instances of the type) are what is actually stored and used. In studying the functional architecture, the task is to abstract from the individual cases to the general type, in order to discover the structure of the mind.

The functional architecture also includes different types of processes. In order for computations to be performed, stored data must be able to be accessed, compared, and modified. Processes operating on structures are the *means* by which computations are actually carried out. Any given computation is carried out by use of one or more processes. It is often implicitly assumed that these processes are stored as instructions to a processor (or processors), just as in a von Neumann computer. However, the process need not be stored separately from the representation, but rather may be something the representation itself does: The fading of invisible ink shortly after it is written is like this; there is no separate "erasure processor," the ink just fades. This last possibility is decidedly non-von Neumann, given that there would be nothing akin to a CPU or separate processor. Empirical research on mental representation will tell us which sorts of processes are used in which functional modules in the brain (and it would not be surprising if more than one type of process is used, with different types performing different kinds of computations).[2]

Processes also differ with respect to their degree of *articulation* and *scope*. With regard to articulation, processes can be described at a very simple, molecular level or at a more complex, macro level. For example, Newell and Simon (1972) discuss very simple "elementary information processes," which are akin to a computer's basic machine operations, whereas Anderson and Bower (1973) and Kosslyn (1980) discuss more complex processes, somewhat akin to subroutines in a large computer program.

In von Neumann computers, more articulated processes are built up by concatenating the primitive machine operations. There is no reason why this need be the way the brain does it, however; a very articulated process may or may not be divisible into more simple processes.

With regard to scope, some processes may be very local, operating only in very specific situations, whereas others may be more global, operating on complex input from numerous sources. One functional architecture that posits only local processes is Newell and Simon's (1972) *production system*, in which "IF/THEN" conditional statements are stored in long-term memory. When the condition (the statement immediately following the IF) is present in a limited-capacity short-term storage medium, the instructions following the THEN are executed (see the chapters in this volume by Anderson and by Glass for examples of production systems). In this architecture, the sequence of activity is determined by the conditions and actions of each production, not by any overriding global process.

In contrast, in the usual functional architecture of a computer, some processing may be quite global. For example, an *executive* process might orchestrate the operation of other processes being

[2]For processes like those that occur in a von Neumann computer, it is useful to distinguish between the *data-access* processes that confer structure on stored data and the *data-use* processes that compare and transform representations. Recall that in the computer the same data could be organized into an array or a list—with the items in any desired order—all depending on how the CPU accesses the data. Similarly, if there are structures having different organizations in the brain (and there surely must be such structures; e.g., see Lindsay & Norman, 1977), then there may be data-access processes that impose the structure. By analogy, these processes are like a doorman at the entrance to a room full of objects. You can only get the objects by asking him, and he acts as if the objects were arranged into a list; for example, he looks for the objects in order, always starting from the top of the list. No matter what you want to do with the object after you get it, overall performance of the task (e.g., time to classify the object) will be marked by the way the doorman treats the contents of the room (e.g., more time will be taken for items further down the list before any other processing can commence). The operation of the doorman imposes a functional structure on the data. Assumptions about these sorts of processes are implicit in claims about the structural properties of representation types (when processing is of the von Neumann type; when it is not, the distinction between the two sorts of processing may not exist).

used to accomplish a particular task. Or, in a different kind of system, a search process might access all of memory in parallel, comparing an input with stored data (something like a holographic memory system; cf. Hinton and Anderson, 1981).

Finally, in most theories of the functional architecture of the brain, there are some assumptions about organization among processes. For example, there may be requirements that one process must use the output from certain others, or two processes may have to work together. In our automated bank teller analogy, the process that displays a string of characters must wait for other processes to determine what should be displayed. In a psychological theory, Kosslyn (1980) claims that an inspection process must be used whenever an image is rotated, with this inspection process being used to tell when the image has rotated far enough. Such organization can be conferred by rules that are embodied in an executive or as input/output characteristics of specific local processes.

A major difficulty in discovering the functional architecture of the mind, over and above the difficulties of discovering representation and process types from observing particular tokens, is the possibility of "structure/process tradeoffs" (see Anderson, 1978; Hayes-Roth, 1979; Pylyshyn, 1979). That is, by adjusting the theory of the process, the theory of the structure can be varied and yet still provide accounts for the data. For example, consider a propositional and depictive theory of "mental rotation." Shepard and Cooper (1982) describe numerous experiments showing that the time to "rotate" an image increases with the amount of rotation performed. Kosslyn (1980) explains these findings by positing that images are represented as depictions in a functional array, and the points are shifted through the medium (there is a detailed theory of why they must be shifted incrementally, but that does not concern us here). In contrast, Anderson (1978) explains these findings by positing that images are represented as propositional descriptions of shapes, with descriptions of the angles connecting the shapes together (e.g., the way various lines and arcs are connected to form a letter). When the image is rotated, the angles are updated a little at a time. Thus, in the depictive theory, the point-shift process will take more time when points must be shifted farther through the medium, whereas in the propositional theory, the angle update process will take more time when more small updates must be made (see also Palmer, 1978). Differences in the theories of processing compensate for differences in the theories of representation.

This sort of structure/process tradeoff is easy to do if one is only trying to explain data from one task. However, when a given structure or process is supposed to be used in numerous different tasks, this kind of facile adjustment is more difficult to accomplish, especially if a premium is placed on keeping the number of putative structures and processes to a minimum (cf., Hayes-Roth, 1979; Pylyshyn, 1979).

The Algorithm The most particular level of analysis of information-processing in the brain specifies how individual tasks are carried out. An *algorithm* is a set of steps that are defined so precisely that they can be carried out automatically, without the use of human understanding or intuition (say, by a computer). In addition, provided the correct input is used, an algorithm is guaranteed to produce a specific output. Although algorithms are often contrasted with *heuristics*, which are steps that are not guaranteed to produce the result (being more like "rules of thumb"), we will not make this distinction here. The important point is that an algorithm defines an explicit procedure, a set of steps that describe a sequence of processing. For example, a flow chart specifying the steps our automated bank teller goes through when looking up an account number describes an algorithm. Algorithms carry out computations, and they do so within the confines of the functional architecture.

It is useful to distinguish between algorithms that merely describe processing and those that are actually followed in a process. In the first case, the system is *rule-described*, in the second it is *rule-following*. For example, the motions of the planets are *described* by Kepler's laws, but the planets do not consult those laws before deciding on their next move, whereas the wise amateur cook *follows* the rules laid down by a recipe. In rule-described algorithms, the output from one process may evoke another process, and its output may evoke yet another process, and so on, like dominoes falling. Alternatively, the algorithm may describe the steps taken by a single, very articulated process. In all rule-described algorithms, the algorithm describes what is being accomplished by processing, but the algorithm is not actually stored and consulted. For example, light striking the retina initiates a sequence of processing whereby figures are segregated from each other and the background. This sequence of processing, or individual portions of it, can be described in terms of an algorithm—even though the algorithm itself is not stored and followed as such.

Unlike processing that is merely described by an algorithm, rule-following processing actually is governed by a rule that is represented as such (as a representation token, as would occur if you memorized a recipe and used it from memory while cooking). For problem solving and the like, these rules specify the steps one must go through mentally to perform a specific computation or set of computations. In fact, some of the research on specific task performance, such as that on expert chess players (Chase & Simon, 1973), is aimed in part at understanding what rules are used to guide processing.

In general, however, when studying mental events the point of trying to formulate algorithms is *not* to understand how people perform given tasks. There are simply too many tasks that humans can perform, and too many ways we can perform them, to study each task in its own right. Rather, the usual goal is to induce general properties of the system, namely, (1) the availability of specific types of structures and processes, and (2) general principles of how algorithms are composed. The principles of composition presumably reflect in part the inherent constraints on combining processes (e.g., needing to use an inspection process to monitor a mental rotation operation) and the inherent limitations and predilections of the system (due to such properties of the functional architecture as the capacity limitations of various media).

In summary, theories of the computation specify what is computed from what input, for what purposes, and under what circumstances the computation will be successful. Theories of the functional architecture specify a "library" of media, representation types, and process types (which may embody rules of how processes can or must be combined). Theories of the algorithm specify the steps whereby a given computation is actually carried out in real time. It is important to note that for every theory of a computation, numerous theories of the functional architecture could be used to explain actual processing. For example, the bookkeeping module could represent digits in numerous ways and process these representations in numerous ways. Furthermore, given a theory of the functional architecture, numerous different algorithms are possible within its confines (varying, for example, in the order in which specific operations are performed).

Although the different levels of theorizing about the brain's functioning are to some degree independent, they do put constraints on one another. The functional architecture must include structures and processes that can be used by an algorithm that can both *perform* the necessary computations, and *account* for the empirical data (processing times, amount and types of errors, and so on). In addition, the problem that a computation must solve is determined in part by the functional architecture. For example, if the functional architecture provides a "mental rotation" process, representations of perceived shapes can be "rotated" to some standard orientation (e.g., upright) before one attempts to recognize them. If no such process is possible, there is a problem of how to represent perceived shapes so that they are in a "standard form" that can be easily compared to representations stored in memory. The point is that the requirements on a computation or set of computations (e.g., for "recognizing" shapes) depend in part on the resources provided by the functional architecture.

Neurophysiological Explanations

One conceivably could pose answers to questions about how information is stored and used in terms of brain activity per se. In fact, many physiological psychologists have as their goal this very reduction. However, a description of how function is embodied in neurophysiology will not supplant a functional description; we will always want to know what a given part or parts of the brain actually *do*, and that is what a theory cast at the functional level of analysis tells us. For example, even if we had a complete neuroanatomical map of the cerebellum, we would not feel that we understood that anatomical structure until we knew what the various circuits do. By analogy, if we want to know why a square peg will not fit in a round hole, we do not want an answer in terms of subatomic particles. Such an explanation would confuse what Putnam (1973) calls the "parent of the explanation" with the explanation. We are asking about pegs and holes, and we want our answer to specify the relevant properties of pegs and holes—such as their shape and rigidity. Similarly, although the functional properties of the brain clearly depend on the workings of its neurophysiology, a description of brain cells and their operation is the parent of the explanation for present purposes—we want to know what that "wet-ware" does in terms of storing and processing information.

The study of neurophysiology produces three kinds of data that bear on theories of mental representation: First, basic facts about brain operation itself. The brain must be able to carry out the processing posited by the theory of information processing. For example, if it turns out that the brain is essentially a parallel-processing device, and is used only awkwardly to perform serial processing, then theories of mental representation that posit only serial processing are rendered implausible (see Ballard, Hinton, & Sejnowski, in press; Feldman & Ballard, 1983).

Second, data produced by behavioral changes following brain damage also bear on theories of mental representation. Specific deficits implicate specific structures and processes in the functional architecture. In these cases only part of an ability may be disrupted, and the disruption may point to loss of some structure or process used by particular algorithms. For example, Bisiach and Luzzatti (1978) found patients who had damage to their right parietal lobes who ignored only the left half of their mental images. The subjects were not blind on the left side; they simply ignored what was there. If they had been blind, that would have suggested that the functional spatial medium was damaged, so the left half could not store depictive representations; but the actual findings suggested that the "inspection" process that interprets patterns was defective, only operating over half the medium.

A third kind of relevant data comes from studies of patterns of activation in normal brains while subjects are performing specific tasks. Evoked potentials, EEG, PET (positron emission tomography), Xenon–133 regional cerebral bloodflow, NMR (nuclear magnetic resonance) and similar techniques can be used to chart actual activity in the working brain. Theories of the functional architecture and algorithms should specify when various structures and processes are used in various tasks, and tasks that putatively recruit many of the same features of the architecture should result in more similar patterns of activity (all else being equal) than tasks that putatively share few features of the architecture.

CONCLUSIONS

The study of mental representation begins by treating the brain as a kind of information-processing system. The system is conceptualized as carrying out various computations, and "mental activity" is the processing of stored representations. A computational analysis can be cast at three levels of abstraction, namely: specification of the computation (what is its purpose, its input, what is actually computed, and the assumptions that must be met for it to operate successfully), the functional architecture (the varieties of available media, representation types, and process types), and the algorithm (the steps taken to perform the computation). All three levels must be studied at once; without a theory of the computation, one will not have good reasons for positing particular processing components; without a theory of the functional architecture, one will have difficulty in defining the problem that must be solved by a computation, and will have few constraints on the basic machinery used by the algorithms; and without a theory of at least some algorithms, one will be unable to test the other levels of theorizing—for it is the algorithms that actually produce the observable behaviors. Furthermore, theories of brain function must be consistent with the observed facts about the brain itself.

To date, theorizing about mental representation has been aided enormously by our understanding of modern digital computers. However, the von Neuman design of such machines is almost certainly not like that of our brains, and there is danger in pressing the analogy too far. In fact, although the vocabulary of information processing borrowed from computers has proven useful, it may also be misleading. For example, many of the brain's processes may be inherent characteristics of the representations themselves, in the way that invisible ink fades of its own accord. Furthermore, much mental processing may rely on parallel computations (see Hinton & Anderson, 1981), which are only awkwardly conceptualized by analogy to standard computer processing. The important point is that theories of mental representation analyze how the brain functions to perform mental activity, and the ultimate vocabulary for discussing said functioning should be appropriate for the brain, not an arbitrary piece of hardware. However, it is clear that scientific theories of mental representation can be formulated, and this chapter has presented what I take to be the conventional view of how such theorizing is proceeding.

REFERENCES

Anderson, J. R. *Language, memory, and thought.* Hillsdale, N.J.: Lawrence Erlbaum Associates, 1976.

Anderson, J. R. Arguments concerning representations for mental imagery. *Psychological Review,* 1978, *85,* 249–77.

Anderson, J. R. Further arguments concerning representations for mental imagery: A response to Hayes-Roth and Pylyshyn. *Psychological Review,* 1979, *86,* 395–406.

Anderson, J. R. *The Architecture of Cognition.* Cambridge, Mass.: Harvard University Press, 1983.

Anderson, J. R., & Bower, G. H. *Human associative memory.* New York: V. H. Winston, 1973.

Ballard, D. H., Hinton, G. E., & Sejnowski, T. J. Parallel visual computation. *Nature,* in press.

Bisiach, E., & Luzzatti, C. Unilateral neglect of representational space. *Cortex,* 1978, *14,* 129–33.

Block, N. (Ed.), *Readings in the philosophy of psychology. Vol 2.* Cambridge, Mass.: Harvard University Press, 1981.

Chase, W. G., & Simon, H. A. The mind's eye in chess. In W. G. Chase (Ed.), *Visual information processing.* New York: Academic Press, 1973.

Chomsky, N. *Syntactic structures.* The Hague: Mouton, 1957.

Chomsky, N. Review of *Verbal behavior* by B. F. Skinner. *Language,* 1959, *35,* 26–58.

Chomsky, N. *Aspects of the theory of syntax.* Cambridge, Mass.: MIT Press, 1965.

Chomsky, N. Rules and representations. *Behavioral and Brain Sciences,* 1980, *3,* 1–62.

Dennett, D. C. *Brainstorms.* Montgomery, Vt.: Bradford Books, 1978.

Estes, W. K. The statistical approach to learning theory. In S. Koch (Ed.), *Psychology: A study of a science.* New York: McGraw-Hill, 1959.
Feldman, J. A. & Ballard, D. H. Four frames suffice. *Cognitive Science*, 1983, *9*, 205–254.
Fodor, J. A. *Psychological explanation: An introduction to the philosophy of psychology.* New York: Random House, 1968.
Fodor, J. A. *The language of thought.* New York: Crowell, 1975.
Fodor, J. A. Methodological solipsism considered as a research strategy in cognitive psychology. *Behavioral and Brain Sciences*, 1980, *3*, 63–110.
Goodman, N. *Languages of art: An approach to a theory of symbols.* Indianapolis, Ind.: Bobbs-Merrill, 1968.
Grice, H. P. Utterer's meaning, sentence-meaning, and word-meaning. *Foundations of Language*, 1968, *4*, 225–42.
Hayes-Roth, F. Distinguishing theories of representation: A critique of Anderson's "Arguments concerning mental imagery." *Psychological Review*, 1979, *86*, 376–82.
Hinton, G. E., & Anderson, J. A. (Eds.). *Parallel models of associative memory.* Hillsdale, N.J.: Lawrence Erlbaum Associates, 1981.
Kolers, P. A., & Smythe, W. E. Images, symbols, and skills. *Canadian Journal of Psychology*, 1979, *33*, 158–184.
Kosslyn, S. M. *Image and mind.* Cambridge, Mass.: Harvard University Press, 1980.
Lindsay, P., & Norman, D. A. *Human information processing: An introduction.* New York: Academic Press, 1977.
Luce, R. D., Green, D. M., & Weber, D. L. Attention bands in absolute identification. *Perception & Psychophysics*, 1976, *20*, 49–54.
Marr, D. *Vision.* San Francisco: W. H. Freeman, 1982.
Marr, D., & Nishihara, H. K. Visual information processing: Artificial intelligence and the sensorium of sight. *Technology Review*, 1978, *81*, 2–23.
McCloskey, M. Intuitive physics. *Scientific American*, 1983, *248*, 122–30.
McDermott, D. V. Artificial intelligence meets natural stupidity. In J. Haugeland (Ed.), *Mind design.* Cambridge, Mass.: MIT Press, 1981.
Newell, A., & Simon, H. A. *Human problem solving.* Englewood Cliffs, N.J.: Prentice-Hall, 1972.
Palmer, S. E. Fundamental aspects of cognitive representation. In E. Rosch & B. B. Lloyd (Eds.), *Cognition and categorization.* Hillsdale, N.J.: Lawrence Erlbaum Associates, 1978.
Pinker, S. Mental imagery and the third dimension. *Journal of Experimental Psychology: General*, 1980, *109*, 354–71.
Posner, M. I. *Chronometric explorations of mind.* Hillsdale, N.J.: Lawrence Erlbaum Associates, 1978.
Putnam, H. Minds and machines. In S. Hook (Ed.), *Dimensions of mind.* New York: New York University Press, 1960.
Putnam, H. Reductionism and the nature of psychology. *Cognition*, 1973, *2*, 131–41.
Pylyshyn, Z. W. Validating computational models: A critique of Anderson's indeterminancy of representation claim. *Psychological Review*, 1979, *86*, 383–94.

Pylyshyn, Z. W. Computation and cognition: Issues in the foundations of cognitive science. *Behavioral and Brain Sciences*, 1980, *3*, 111–33.

Pylyshyn, Z. W. The imagery debate: Analogue media versus tacit knowledge. *Psychological Review*, 1981, *88*, 16–45.

Schwartz, R. Imagery—there's more to it than meets the eye. In N. Block (Ed.), *Imagery*. Cambridge, Mass.: MIT Press, 1981.

Shepard, R. N. Psychophysical complementarity. In M. Kubovy & J. R. Pomerantz (Eds.), *Perceptual organization*. Hillsdale, N.J.: Lawrence Erlbaum Associates, 1981.

Shepard, R. N., & Cooper, L. A. *Mental images and their transformations*. Cambridge, Mass.: MIT Press, 1982.

Stevens, S. S. *Psychophysics: Introduction to its perceptual, neural, and social prospects*. New York: Wiley, 1975.

Tversky, A. Features of similarity. *Psychological Review*, 1977, *84*, 327–52.

Ullman, S. *The interpretation of visual motion*. Cambridge, Mass.: MIT Press, 1979.

Wickelgren, W. A. The long and short of memory. *Psychological Bulletin*, 1973, *80*, 425–38.

Winograd, T. *Understanding natural language*. New York: Academic Press, 1972.

Wittgenstein, L. *Philosophical investigations*. New York: Macmillan, 1953.

5

EFFECT OF MEMORY SET ON REACTION TIME

Arnold Lewis Glass
Rutgers University

In 1966 Saul Sternberg published a paper that was to have a wide impact on the emerging field of cognitive psychology. Sternberg asked his subjects to remember from one to six randomly selected digits. He then presented a single probe item and measured how long it took to respond as to whether or not the probe was in the memory set. As can be seen from the idealized graph in Figure 5-1, his results are defined by three parameters. First, reaction time (RT) increases linearly with the size of the memory set, a result obtained for both memory set items (targets) and items not in the memory set (distractors). Second, the slopes for targets and distractors are equal. Third, the intercept for distractors is greater than the intercept for targets. All three of these aspects of the results have since been replicated many times. However, Sternberg's initial exposition did not report the intercept difference, and subsequent research was devoted almost exclusively to explaining the first two parts of the results. The intercept difference has been neglected by experimentalists and theorists alike.

The research reported here was supported by an NIH grant (HD 12278–02). The chapter was written while the author was a Visiting Scholar at Harvard University. The author is indebted to William Estes, whose stimulating discussion of the topic inspired the development of the model described herein, and to Joel Angiolillo-Bent and Gregg Ashby, whose suggestions and emendations are reflected throughout the report.

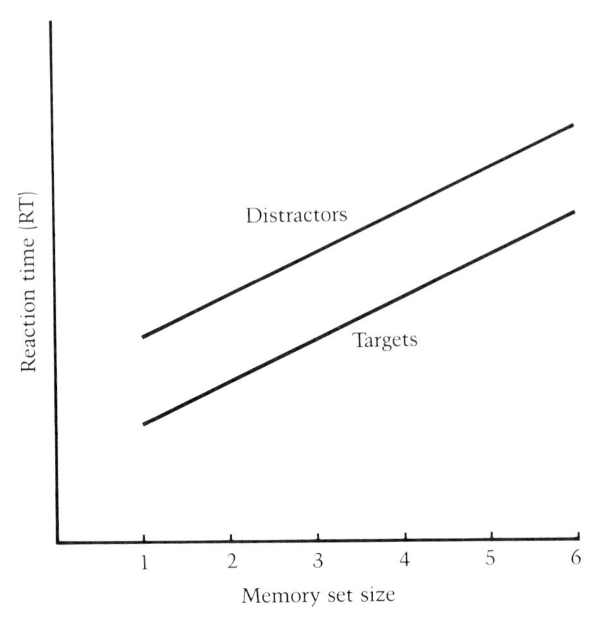

FIGURE 5–1 Reaction time to determine whether a probe is a target or a distractor, as a function of the memory set size (varied set procedure).

Two straight, parallel lines is a deceptively simple-looking result, but no plausible explanation for them was immediately apparent. As Sternberg (1969a) later pointed out, a linear increase in RT as a function of memory set size is predicted by a serial comparison model. If a subject compares the probe to items in the memory set, then on the average, the time it takes to compare it to two items should be twice as long as the time to compare it to one item; the time to compare the probe to three items should be three times as long as the comparison time for one item; and so on. However, a serial comparison is not a plausible model of how such input is identified in human memory. If you were asked whether the letter string "dog" or "tangent" or "apogee" is a word, you surely would not serially compare it to each word in your memory to decide whether or not it is in the set of words. If you knew 50,000 words and took a millisecond to make each comparison (which is about as fast as a neuron can transmit information), it would take 50 seconds to compare such an input to every word in memory. Yet people can decide whether a string of letters is a word in less than a second. If you do not use a serial comparison strategy for memory sets greater than six items, but rather use some much faster method, there is little reason to believe that you would suddenly resort to this very slow decision-making process for small sets of six items or less.

Why then, are the graphs linear; and furthermore, why are they parallel? These questions fascinated experimental psychologists, many of whom contributed to the hundreds of studies of the task. This research effort led to several new findings, but contrary to early hopes, these newer results have not led directly to a convincing explanation of Sternberg's original findings. So an air of paradox remains over the area.

The purpose of this review is to present the findings that I think are most enlightening and to dispel some of the paradox that surrounds the task. After the basic findings are presented, a model will be introduced. The model consists of a set of assumptions, each of which can be incorporated into other information-processing models and each of which has independent empirical support. It will be shown that most of the results obtained in the memory set task can be accounted for within the framework provided by these assumptions. In some cases, the result will follow directly from the assumptions. In other cases, it will only be possible to show how the assumptions might account for the result, since research on this topic continues to this day and some critical investigations have not been performed. Nevertheless, the range of possibilities can be narrowed sufficiently to show that the explanation of the effects of a memory set fits within the framework of contemporary cognitive theory.

The final part of the paper will examine the impact of memory set research and its theoretical implications on general cognitive theory. Three issues will be discussed. First, empirical support from other tasks for the assumptions necessary to describe the effects of a memory set will be summarized. Second, some of the remaining questions will be raised. Finally, alternative approaches to explaining the task will be evaluated.

BASIC FINDINGS

In the memory set paradigm, a set of from one to six items (e.g., digits) has to be retained. Then a single item is presented and the subject must press one of two response keys to indicate whether or not the probe is a member of the memory set. Probes that are set members are called targets and probes that are nonmembers are called distractors. The following list summarizes the findings on reaction time (RT) that are usually obtained.

F1 There is a linear increase in RT with an increase in set size for both targets and distractors (Sternberg, 1975; Schneider & Shiffrin, 1977).

F2 The slope of the increase in RT with set size for distractors is equal to the slope for targets, that is, the lines are parallel (Sternberg, 1975).

F3 The slope of the RT function for set size is greater for distractors that are similar to at least one of the memory set items than for distractors that are dissimilar to the memory set (Wescourt & Atkinson, 1976).

F4 Subjects take the same time to reject distractors that are similar to one item in the memory set as those that are similar to every item in the memory set (Huesmann & Woocher, 1976).

F5 The immediate memory span for different kinds of items increases monotonically with the slope of their RT function (Cavanaugh, 1972).

F6 Concurrent task manipulations that use capacity increase the slope of the RT function (Forrin & Morin, 1969; Howard, 1975; Krueger, 1975; Sternberg, 1969b).

Some findings in the memory set task depend on whether the targets and distractors are drawn from the same pool of test items or from separate pools. In the fixed set procedure, the same memory set is tested over a series of trials, so the pool of targets and distractors is disjointed. For example, the targets might always be drawn from the set 0, 2, 4, 6, and 8 and the distractors from the set 1, 3, 5, 7, and 9. In the varied set procedure, targets and distractors are drawn from the same pool of test items and the target set is changed on every trial. For example, both targets and distractors might be drawn from the set 0, 1, 2, 3, 4, 5, 6, 7, 8, and 9, so that on one trial the memory set might be 5, 1, and 6, and the probe 6 might be a target. On another trial the memory set might be 5 and 8, and the probe 6 might be a distractor. As the following list indicates, some findings are obtained only when one procedure or the other is used.

F7 In the fixed set procedure, there are no serial position effects for items in the memory set (Sternberg, 1969b).

F8 With the fixed set procedure, the RT slope for memory set size decreases with practice (Schneider & Shiffrin, 1977).

F9 With the varied set procedure, the RT slope for memory set size does not change with practice (Kristofferson, 1972a).

F10 After extended practice with a fixed set procedure, introducing new distractors does not influence RT for either targets or distractors (Atkinson & Juola, 1974).

THE BASIC ASSUMPTIONS

These are the basic assumptions of the *limited-capacity parallel* model that I propose:

A1 Feature Assumption. A probe is first analyzed into a set of features. Features are serially extracted from the probe by a feature analyzer.

A2 Parallel Assumption. Each memory set item is represented in memory by a processor that compares it to the probe. Following common practice, this processor will be called a *logogen*. (Morton, 1969). As features are extracted from the probe, they are simultaneously sent to and processed by the logogens for each item in the memory set. Hence, in the parlance of the memory set experiment, the probe is compared to the memory set in parallel.

A3 Logogen Assumption. Each logogen contains a list of features, which it compares to features from the probe. Let F be the number of feature comparisons made, and let M be the number of matches found between logogen features and probe features. Some criterion number of features, C_1, is set so that if $M = C_1$, a match signal is emitted and a positive response is made. A second criterion, C_0, is also set so that if $F - M = C_0$, a no-match signal is emitted.

A4 Negative Criterion Assumption. When every logogen signals no match, a negative response is made.

A5 Limited Capacity Assumption. The time it takes the logogen of a memory set item to emit a signal is constrained by the equation

$$T = \frac{F}{Ca}$$

where F is the total number of features compared and Ca is the capacity available to logogen for feature comparison at a moment of time.

A6 Divided Capacity Assumption. Ca is determined by the equation

$$Ca = \frac{A}{N}$$

where A is the capacity available to all logogens and N is the number of logogens drawing on capacity, and that is, the number of items in memory set.

A7 Noise Assumption. The feature comparison process described by A3 sometimes results in mistakes. A logogen may fail to find a match for a probe feature that is on its list or may incorrectly match a probe feature that is not on the list.

DERIVATION OF FINDINGS FROM BASIC ASSUMPTIONS

Let us review assumptions A1 through A4 about the way in which a probe is compared to the items in the memory set. A probe is compared by a logogen to a memory set item until either C_1 features are found to match or C_0 features are found that do not match its feature list (Morton, 1969). During a test trial, the probe is simultaneously compared to logogens for all of the items in the memory set. As soon as a match signal is generated by any logogen, a positive response is made. However, if all of the logogens emit a no-match signal, a negative response is made. Thus, these four assumptions predict that RT will not increase with set size for targets, a prediction that violates F1.

So far it has been assumed that each logogen has an independent capacity for processing information, just as six battery-powered radios side by side are unaffected by each other's performance. However, it is also possible to imagine a situation in which the six radios are plugged into a common power source and thus have a common capacity. In this case, as more radios are plugged into the common capacity, the power available for each individual radio, and hence possibly the volume at which it will operate, will be reduced. Both Kahneman (1973) and Norman and Bobrow (1975) have suggested that the brain exhibits this kind of shared capacity between different mental processes, a situation that would sometimes restrict task performance. Applying this hypothesis to the memory set task, let us consider the validity of A5, that capacity is limited, and of A6, that capacity is divided.

One way to understand the role of A5, the Limited Capacity Assumption, in a process model is to suppose that features (from the feature analyzer) are arriving at the logogen faster than it can process them. Thus, the processing speed of the logogen is a limiting factor. The logogen takes a certain amount of time to compare each feature of the probe to the feature list, and the time it takes is determined by the capacity available for the comparison. For example, when more capacity is available for the comparison, perhaps the test feature is compared to several list features at a time, so that a semiparallel comparison is employed. But when less capacity is available, the test feature must be compared to the list features one at a time.

A6, the Divided Capacity Assumption, states that all the target logogens share a common pool of capacity, which they divide up evenly. By assumptions A2, A5, and A6, the following equation will determine RT in a memory set experiment:

$$\mathrm{RT} = \frac{F}{(A/N)} + K \qquad \text{(E1)}$$

where F is the total number of features the logogen compares, A is the total common capacity available to all logogens for feature comparison, N is the number of items in the memory set, and K is the time for all other perceptual and response processes.

The terms of equation E1 may be rearranged as follows:

$$\begin{aligned} \mathrm{RT} &= \frac{F}{(A/N)} + K \\ &= F\left(\frac{N}{A}\right) + K \\ &= \frac{FN}{A} + K \\ &= N\left(\frac{F}{A}\right) + K \end{aligned} \qquad \text{(E1')}$$

To summarize, equation E1′ is derived from assumptions A2, A3, A5, and A6, and it predicts that RT will increase linearly with set size for targets, a prediction supported by F1.

Target and Distractor RT Slopes are Equal

Equation E1 states that for a given set size (N), RT is a function of the number of features (F) that must be compared to determine whether the probe is a target or a distractor. Let F_1 be the number of feature comparisons required on the average to satisfy C_1, the target criterion defined in A3. Also, let F_0 be the number of feature comparisons required on the average to satisfy C_0, the distractor criterion defined in A4. If $F_1 = F_0$, then equation E1′ predicts that the RT functions for targets and distractors will be linear and parallel.

Thus, assumptions A3 and A4 extend E1′ to distractors. Sternberg (1969a) has pointed out that if the time it takes a logogen to compare F features is variable, the set size RT function for distractors may not be linear or parallel to the positive function. This is because the RT for distractors is determined by the finishing time of the last logogen to emit a no-match signal. If the finishing times of logogens are spread over some distribution, then the larger the set size, the greater will be the probability of a slow finishing time being included. However, according to A2, the Parallel Assumption, on a given trial all the logogens receive features from the feature analyzer and compare them in lock step. Thus, all the logogens will compare the ith probe feature at the same moment in time. So if decisions about both targets and distractors are made after those about F features, the RT functions for both targets and distractors will be linear and parallel.

The qualification that the average number of feature comparisons must be the same for targets and distractors is obviously a major one. Since the RT slopes for targets and distractors are usually found to be parallel, it must be shown to be plausible that $F_1 = F_0$ for the conditions under which most experiments are run.

Let us now consider three interrelated factors that influence F—the amount of noise in the feature comparison process, the response criterion, and the similarity of the distractors to the targets. Suppose that the feature comparison process was absolutely noiseless and errorless. Then, the target criterion C_1 would equal the minimal number of features necessary to discriminate a target from all possible distractors. The distractor criterion C_0 would equal one because in a noiseless comparison process, if even a single probe feature does not match a logogen feature, it is sufficient evidence that the probe is not the target of that logogen.

The probes for a memory set experiment are often drawn from the set of alphanumeric characters. It seems to me that each character in this set cannot be distinguished from all the others by a unique feature. If this assumption is true, then C_1 would be greater than one even if the comparison process was errorless and noiseless. If a random sampling process for the probe features is assumed, then F_1 would be larger than F_0 for the alphanumeric character set. Therefore, a noiseless comparison process predicts different RT slopes for targets and distractors in the typical memory set experiment.

If there is even a small amount of noise in the comparison process, however, the criterion necessary for accurate responses changes radically. In a noisy comparison, there is some probability of a logogen failing to match a target feature. In this case, if C_0 is set to one, a target will be erroneously classified as a distractor every time a single feature from a target does not match its logogen. To reduce these incorrect classifications, C_0 must be increased. Now, the larger C_0 becomes, the fewer errors will be made when targets are presented. But the higher distractor criterion also produces a larger mean RT for distractors. Hence, a speed/accuracy trade-off curve would emerge, and this curve would be influenced by the similarity between the targets and distractors. The more similar a distractor is to the targets, the more feature comparisons are required to detect each feature mismatch. Hence, an increase in C_0 causes an increase in F_0, which, increases the slope of the RT function.

If a noisy comparison process also causes incorrect feature matches, then a parallel argument can be made to show that as C_1 varies, it traces out a speed/accuracy trade-off function between target detection speed and distractor detection accuracy. Again, this curve is influenced by target–distractor similarity.

Let us assume there is some noise in the comparison process. Then the times to identify targets and distractors will be influenced by the position in the speed/accuracy trade-off functions that people adopt for positive and negative decisions. The error rates for targets and distractors are usually quite similar. Unfortunately, the feature analysis described here has not been explored in sufficient detail to know whether trying to hold error rates constant leads to $F_1 = F_0$, which would predict equal slopes for target and distractor functions. All that can be said at this point is that assumptions A1 through A7 are not apparently inconsistent with F2.

The Effect of Similarity

Recall that the Logogen Assumption, A3, implies that the more similar a distractor is to a target, the greater will be F_0, the average number of feature comparisons before the mismatch criterion is exceeded. The greater F_0 is, the greater will be the memory set RT function for those trials on which the distractor is presented. Conversely, if the distractor is very dissimilar to the memory set, F_0 will be small, and the memory set function will be shallow on the trials for which it is the probe.

The results of experiments on the effect of varying the similarity of distractors to the memory set comprise finding F3. As predicted by assumption A3, dissimilar distractors produced smaller slopes than either similar distractors or targets (Ellis & Chase, 1971; Foss & Dowell, 1971; Lively & Sanford, 1972; Wescourt & Atkinson, 1976). Thus, assumption A3 predicts finding F3.

Now, let us consider what happens when a distractor is similar to a single target in the memory set. By assumption A4, a negative response will not be made until the logogen for the target to which it is most similar emits a no-match signal. Hence, it should make no difference whether a distractor is similar to only one target in the memory set or to all the items in the memory set. If the distractor is compared to the targets in parallel, the RT for these two conditions should be equal. In contrast, if the distractor is compared serially to the targets, the RT should be much greater when it is similar to all the targets, since the times for each probe–target comparison are additive. Huesmann and Woocher (1976) in fact found no difference in RT whether the distractor was similar to one or all the targets (F4). On this basis they proposed a model that included assumptions A2 and A3. It is difficult to see how any serial model could account for Huesmann and Woocher's findings.

The Logogen Assumption, A3, also predicts that the slope of the set size function for targets and distractors will be positively correlated with the similarity of the distractors to the targets. The more similar the distractors are to the targets, the more features will have to be compared to distinguish them. By equation E1′, the more features that have to be compared, the greater will be the slope. The critical memory set experiment, comparing RT slopes for two sets of items that differ only in the similarity between their targets and distractors, has yet to be done.

Neisser (1963) has reported that similar distractors do lead to steeper RT slopes in a visual search task, in which a display containing more than one item is searched for the target. Other results also imply that RT functions will increase with the similarity of the distractors to the targets. For example, Conrad (1964) and Lee and Estes (1977) have found that in a short-term retention task, the more similar two items are to each other, the more likely they are to be confused. When this result is combined with the basic assumptions of their perturbation model (Estes, 1972; Lee & Estes, 1977), it can be predicted that the length of a string of items that can be correctly recalled in order will be inversely related to the similarity of the string items. That is, the more similar a set of items is, the shorter will be its span. These results suggest that finding F5, the correlation that Cavanaugh (1972) found between memory set RT and memory span, is the result of a common effect of item similarity in both tasks. Suppose it is assumed that the more similar the memory set items are, the more features that must be encoded to distinguish them in memory; hence, the more capacity they will occupy. Then, the relationship between similarity and memory span would be described by the equation

$$S = \frac{A}{I} \qquad \text{(E2)}$$

where S is the memory span, A is the total available capacity, and I is the similarity of the items, with $I > 1$; the larger I is, the greater the similarity. Of course, by A3, the Logogen Assumption, the number of features that it is necessary to encode for the memory set items will be directly related to their similarity as described by the equation

$$F = ZI \qquad \text{(E3)}$$

where F is the number of features encoded, Z is a constant, and I represents item similarity. Equation E3 may be rearranged as $I = F/Z$ and then substituted in E2 to form equation E2′:

$$S = \frac{A}{(F12)} \qquad \text{(E2')}$$

This equation can be rearranged as

$$Z\left(\frac{1}{S}\right) = \frac{F}{A} \qquad \text{(E2'')}$$

Equation E2″ implies finding F5 (Cavanaugh, 1972), that the larger the immediate memory span for a set of items, the more shallow the slope for that set of items in a memory set experiment. That is, the slope of the memory set RT function (F/A) is directly related to the reciprocal of the memory span.

The Effect of Concurrent Tasks

Turning to A5 and A6, that processing capacity is both limited and divided, these assumptions clearly predict that if another task is performed concurrently with the memory scanning task, then this secondary task should use capacity and increase the slope of the RT. This finding, F6, has been observed several times (Forrin & Morin, 1969; Howard, 1975; Krueger, 1975; Sternberg, 1969b). It is also worth noting that the Limited Capacity assumption A5 implies that when two stages of a process, such as feature extraction and feature comparison, are going on concurrently, these separate stages may also share capacity. When this implication is combined with Sternberg's (1969a) analysis of how factors influencing different processing stages will affect the RT slope, we can predict that the intercept as well as the slope should be elevated. This result was observed in the four cited experiments above. Results from other experiments also suggest that different processing stages share capacity (Shulman & Greenberg, 1971).

Lack of Serial Position Effects

Next, consider finding F7, that the RT for a target does not depend on its serial position within the memory set. This result follows directly from assumption A2, that each logogen processes the probe in parallel. As Sternberg (1975) noted, serial position effects only occur if the varied set procedure is used and if the interval between the presentation of the memory set and the target is brief. This restriction suggests that when serial position effects do occur, they are the result of short-lived peripheral processes (e.g., iconic storage). Such processes are outside the scope of the theory presented here and will not be discussed further.

A second explanation for serial position effects is that capacity is distributed unequally among items of the memory set. If more capacity were allocated to the items presented first and last in the memory set, then RT for these items when they were used as targets should be faster. The results of certain experiments support this explanation. Seamon and Wright (1976) asked subjects to subvocally rehearse one to four targets cyclically at a self-paced rate until the probe was presented. When the item rehearsed last matched the probe, RTs were faster than when it differed (see also, Seamon, 1976, 1978). Seamon's explanation for this effect is that the most recent rehearsal facilitates the encoding stage by activating a representation of the target. But these results are also consistent with the assumption that as a memory set item is rehearsed, the amount of capacity allocated to it is momentarily increased. This assumption also explains Baddeley and Ecob's (1973) finding that if a target occurs more than once in the memory set, it is responded to more rapidly, since it is surely the case that a repeated item will be rehearsed more often.

Extending the Basic Model: The Effect of Practice and the Critical Feature Hypothesis

Next, let us consider why the slope of the RT function decreases with practice on a fixed set (F8), but not with practice on a varied set (F9). First, suppose that one or more items in the memory set contain features that do not match any of the potential distractors. Then, the set of features that must be compared to a probe by the logogen of this memory set item may be restricted to this residual set of critical features without falsely rejecting any targets or accepting any distractors. Clearly, if the number of features a logogen contains is reduced, then the number of feature matches, M, that must be made between a probe and that logogen before it emits a match response will also be reduced (let us call this reduced number M'). Further assume that the feature extraction process can be modified over time, so that the critical features contained in the logogens are extracted from the probes first. Then the number of feature comparisons necessary to yield M' matches for targets can also be reduced. There is already considerable evidence that subjects extract critical features first and use them to discriminate targets from distractors (Biederman, 1972; Robinson, 1969). Thus, in the fixed set procedure, if the target set can be discriminated from the distractor set by critical target features, the slope of the RT function will decrease with practice (F8). Clearly, in the varied set procedure, since the targets and distractors are the same set of items, the set of critical features that distinguishes them is empty, and the slope of the RT function will not decrease (F9).

The supposition that there must be some target feature not possessed by any distractor is a strong one that can be tested by constructing a set of targets for which this is not the case. Suppose a set of targets were constructed for which there was no set of features that characterized only targets. If the explanation just presented for the decline in RT with practice is correct, then even after extended practice in which half of the set was used for the targets and the other half was used for the distractors, the RT function should not decline. Hence, this hypothesis predicts that with the appropriate set of items, RT will not decline after extended practice with a fixed set. This prediction has not yet been tested in a memory set experiment.

The critical feature explanation of the fixed set practice effect can account for F10, that adding new distractors does not affect RT. Any probe that lacks a sufficient number of the features contained by targets will be rejected according to the hypothesis, whether or not it has been presented before. Hence, new distractors will be rejected as rapidly as old distractors, as long as they are as dissimilar from the targets as were the old distractors.

EVALUATION OF THE LIMITED-CAPACITY PARALLEL MODEL

The basic assumptions of the present model are actually general assumptions about information processing for which there is empirical support from tasks other than those involving a memory set. The notion that visual inputs are analyzed into features (A1) is virtually the cornerstone of modern research on letter and word recognition (Neisser, 1967). When the time it takes to identify an item is considered along with the size of the set of items it must have been compared against, it appears that the comparison process must have been "featural" (A1) or parallel (A2) or both.

First, Neisser (1974), Neisser, Novick, and Lazar (1963), and Sperling, Budiansky, Spivak, and Johnson (1971) have shown in visual search tasks that given a fixed memory set, search for any item of that set proceeds only as fast as the search rate for the slowest target alone. For example, suppose that the search rate for the letter *a* is slower than for the letters *f* and *h*. Then, practiced subjects could search for an *a*, *f*, or *h* only as fast as they could search for an *a* alone. This result implies that when any item for the set is being searched for, either (1) the search is based on the intersection of features of the individual items or (2) a display item is compared to the memory set items in parallel.

Second, compare the amount of information that can be scanned in 1 second to the neuronal transmission time. It takes about a millisecond for a neuron to transmit a signal. If it is assumed that every neuron represents a different item, the neural transmission mechanism thus limits the serial scanning rate to something less than 1000 items per second. But letter strings can be classified as words or nonwords in a lexical decision task in much less than a second, and the class of words that can be so identified clearly has more than 1000 members. So it must be the case that features of the letter string are used to limit search to subsets of words that have the same features (A1) or that the letter string is compared to more than one word at a time (A2) or both.

The logogen model (A3) also has considerable empirical support (e.g., Hillinger, 1980). In addition, evidence for a terminating, feature-testing comparison process (A3) comes from tasks similar to the memory set task discussed here. Such tasks include a same or different judgment on a pair of items (Robinson, 1969) and an item classification task (Biederman, 1972). A classification task differs from a memory set task only in that in the former the memory set is fixed and the response required is to classify the probe into one of several categories rather than as either a target or a distractor.

There is also support from a variety of other tasks (Hitch & Baddeley, 1976; Kahneman, 1973; Larkin & Burns, 1977; Okada & Burrows, 1978) that human information processing draws on a resource of limited capacity (A5, A6). The mere fact that two tasks interfere with each other (Brooks, 1968; Segal & Fusella, 1970) implies that they share a limited capacity.

The assumptions presented here are consistent with previous suggestions that a parallel model could account for the effects of memory (Atkinson, Holmgren, & Juola, 1969; Moray, 1967; Shulman & Greenberg, 1971; Townsend, 1971). These basic assumptions are much more explicit and detailed than previous descriptions, so many more findings can be accounted for. For example, the parallel models mentioned directly above all consist of only assumptions A2 and A6 in some form. The Huesmann and Woocher (1976) model includes A1, A2, and A3, but lacks A4, A5, and A6.

OTHER EXPLANATIONS

There are explanations of the effect of memory set whose assumptions contradict most of the basic assumptions made here. These models, like Sternberg's original proposal, assume a serial search of the memory set. The proposal in this review need only be compared to Schneider and Shiffrin's (1977) model, since it represents the most successful example of the alternative point of view.

Schneider and Shiffrin (1977) proposed that two separate processes were involved in comparing a probe to a memory set. Initially a slow, serial scan is required. But if a probe item is consistently used as a target, then it comes to be matched automatically to its representation in the memory set whenever it appears in the visual display. Hence, for these targets, the comparison time is independent of the number of items in the memory set. The Schneider and Shiffrin model can account for findings F1, F2, F7, F8, F9, and F10. However it cannot account for the effect of similarity (F3, F4).

Although both the limited-capacity parallel model presented here and Schneider and Shiffrin's model predict the shape of the set size RT function in a variety of conditions, the assumptions predicting the actual functions are very different. Schneider and Shiffrin observe that the RT slopes for targets and distractors are linear when the memory set is varied. They reported that the slope for the distractors is twice that of the targets when the visual display contains more than one item, but that they are equal when the visual display contains just one item. They concluded that the comparison process is serial and that when the slope of the distractors is twice that of the targets, it is self-terminating; when it is equal to the targets, it is exhaustive; and when the slope falls between those values, search is sometimes serial and sometimes exhaustive. Schneider and Shiffrin account for the declining negatively accelerated set size RT functions observed with fixed sets by assuming a mixture of serial and automatic (essentially parallel) comparisons.

While these assumptions describe the data, they are also ad hoc. If tasks other than those involving a small memory set are considered, the amount of evidence suggesting serial character comparison simply is not equivalent to the large body of evidence for featural and parallel processing. Also, there is the issue of parsimony. At one point, Schneider and Shiffrin argue against a feature processing explanation of the negatively accelerated RT function by pointing out that if it can be predicted from the serial and parallel searches they had already proposed, there is no need to invoke another process. This argument can be turned against them. If the single parallel comparison process described here can account for all the RT functions, and in addition, if there is independent support for both featural and parallel processing from other tasks, there is no need to invoke a serial comparison process just for small, unpracticed memory sets.

To summarize, there are important differences between the models. The Schneider and Shiffrin model assumes that a probe is compared holistically to each memory set item. This basic assumption requires further assumptions of both serial and parallel comparison processes in order to account for the decrease in the slope with practice. In contrast, the limited-capacity parallel model assumes a featural comparison of the probe to the memory set. This assumption makes it possible for a single parallel comparison process to account for the decline in the RT function with practice. Together, the two models map the boundaries of a theoretical landscape that contains a range of possibilities between them.

The explanation of the memory set RT function has been the major stumbling block for the general acceptance of a parallel, feature-testing model as a general model of human information processing. However, more than 10 years of effort in solving the problem has begun to pay off. A plausible explanation of the set size function now seems to be within the scope of the model's basic assumptions. Certainly, more tests of its assumptions remain to be done and an unexpected disconfirmation may yet derail the model. But if the proposed experiments yield their predicted results, the solution to the memory set conundrum may be at hand.

REFERENCES

Atkinson, R. C., Holmgren, J. E., & Juola, J. F. Processing time as influenced by the number of elements in a visual display. *Perception and Psychophysics*, 1969, *6*, 321–26.

Atkinson, R. C., & Juola, J. F. Search and decision processes in recognition memory. In D. H. Krantz, R. C. Atkinson, R. D. Luce, & P. Suppes (Eds.), *Contemporary developments in mathematical psychology* (Vol. 1). San Francisco: Freeman, 1974.

Baddeley, A. D., & Ecob, J. R. Reaction time and short-term memory: Implications of repetition effects for the high-speed exhaustive scan hypothesis. *Quarterly Journal of Experimental Psychology*, 1973, *25*, 229–40.

Biederman, I. Human performance in contingent information-processing tasks. *Journal of Experimental Psychology*, 1972, *93*, 219–38.

Brooks, L. R. Spatial and verbal components of the act of recall. *Canadian Journal of Psychology*, 1968, *22*, 349–68.

Briggs, G. E. On the predictor variable for choice reaction time. *Memory and Cognition*, 1974, *2*, 575–80.

Cavanaugh, J. P. Relation between the immediate memory span and the memory search rate. *Psychological Review*, 1972, *79*, 525–30.

Conrad, R. Acoustic confusion in immediate memory. *British Journal of Psychology*, 1964, *55*, 75–84.

Egeth, H., & Smith, E. E. On the nature of errors in a choice reaction task. *Psychonomic Science*, 1967, *8*, 345–46.

Ellis, S. H., & Chase, W. G. Parallel processing in item recognition. *Perception and Psychophysics*, 1971, *10*, 379–84.

Estes, W. K. An associative basis for coding and organization in memory. In A. W. Melton & E. Martin (Eds.), *Coding processes in human memory*. Washington, D.C.: V. H. Winston & Sons, 1972.

Forrin, B., & Morin, R. E. Recognition times for items in short- and long-term memory. *Acta Psychologica*, 1969, *30*, 126–41.

Foss, D. J., & Dowell, B. E. High-speed memory retrieval with auditorily presented stimuli. *Perception and Psychophysics*, 1971, *9*, 465–68.

Hillinger, M. L. Priming effects with phonemically similar words: The encoding-bias hypothesis reconsidered. *Memory and Cognition*, 1980, *8*, 115–23.

Hitch, G. J., & Baddeley, H. Verbal reasoning and working memory. *Quarterly Journal of Experimental Psychology*, 1976, *28*, 603–21.

Howard, J. H., Jr. The attentional demands of negation in a memory-scanning task. *Memory and Cognition*, 1975, *3*, 319–24.

Huesmann, L. R., & Woocher, F. D. Probe similarity and recognition of set membership: A parallel-processing serial-feature-matching model. *Cognitive Psychology*, 1976, *8*, 124–62.

Kahneman, D. *Attention and effort*. Englewood Cliffs, N.J.: Prentice-Hall, 1973.

Kristofferson, M. W. Effects of practice on character classification performance. *Canadian Journal of Psychology*, 1972, *26*, 54–60. (a)

Kristofferson, M. W. When item recognition and visual search functions are similar. *Perception and Psychophysics*, 1972, *12*, 379–84. (b)

Krueger, L. E. The effect of an extraneous added memory set on item recognition: A test of parallel dependent vs. serial comparison models. *Memory and Cognition*, 1975, *3*, 485–95.

Larkin, W., & Burns, D. Sentence comprehension and memory for embedded structure. *Memory and Cognition*, 1977, *5*, 17–22.

Lee, C. L., & Estes, W. K. Order and position in primary memory for letter strings. *Journal of Verbal Learning and Verbal Behavior*, 1977, *16*, 395–418.

Lively, B. L., & Sanford, B. J. The use of category information in a memory search task. *Journal of Experimental Psychology*, 1972, *93*, 379–85.

Moray, N. Where is capacity limited? A study and a model. *Acta Psychologica*, 1967, *27*, 84–92.

Morton, J. Interaction of information in word recognition. *Psychological Review*, 1969, *76*, 165–78.

Neisser, U. Decision time without reaction time: Experiments in visual scanning. *American Journal of Psychology*, 1963, *76*, 376–85.

Neisser, U. *Cognitive psychology*. Englewood Cliffs, N.J.: Prentice-Hall, 1967.

Neisser, U. Practice card sorting for multiple targets. *Memory and Cognition*, 1974, *2*, 781–85.

Neisser, U., Novick, R., & Lazar, R. Searching for ten targets simultaneously. *Perceptual and Motor Skills*, 1963, *17*, 955–61.

Norman, D. A., & Bobrow, D. G. On data-limited and resource-limited processes. *Cognitive Psychology*, 1975, *7*, 44–64.

Okada, R., & Burrows, D. The effect of subsidiary tasks on memory retrieval from long and short lists. *Quarterly Journal of Experimental Psychology*, 1978, *30*, 221–33.

Robinson, J. S. Familiar patterns are no easier to see than novel ones. *American Journal of Psychology*, 1969, *82*, 513–22.

Ross, J. Extended practice with a single character classification task. *Perception and Psychophysics*, 1970, *8*, 276–78.

Schneider, W., & Shiffrin, R. M. Controlled and automatic human information processing: I. Detection, search and attention. *Psychological Review*, 1977, *84*, 1–66.

Seamon, J. G. Effects of generative processes on probe identification time. *Memory and Cognition*, 1976, *4*, 759–62.
Seamon, J. G. Rehearsal, generative processes, and the activation of underlying stimulus representations. *Perception and Psychophysics*, 1978, *23*, 381–90.
Seamon, J. G., & Wright, C. E. Generative processes in character classification: Evidence for a probe encoding set. *Memory and Cognition*, 1976, *4*, 96–102.
Segal, S. J., & Fusella, V. Influence of imaged pictures and sounds in detection of visual and auditory signals. *Journal of Experimental Psychology*, 1970, *83*, 458–74.
Shiffrin, R. M., & Schneider, W. Controlled and automatic human information processing: II. Perceptual learning, automatic attending, and a general theory. *Psychological Review*, 1977, *84*, 127–90.
Shulman, H. G., & Greenberg, S. N. Perceptual deficits due to division of attention between memory and perception. *Journal of Experimental Psychology*, 1971, *88*, 171–76.
Simpson, P. J. High-speed scanning: Stability and generality. *Journal of Experimental Psychology*, 1972, *96*, 239–46.
Sperling, G., Budiansky, J., Spivak, J. G., & Johnson, M. C. Extremely rapid visual search: The maximum rate of scanning letters for the presence of a numeral. *Science*, 1971, *174*, 307–11.
Sternberg, S. High-speed scanning in human memory. *Science*, 1966, *153*, 652–54.
Sternberg, S. The discovery of processing stages: Extensions of Donder's method. In W. G. Koster (Ed.), *Acta Psychologica*, 1969, *30*, 276–316. (a)
Sternberg, S. Memory-scanning: Mental processes revealed by reaction-time experiments. *American Scientist*, 1969, *57*, 421–57. (b)
Sternberg, S. Memory scanning: New findings and current controversies. *Quarterly Journal of Experimental Psychology*, 1975, *27*, 1–32.
Swanson, J. M., & Briggs, G. E. Information processing as a function of speed versus accuracy. *Journal of Experimental Psychology*, 1969, *81*, 223–29.
Townsend, J. T. A note on the identifiability of parallel and serial processes. *Perception and Psychophysics*, 1971, *10*, 161–63.
Wescourt, K. T., & Atkinson, R. C. Fact retrieval processes in human memory. In W. K. Estes (Ed.), *Handbook of learning and cognitive processes 4*. Hillsdale, N.J.: Lawrence Erlbaum Associates, 1976.

6

FACETS OF HUMAN INTELLIGENCE

Robert J. Sternberg
Yale University

In some areas of psychology, investigators find it difficult or impossible to measure the psychological attributes that they wish to study. Consider, for example, motivation. Despite decades of research and countless attempts to measure this attribute (see, e.g., Atkinson, 1958, 1964; Atkinson & Raynor, 1978; Cattell, 1935, 1957; McClelland, 1971), there exists no generally accepted measure of human motivation that seems to predict or define this construct across a variety of tasks and situations. Other examples of such difficult-to-measure constructs include curiosity, creativity, and social competence, to name just a few.

In contrast, contemporary research and practice dealing with the nature and measurement of intelligence is faced with an embarrassing situation: Almost everything works! Differential psychologists have discovered that an extremely wide range of tasks—vocabulary, reading comprehension, mathematical problem solving, analogies, syllogisms, spatial visualization, anagrams, among others—is moderately predictive of performance in criterion situations assumed to require intelligent performance, such as, school and employment (Cronbach, 1970; Schmidt & Hunter, 1977). Experimental psychologists have discovered that tasks ranging in complexity from

Preparation of this chapter was supported by Contract N0001483K0013 to Robert J. Sternberg from the Office of Naval Research, with joint support from the Army Research Institute.

simple reaction time to complex problem solving correlate with scores on the standard psychometric tasks found on intelligence tests. A variety of theoretical frameworks have been proposed to account for why each of these various tasks or classes of tasks measures "intelligence."

This chapter will discuss the issue of what makes behavior "intelligent behavior," and thus, what makes a particular test a measure of intelligence. The chapter is divided into three major parts. The first describes alternative views of the nature of intelligent behavior and the tasks for assessing intelligence that these views have generated. The second part describes a new view of the nature of intelligence. The third applies this new perspective to understanding the existing literature on intelligence, dealing in particular with the question of why so many different tasks seem to measure "intelligence."

ALTERNATIVE VIEWS OF HUMAN INTELLIGENCE

This part of the chapter will be divided into two sections. The first will briefly present alternative differential, or psychometric, views of the nature of human intelligence. These views are the historical precursors of contemporary cognitive views, which will be described in the second section. Although the differential and cognitive views have probably been the most influential in American conceptions of the nature of intelligence, they are not the only views that have been advanced (see, e.g., Hebb, 1949, and Hendrickson, 1982, for two physiological views; and Piaget, 1972, for a genetic-epistemological view). These other viewpoints are not discussed here for lack of space, but a description can be found elsewhere (Eysenck, 1982; Sternberg, 1982a).

Differential Views of the Nature of Human Intelligence

Differential views have in common (with rare exceptions) their attempt to understand intelligence in terms of a set of *factors* which are static latent sources of individual differences. It is proposed that differences in intelligence test performance can be decomposed into individual differences involving such factors, each of which is posited to represent a distinct human ability.

Given that the large majority of differential views have in common the use of factors as a basis for understanding intelligence, one might wonder how these views actually differ from one another. The primary differences are in terms of (a) the number of factors posited by the theory and (b) the geometrical arrangement of the factors with respect to each other. Let us consider how number and geometrical arrangement can form the bases for alternative theories of intelligence.

Variation in Number of Factors

Differential theorists vary greatly in the number of factors they purport to be important for understanding intelligent behavior.

At the lower end of the range, Spearman (1927) proposed that intelligence comprises two kinds of factors, a general factor and specific factors. The ability represented by the general factor permeates performance on all intellectual tasks; the abilities represented by the specific factors each involve only a single task, and hence are not of much psychological interest. Thus, from Spearman's viewpoint, there is just one factor of major psychological interest, the general factor, or *g*, as it has often been called. Spearman made two (not necessarily mutually exclusive) proposals regarding individual differences in *g*: (1) that they might be understood in terms of differences in the levels of mental energy individuals could bring to intellectual task performance, and (2) that they could be understood in terms of differences in people's abilities to utilize three "qualitative principles of cognition": apprehension of experience, eduction of relations, and eduction of correlates (Spearman, 1923). In order to understand what each of these three principles represents, consider an analogy of the form A : B :: C : ? , for example, LAWYER : CLIENT :: DOCTOR : ? . *Apprehension of experience* refers to encoding (perceiving and understanding) each of the given terms of the analogy. *Eduction of relations* refers to inference of the relation between the first two terms; here, LAWYER and CLIENT. *Eduction of correlates* refers to application of the inferred principle to a new domain; here, applying the rule inferred between LAWYER and CLIENT to produce a completion for DOCTOR : ? . The best educed answer to this analogy would presumably be PATIENT. Given that analogies directly embody these principles, it is not surprising that Spearman (1923, 1927) and many others subsequently found analogies to be among the best available measures of *g* (see Sternberg, 1977, for a review of relevant literature).

In a more "middle-of-the-road" position, one finds Thurstone (1938), who proposed that intelligence comprises seven "primary mental abilities." Consider the identity of each of these abilities, and how it is commonly measured:

1 *Verbal comprehension* This ability is typically measured by tests of vocabulary (including both synonyms and antonyms) and reading comprehension.

2 *Verbal fluency* This ability is typically measured by tests that require rapid production of words. For example, the individual might be asked to generate, as quickly as possible and within a limited period of time, as many words as he or she can think of that begin with the letter *d*.

3 *Number* This ability is typically measured by arithmetic word problems that place some emphasis upon both computation and reasoning, but relatively little on prior knowledge.

4 *Spatial visualization* This ability is typically measured by tests requiring mental manipulation of symbols or geometric designs. For example, the individual might be shown a picture of a geometric design in some degree of angular rotation, followed by a set of pictures of the design in various orientations that are either identical (except for degree of rotation) to the original or mirror images of it. The individual would have to indicate whether each item is the same as the original (or, alternatively, is a mirror image).

5 *Memory* This ability is typically measured by a test of serial recall—memory for words or sentences—or by paired-associate recall—names paired with pictures of people.

6 *Reasoning* This ability is typically measured by tests involving analogies and series completions (e.g., 2, 4, 7, 11, ?).

7 *Perceptual speed* This ability is typically measured by tests requiring rapid recognition of symbols (e.g., rapid crossing out of *l*'s that are embedded in a string of letters).

Pretty much at the upper extreme of number of proposed factors is Guilford (1967), who has proposed that intelligence comprises 120 distinct factors. According to Guilford, every mental task involves three ingredients: an operation, a content, and a product. There are five kinds of *operations*: cognition, memory, divergent production, convergent production, and evaluation. There are four kinds of *contents*: figural, symbolic, semantic, and behavioral. And there are six kinds of *products*: units, classes, relations, systems, transformations, and implications. Since the subcategories are independently defined, they are multiplicative; thus, there are $5 \times 4 \times 6 = 120$ different mental abilities. (Guilford & Hoepfner, 1971, report that the number of demonstrated abilities is 98.)

Guilford and his associates have devised tests that measure many of the factors posited by the model. Consider how just a few of these abilities are measured. Cognition of figural relations, for example, is measured by tests such as figure analogies or matrices. Memory for semantic relations is measured by presenting to examinees a series of relationships, such as, "gold is more valuable than iron," and then testing retention in a multiple-choice format. Evaluation of symbolic units is measured by same–different tests, in which subjects are presented with pairs of numbers or letters that are identical or different in minor details. Subjects are then asked to identify each pair as "same" or "different."

Variation in Geometric Structure of Factors

As noted earlier, two models positing the same number of factors—and even the same contents for factors—might still differ because of the different geometrical arrangements of these factors. The four most well-known structures are an unordered arrangement, a cubic arrangement, a hierarchical arrangement, and a radex arrangement.

Unordered arrangements consist of lists of factors, all of which are asserted to be equal in importance to each other. Thurstone's primary mental abilities provide a good example of this kind of arrangement. Thurstone (1938) suggested simply that intelligence could be understood in terms of seven factors. They are not ordered in any particular way; any permutation of the list is as valid as any other.

The most well-known *cubic* theorist is Guilford (1967), who represented the structure of intellect as a large cube composed of 120 smaller cubes. Each dimension of the cube corresponds to one of the three categories (operation, content, product), and each of the 120 possible combinations of the three categories forms one of the smaller cubes.

Hierarchical arrangements are probably most popular in contemporary psychometric literature on intelligence. According to this kind of view, abilities are not of equal importance. Rather, certain abilities are more global, and hence more important, than others. Spearman's factorial model (1927), with one general factor and less important specific factors, might be seen as the original hierarchical model, although it is not clear that Spearman thought of his theory in this way. Holzinger (1938) elaborated upon Spearman's point of view by suggesting that there existed group factors intermediate in generality between the general factor and the specific factors. The group factors permeated performance on some class of tasks (in any case, on more than one task), but were not involved in performance of all mental tasks. Burt (1940) proposed a five-level hierarchical model, with the "human mind" at the top, the "relations level" just below it, associations below that, perceptions below associations, and sensation at the bottom of the hierarchy. Vernon (1971) proposed a more sophisticated hierarchical model, suggesting that *g* could be decomposed into two broad group factors—verbal educational ability and practical-mechanical ability. He further proposed that these broad group factors could be further decomposed into narrower group factors, although this further decomposition is of less importance in his theory.

Finally, Guttman (1965) has proposed a *radex* arrangement for the components of intelligence. A radex can be thought of as a circle. Each subtest found on intelligence tests can be placed somewhere in the circle. Tests nearer the center of the circle measure abilities more "central" to intelligence. Thus, the purest measures of intelligence would be at the center of the circle, and the least pure measures would be at the periphery of the circle.

Summary of Different Views

In sum, then, psychometric, or differential, theories differ primarily in the number of factors they posit and the geometric arrangement of these factors. On their face, the theories *seem* quite different. At a deeper level, however, it is not clear that these differences are terribly consequential. There are at least three reasons for this lack of consequentiality.

First, some of the differences appear, on closer examination, to be in emphasis rather than substance. For example, Spearman's and Thurstone's theories appear to be radically different. But near the end of his career, Spearman was forced to concede the existence of group factors; indeed, he even collaborated with Holzinger on the development of a theory that encompassed group factors as well as the general one. Similarly, Thurstone was forced, by the end of his career, to acknowledge the existence of a higher-order general factor that in some sense incorporated his primary mental abilities. The principal evidence for such a higher-order factor is that the primary mental abilities are not statistically independent, but rather are intercorrelated with each other. People who tend to be proficient in one ability tend to score high in others as well, and people who tend to score low in one ability tend to be low in others as well. When one factor analyzes these factors, one obtains a general, higher-order factor. The main difference between the Spearman and Thurstone theories may thus have been in the emphases they placed on higher-order versus lower-order factors, Spearman emphasizing the former, Thurstone the latter.

Second, the alternative theories are, in many cases, mathematically equivalent. Factors can be represented in a "factor space," where each factor is a dimension in the space. When a factor analysis is performed, the locations of points (tests) in the factor space are fixed, but the locations of the factor axes are not. In other words, it is possible to have many—indeed, infinite—orientations of the factor axes. It turns out that many of the theories differ from one another almost solely in terms of orientation of factor axes. Hence, each theory is equally good from a mathematical point of view. The different theories simply say the same things in different ways (see Sternberg, 1977, for an elaboration of this point of view).

Third, recent cognitive-experimental research suggests that the various factorial theories can all be mapped into a common set of information-processing components of task performance (see, e.g., Sternberg, 1980a, 1980c). In other words, no matter what factor structure one uses, the basic processes contributing to the factors are the same. In order to understand more about these processes, we need to consider just what information-processing research has to say about what makes behavior intelligent.

Cognitive Views of the Nature of Human Intelligence

Cognitive views of intelligence have in common their attempts to understand intellectual functioning in terms of the mental processes that constitute task performance. A primary difference among these views is the level of cognitive functioning they emphasize. At one extreme, there exist investigators who have proposed to understand intelligence in terms of sheer speed of information processing; they use the most simple tasks they can devise in order to measure speed uncontaminated by other variables. At the other extreme, there are investigators who have studied accuracy and strategy in very complex forms of problem solving; they deemphasize or discount speed of functioning in mental processing. Let us now consider a sampling of the range of levels of processing that have been studied.

Pure Speed

Proponents of the notion that individual differences in intelligence can be traced back to differences in speed of information processing have tended to use simple reaction time (RT) and related tasks to make their point. In a simple RT paradigm, the subject is required simply to make a single overt response as quickly as possible following presentation of a stimulus. Since the days of Galton, this paradigm has been widely used as a measure of intelligence (Berger, 1982). Although Galton (1883) and Cattell (1890) were strong supporters of the importance of sheer speed in intellectual functioning, the levels of correlation obtained between measures of simple RT and various standard measures of intelligence (e.g., IQ test scores, school grades, and the like, none of which are perfect in themselves) have been rather weak. Wissler (1901) obtained correlations close to 0, as did Lemmon (1927–28). Lunneborg (1977) obtained correlations with eight psychometric measures of intelligence ranging from −.17 to −.42, with a median of −.38. (Negative correlations would be expected since longer RTs are presumed to be associated with lower levels of intelligent performance.) In my view, the most trustworthy results are those attributable to

Jensen (1982) (see also Jensen, 1980), who has reported correlations for two samples: one in the mid −.20s, the other around .10. Clearly, if there is any relationship at all between measures of pure speed and of psychometrically measured intelligence, it is a weak one.

Choice Speed

A slight complication of the above view is that intelligence derives not from simple speed of processing, but rather from speed in making choices or decisions about simple stimuli. In a typical choice-RT paradigm, the subject is presented with one of two or more possible stimuli, each requiring a different overt response. The subject has to choose the correct response as rapidly as possible following stimulus presentation. Correlations with psychometric measures of intelligence have been higher than those obtained for simple reaction time (Berger, 1982). Lemmon (1927–28) found a correlation of −.25 between choice reaction time and measured intelligence. Lunneborg (1977) found variable correlations. In one study, correlations ranged from −.28 to −.55, with a median of −.40. In a second study, however, the correlations were trivial. Jensen (1982) reported a correlation of −.30 for one sample, but a correlation close to 0 for another. Lally and Nettelbeck (1977) obtained a correlation of −.56, but in a sample with a very wide range of IQ (57 to 130); such samples tend to elevate correlations spuriously.

An interesting finding in the research of both Jensen (1979, 1982) and Lally and Nettelbeck (1977) is that the correlation between choice reaction time and IQ tends to increase with the number of stimulus-response choices involved in the task. In fact, these investigators found a roughly linear relation between the level of correlation obtained and the log to the base two of the number of choices (bits) in the task, at least through eight choices (three bits). But the correlations for typical ranges of subject ability nevertheless seem to peak at slightly over the −.40 level. Thus, increasing the number of choices in a choice-RT paradigm seems to increase correlation with IQ, but the task is still far from providing what would seem to be a causal account of individual differences in psychometrically measured IQ. Speed of decision making in the choice-RT paradigm may be one contributor to individual differences in intellectual performance, but it does not seem to be a really major one.

Speed of Lexical Access

Hunt (1978) has proposed that individual differences in verbal intelligence may be understandable largely in terms of differences in speed of access to lexical information in long-term memory. According to this view, individuals who can access information more quickly profit more per unit time of presented information, and hence are able to perform better on a variety of tasks, especially verbal ones. Hunt, Lunneborg, and Lewis (1975) initiated a paradigm for testing this theory that makes use of a letter-comparison task (Posner & Mitchell, 1967). Subjects are presented with pairs of letters—such as, *AA*, *Aa*, or *Ab*—that may be the same (or different) either physically or in name. For example, *AA* are the same both physically and in name, *Aa* are the same in name only, and *Ab* are the same neither in name nor in physical appearance. The subject's task is to indicate as rapidly as possible whether the two letters are a match. In one condition, subjects respond with respect to whether the letters are a physical match; in another condition, the same subjects respond with respect to whether the letters are a name match. The measure of interest is each subject's average name match time minus physical match time. This measure is taken to be an index of time of access to lexical information in long-term memory. Physical match time is subtracted from name match time in order to obtain a relatively pure measure of lexical access time, uncontaminated by speed of responding. Thus, whereas those who study simple reaction time are particularly interested in sheer speed of responding, Hunt and his colleagues do what they can to eliminate this element.

A number of investigators have used this paradigm as a basis for understanding individual differences in verbal intelligence (Hunt et al., 1975; Jackson & McClelland, 1979; Keating & Bobbitt, 1978). Unlike the simple and choice reaction time tasks, the lexical-access task yields a remarkably consistent picture with respect to its relationship to measured intelligence: Correlations with scores on verbal IQ tests are typically about −.30. Thus, lexical access time seems to be related at some level to intellectual performance. But again, it is at best, only one contributor to individual differences in what standard psychometric IQ tests measure. The correlation is simply too weak to make strong causal statements.

Components of Reasoning and Problem Solving

A number of investigators have emphasized the kinds of higher-order processing involved in reasoning and problem solving in their attempts to understand intelligence (e.g., Pellegrino & Glaser, 1980, 1982; Simon, 1976; Sternberg, 1977; Sternberg & Gardner, 1983; Whitely, 1980). Following in the tradition of Spearman's information-processing "principles of cognition," these investigators have sought to understand individual differences in intelligence in terms of individuals' differential processing of information in tasks involving analogies, series completions, syllogisms, and the like. There have been two main emphases in this work, namely, on performance processes and on executive processes. Let us consider each in turn.

Investigators seeking to understand intelligence in terms of *performance processes* seek to discover the processes individuals use in problem solving from the time they first see a problem to the time they respond. Consider, for example, the widely studied task involving an analogy item. In a typical theory of analogical reasoning, performance on the analogy item is decomposed into component processes such as *inferring* the relation between the first two terms of the analogy, *mapping* the higher-order relation that connects the first half of the analogy to the second half, and *applying* the relation inferred in the first half of the analogy to the second half of the problem (Sternberg, 1977). The motivating idea is that individuals' skills in solving these problems derive from their ability to execute each of these processes. Moreover, the processes involved in analogy solution have been shown to be quite general across various kinds of inductive reasoning (Greeno, 1978; Pellegrino & Glaser, 1980; Sternberg & Gardner, 1983). Thus, the component processes are of interest because they are not task-specific, but rather are quite general across a variety of problem-solving tasks (see also Newell and Simon, 1972, for a discussion of similar logic applied to other kinds of complex problems).

How well does the performance-process approach work? For the three components noted above (inference, mapping, application), Sternberg (1977) found median correlations of −.16 for schematic-picture analogies and −.34 for verbal analogies. In a geometric analogies experiment, only application was reliably estimated for individual subjects, and it showed a median multiple correlation (taking into account error rates as well as latencies) with psychometric test performance of .34. Sternberg and Gardner (1983) obtained much more reliable estimates of the reasoning process parameters than had Sternberg (1977). They administered to subjects three different tasks—analogies, series completions, and classifications—with three different contents: schematic picture, verbal, and geometric. Correlations between a combined reasoning component (including inference, mapping, and application) and psychometrically measured intelligence were −.70 for analogies, −.50 for series completions, and −.64 for classifications, averaged over contents. Correlations were −.70 for schematic-picture items, −.61 for verbal items, and −.67 for geometric items, averaged over tasks. This approach seems capable of yielding rather high correlations. Thus, it holds some promise for understanding individual differences in psychometrically measured intelligence, although again, it seems highly unlikely that this approach provides anything close to a full account of individual differences in intelligence. In particular, the approach does not deal with the question of how individuals decide in the first place what performance components to use.

Investigators seeking to understand intelligence in terms of *executive processes* seek to discover the means by which individuals decide (1) what performance components to use in solving various kinds of problems; (2) how to combine the performance components into an overall strategy; (3) how to represent information; and (4) how to trade off speed for accuracy (Brown, 1978; Flavell, 1981; Sternberg, 1980c). For instance, Sternberg (1980c) has proposed that such "metacomponents" (as he calls them) are highly general across tasks involving intelligent performance, and that they are in large part responsible for the appearance of a general factor in mental ability tests. According to this view, what is "general" across the tests is the execution of the metacomponents of task performance. Because metacomponents are difficult to isolate from task performance, existing data regarding the relationship between these metacomponents and psychometrically measured intelligence are spotty, at best. The only data of which I am aware are reported in Sternberg (1981b). Two metacomponents, global planning and local planning, were isolated from a complex inductive-reasoning task. *Global planning* is an indication of general strategic planning of solution approaches across a range of item types. *Local planning* indicates specific strategic planning for an individual item. It was found that global planning scores correlated (.43) with measured intelligence and that local planning scores correlated (−.33) with measured intelligence. Thus, more intelligent individuals tended to spend relatively more time than others in global planning, but relatively less time than others in local planning.

Summary of Cognitive Approaches

All of the cognitive approaches noted above seem to have at least some merit, in that they yield significant correlations with psychometrically measured intelligence. As a result, proponents of these various approaches have tended to view their individual approaches as basically successful. Although none of the approaches has yielded stunningly high correlations, all of them have yielded enough nonnegligible correlations to provide their proponents with encouragement to go on. This, of course, is the same situation as has evolved with psychometric approaches, which have also been remarkably resistant to disconfirmation. The question that arises is whether there might exist some theoretical account that could explain why almost anything seems to work, at least when "working" consists of the generation of moderate correlations with measured IQ. In the next part of the chapter, I present a new theory that seems to account for this embarrassment of riches.

TWO-FACET THEORY

Motivation

All of the accounts presented above—both psychometric and cognitive—suffer from a common flaw: they are post hoc. Investigators have started with a class of tasks, and then claimed that intelligence is whatever it takes to do well on those tasks.

Consider first the psychometric theories. The "factors of intelligent behavior" that emerge from factor analysis are largely determined by the tasks that are entered into the analysis. For example, "spatial ability" can appear as a factor of intelligence only if spatial-type tasks are included in the test battery. If such tasks are not included, there is no way for a spatial factor to emerge. But how does one decide to include spatial, or any other particular kind of task, in one's test battery? Unfortunately, psychometric theorists never provided any *a priori* guidelines for task selection. Rather, they chose tasks that they thought would "work," in some sense of the word. As time progressed, the major basis for task selection seems to have become past use. Tasks were used that were similar or identical to tasks that had been used before. But tradition scarcely constitutes an *a priori*, theoretical basis for choosing tasks that measure intelligence.

Consider cognitive theories next. As Newell (1973) has observed, task selection in cognitive-psychological research has scarcely been theoretically motivated. On the contrary, it appears to have been at least as haphazard as task selection in psychometric research. Tasks have been selected for any number of reasons, but theoretical motivation does not appear to be one of them. At times, cognitive psychology has seemed to be "a psychology of tasks" (Sternberg, 1979), in which interrelationships have been only vaguely understood. Cognitive psychologists studying intelligence seem to have picked up well-worked standard tasks, and then developed theories that happened to suit. For example, Hunt's early work (1978) was based on the standard tasks being used in the cognitive psychologists' laboratory, just as Sternberg's early work (1977) was based on the standard tasks used in psychometric tests of intelligence.

The theory proposed below differs from these earlier ones in starting with a specification of the attributes of tasks or situations that lead to their measuring intelligence. No attempt is made to specify the particular tasks or situations that should be used. Indeed, from the present viewpoint, the proper choice of tasks and situations will vary across persons and groups of persons. Thus, what matters is not the particular tasks or situations used, but what they measure for a given individual. Prior theorizing has been misguided in starting with tasks rather than with the skills a task should measure. The kinds of skills proposed as important here could, in fact, apply to almost any task or situation, given the right circumstances.

The two-facet theory proposes that a task measures "intelligence" to the extent that it requires either or both of two skills: (1) the ability to deal with novel kinds of task and situational demands and (2) the ability to automatize information processing. Let us consider each of these skills in turn.

Ability to Deal with Novel Task and Situational Demands

Novel Tasks

The idea that intelligence involves the ability to deal with novel task demands is itself far from novel (Cattell, 1971; Horn, 1968; Kaufman & Kaufman, 1983; Raaheim, 1974; Snow, 1981; Sternberg, 1981b, 1982b, 1982c). Sternberg (1981b) has suggested, in fact, that intelligence is best measured by tasks that are "nonentrenched" in the sense that they require types of information processing from outside a person's everyday experience. The task may be nonentrenched in either the kinds of operations or the kinds of concepts it requires the individual to utilize. According to this view, then, intelligence involves

> not merely the ability to learn and reason with new concepts but the ability to learn and reason with new kinds of concepts. Intelligence is not so much a person's ability to learn or think within conceptual systems that the person has already become familiar with as it is his or her ability to learn and think within new conceptual systems, which can then be brought to bear upon already existing knowledge structures (Sternberg, 1981b, p. 4).

It is important to note that the usefulness of a task in measuring intelligence is not a linear function of task novelty. The task that is presented should be novel, but not totally outside the individual's past experience (Raaheim, 1974). If the task is too novel, then the individual will have no cognitive structures to bring to bear upon the task, and as a result, the task will simply be outside of the individual's range of comprehension. Calculus, for example, would be a highly novel field of endeavor for most 5-year-olds. But calculus tasks would be so far outside their range of experience that such tasks would be worthless for the assessment of intelligence in this age group. In Piagetian terms, the task should primarily require accommodation, but must require some assimilation as well (Piaget, 1972).

Implicit in the above discussion is the notion that novelty can be of two kinds, either or both of which may be involved in task performance. The two kinds of novelty might be characterized as involving (a) comprehension of the task and (b) acting upon one's comprehension of the task. Let us consider the meaning of each of these two kinds of novelty.

Novelty in comprehension of the task refers to the novelty that is inherent in understanding the task confronting oneself. Once one understands the task, acting upon it may or may not be challenging. Consider, for example, the "conceptual projection" task used by Sternberg (1981b, 1982c). Subjects were presented with elaborate scenarios regarding objects that change their properties over time and space. In one scenario, certain objects change colors in the year 2000, and others do not. Subjects are required to learn how to make judgments concerning what has happened with regard to the colors of certain of the objects in 2000. In another scenario, some objects change consistency (from liquid to solid, or vice versa) when transported from one side of the equator of a distant planet to the other, while other objects do not undergo such changes. Again, subjects must learn how to make judgments regarding what has happened to the consistencies of certain objects that have been transported, in this case over space as well as time. Learning how to perform the task is quite difficult and takes subjects a fair amount of time. But once subjects learn how to perform the task, their error rates are quite low, generally under 5 percent. In this particular task, difficulty due to task novelty seems to inhere primarily in learning the nature of the task and in the rather bizarre concepts employed in the task. Once subjects succeed in this learning, however, performance is almost error-free.

Novelty in acting upon one's comprehension of the task refers to novelty in acting upon a problem rather than in learning about the problem or in learning how to solve it. Consider, for example, an example of the insight problems used by Sternberg and Davidson (1982, 1983).

> Water lilies double in area every 24 hours. At the beginning of the summer there is one water lily on a lake. It takes 60 days for the lake to become covered with water lilies. On what day is the lake half covered?

People generally have little difficulty comprehending what problems such as this one are saying. Indeed, many have encountered superficially similar problems during their school careers. But people often have considerable difficulty in coming up with the insights needed to solve such a problem. Thus, their difficulty is in acting upon their understanding of the problem, rather than in understanding the problem itself. In the present instance, they have to infer that the fact that the water lilies double in area every 24 hours implies that 24 hours before the lake became fully covered (on the 60th day), it was half covered. The answer to the problem is thus the "59th day." In this particular kind of task, subjects were able to solve only about 40 percent of the problems correctly.

It is possible, of course, to formulate problems involving novelty in both comprehension and execution of a particular kind of task, as well as those that involve novelty in neither comprehension nor execution. The present account would suggest that problems of these two kinds might be less satisfactory measures of intelligence than those involving novelty in either comprehension or execution, but not in both. The reason for this supposition is that the former problems might be too novel, whereas the latter problems might not be novel enough to provide optimal measurement of intelligence.

The two-facet theory does not specify the mental mechanisms involved in dealing with novel tasks. Such a specification is left to mechanistic theories of intelligence. In my own "componential" theory (Sternberg, 1980b), for example, the ability to deal with novelty would be understood largely in terms of the application of such "metacomponents" as identification of the problem, selection of components for solving the problem, selection of a strategy for combining components, and so on; and in terms of "knowledge-acquisition" components, such as selective encoding of relevant information to be learned, selective combination of information in an optimal way, and selective comparison of new information to old information.

The theory also does not specify the relevant range of tasks in which expeditious processing of novelty is relevant to the understanding of intelligence. For example, learning how to juggle with one's eyes closed would probably be a novel task for most people, but might not provide a particularly good assessment of intelligence. The relevant range of tasks must be described in terms of a "contextual" theory of intelligence (Sternberg, in press-a), one that specifies what classes of mental and observable behaviors are considered intelligent in the context of a given sociocultural milieu.

Novel Situations

The notion that intelligence is measured particularly well in situations that require adaptation to new and challenging environmental demands encompasses both expert and lay notions of the nature of intelligence ("Intelligence and its measurement," 1921;

Sternberg, Conway, Ketron, & Bernstein, 1981). The idea is that a person's intelligence is best shown, not in run-of-the-mill situations that are encountered regularly in everyday life, but rather in extraordinary situations that challenge the individual's ability to cope with the environment. Almost everyone knows someone (perhaps oneself) who performs well when confronted with tasks that are presented in a familiar milieu, but who falls apart when presented with similar or even identical tasks in an unfamiliar milieu. For example, a person who performs well in his or her everyday environment may find it difficult to function in a foreign country, even one that is similar in many respects to "home." In general, some people can perform well, but only under situational circumstances that are highly favorable to their getting their work done. When the environment is less supportive, their efficacy is greatly reduced.

Essentially the same constraints that apply to task novelty also apply to situational novelty. First, too much novelty can render the situation nondiagnostic of intellectual level. Moreover, there may exist situations in which no one could function effectively (this is perhaps epitomized by the situation confronted by the protagonist of Sartre's *No Exit*). Second, situational novelty can inhere either in understanding the nature of the situation or in performing within the context of that situation. In some instances, it is figuring out just what the situation is that is difficult; in others, it is operating in that situation once one has figured out what it is. Third, the two-facet theory does not specify the mechanisms that lead to greater or lesser efficacy in situational adaptation. A mechanistic theory is needed for this purpose. Fourth and finally, the theory presented here does not specify the range of novel situations to which adaptation would be considered "intelligent." Waking up one morning and finding that people only drive their cars in reverse gear might be quite a novel experience, but being able to function in such an environment might not provide a very good index of intelligence.

Interactions Between Tasks, Situations, and Persons

It is important to take into account the fact that tasks or situations that are novel for some persons may well not be novel for others. Thus, a given task or situation will not necessarily measure "intelligence" to the same extent for some people that it does for others. From the present viewpoint, it is the novelty of the task, rather than the task itself, that makes it a measure of intelligence, and level and type of novelty can differ widely for performers of a given task. Similarly, people vary widely in the extent to which various kinds of situations are novel in their experience. Not only do task and situation interact with person, but they can interact with each other as well. A task that is novel in one situation might not be novel in another situation. Finally, at the level of "third-order" interaction, a task may be novel (or mundane) for some persons in one situation but not a second situation, whereas the same task would be novel (or mundane) for other persons in the second situation but not the first. In sum, one needs to take into account interactions among these variables as well as their main effects.

Ability to Automatize Information Processing

Automatization as a Function of Task

Many kinds of tasks requiring complex information processing seem so intricate that it is a wonder we can perform them at all. Consider reading, for example. The number and complexity of operations involved in reading is staggering, and what is more staggering is the rate at which these operations are performed (Crowder, 1982; Just & Carpenter, 1980). Performance of tasks as complex as reading would seem to be possible only because a substantial proportion of the operations required are automatized and thus require minimal mental effort. (See Schneider and Shiffrin, 1977, and Shiffrin and Schneider, 1977, for a discussion of the mental requirements for tasks involving controlled and automatized information processing.) Deficiencies in reading have been theorized to result in large part from failures in automatization of operations (LaBerge & Samuels, 1974; Sternberg & Wagner, 1982).

The proposal being made here is that complex verbal, mathematical, and other difficult tasks can feasibly be executed only because many of the operations involved in their performance have been automatized. Failure to automatize such operations, either fully or in part, results in a breakdown of information processing and hence less intelligent task performance. Intellectual operations that can be performed smoothly and automatically by the more intelligent individuals are performed only haltingly and under conscious control by less intelligent individuals.

As in the case of novelty, automatization can occur either in task comprehension, task execution, or both. Let us consider how each of these kinds of automatization operates in various kinds of tasks.

The standard synonyms test used to measure vocabulary is familiar to most middle-class students at or above the secondary-school level. Indeed, when confronted with a multiple-choice synonyms test, about the only things such students need to check are whether the test is in fact one of synonyms (as opposed to, say, antonyms) and whether there is a penalty for guessing. But examinees can usually read the directions to such a test cursorily, and could probably skip them altogether if they were merely told the name of the task. Comprehension of what is required is essentially automatic. But solution of individual test items may be far from automatic, especially if the test requires discriminating relatively fine shades of meaning. Students may find they have to give a fair amount of thought to the individual items, whether because they need to discriminate shades of meaning or because they are unsure of the meaning of particular words, and have to employ strategies to guess the best answers for such items. In the standard synonyms task, comprehension of task instructions is essentially automatic (or nearly so), but solution of test items (beyond the simplest ones) probably is not.

In contrast, experimental tasks used by cognitive psychologists seem to present the opposite situation, in at least one respect. Tasks such as the letter-matching task used by Posner and Mitchell (1967) and the fixed-set memory-scanning task of S. Sternberg (1969) are probably unfamiliar to most subjects when they enter the cognitive psychologist's laboratory. The subjects do not automatically know what is expected of them and have to listen reasonably carefully to the instructions. But after the task is explained and the subjects have had some practice in performing the tasks, it is likely that task performance becomes rapidly automatized. The tasks come to be executed almost effortlessly, with little conscious thought.

It is possible, of course, for task performance to be fully automatized, or not to be automatized at all. When one gets hold of a mystery story to read, one knows essentially what one is going to do and how one is going to do it. Comprehension of the task and then performance of it are both quite automatized. In contrast, learning how to solve a new kind of mathematics problem, such as a mixture or a work problem, is probably automatized with respect to neither comprehension nor task execution.

The proposed theory specifies neither the mechanisms by which automatization occurs (but see Schneider & Shiffrin, 1977; Shiffrin & Schneider, 1977; Sternberg, 1981a, in press-b) nor the range of tasks for which automatization of performance is relevant (but see Sternberg, in press-a). Such specifications are left to mechanistic and contextual theories, respectively.

Automatization as a Function of Situation

Very little is known about how situations affect automatization of task performance. Clearly, one wishes to provide as much practice on the task to be automatized as possible, and to use a fixed-set rather than a varied-set mode of presentation (Shiffrin & Schneider, 1977). Presumably, one might wish to minimize distraction from the task in order to allow the individual to concentrate on learning the task and eventually automatizing it.

Interactions Between Tasks, Situations, and Persons

As was the case with response to novelty, interactions can exist in promotion of automatization between tasks and situations; between tasks and persons; between situations and persons; and between tasks, situations, and persons. Much of the literature on aptitude-treatment interactions in task performance can be viewed as an attempt to understand how different kinds of environments promote or retard learning on specific classes of tasks as a function of aptitude characteristics of the learner. In general, replicable findings in the aptitude-treatment interaction literature are hard to come by (Cronbach & Snow, 1977). But sufficient evidence has been accumulated to suggest that such interactions do indeed exist.

In the domain of laboratory tasks, MacLeod, Hunt, and Mathews (1978) and Mathews, Hunt, and MacLeod (1980) found that the optimal strategy for promotion of rapid performance on sentence-picture comparison items was a function of the individual's level of spatial ability. A spatial strategy worked better for some individuals, whereas a linguistic strategy worked better for others whose scores on spatial ability tests were relatively lower. Sternberg and Weil (1980) obtained a similar result for linear syllogisms: Optimality of a linguistic, spatial, or a mixed strategy depended upon an individual's pattern of verbal and spatial aptitudes. In the domain of more commonly performed, real-world tasks, it seems highly likely that certain methods of teaching reading lead to better performance, including fuller skill automatization, than do other methods (Baron & Strawson, 1976; Cronbach & Snow, 1977; Crowder, 1982; Spache & Spache, 1973). The whole-word method seems better suited to certain ability patterns, and the phonics method to others. Similarly, different methods of foreign-language instruction seem to be differentially effective for individuals with different aptitude patterns, but it is not yet clear just what the nature of the interaction is (Carroll, in press; Diller, 1978). Tentatively, one might venture that grammar-intensive and learning-from-context methods may work better for those with higher general intelligence but only average abilities specialized for language learning; mimicry and memorization methods may work better for those with higher specialized language-learning abilities but only average general intelligence.

Relationship between Abilities to Deal with Novelty and to Automatize Processing

For many (but probably not all) kinds of tasks, the ability to deal with novelty and to automatize information processing may occur along an experiential continuum. When one first encounters a task or kind of situation, ability to deal with novelty comes into play.

The more intelligent person will be more rapidly and fully able to cope with the novel demands being made. As experience with the task or kind of situation increases, novelty decreases, and the task or situation will become less appropriate in its measurement of intelligence from the standpoint of processing of novelty. However, after some amount of practice with the task or in the situation, automatization skill may come into play, making the task a more appropriate measure of automatization skill. Thus, a given task or situation may continue to provide appropriate measurement of intelligence over practice, but for differing reasons at different points in practice: Early in the person's experience, the ability to deal with novelty is assessed; later, the ability to automatize information processing is assessed.

WHAT TASKS MEASURE INTELLIGENCE, AND WHY?

The proposed two-facet theory suggests what kinds of tasks should be used to measure intelligence and what kinds of tasks should not be so used. This theory also accounts for why some measures of intelligence are better measures than others. Let us consider some of the tasks most frequently used, and the implications of the theory for understanding why these tasks are more or less successful.

Laboratory Tasks

According to the present view, the simpler tasks, such as simple reaction time, choice reaction time, and letter identification, have some validity as measures of intelligence because they primarily measure automatization of various kinds. For example, simple reaction-time tasks measure in part the extent to which an individual can automatize rapid responses to a single stimulus, and letter-identification tasks measure in part the extent to which access to highly overlearned codes stored in long-term memory is automatized. Speed is a reasonable measure of intellectual performance because it is presumably highly correlated with degree of automatization; but it is only an indirect measure of this degree of automatization, and hence provides an imperfect measure of it. One might expect some increase in correlation of task latencies with measured intelligence as task complexity increases, even at these very simple levels, because of the increased element of novelty in the higher levels of even simple tasks. Thus, choice reaction time introduces an element of uncertainty that is absent in simple reaction time, and the amount of uncertainty, and hence the novelty, increases as the number of response choices increases.

The more complex laboratory tasks, such as analogies, classifications, syllogisms, and the like, probably measure both degree of automatization and response to novelty. To the extent that subjects have had past practice on these test item formats, their selection and implementation of strategies will be partially automatized when they start the tasks. But even if they have had little or no prior experience with certain kinds of items, the formats tend to be repetitive. In the large numbers of trials typical of cognitive-psychological experiments, subjects are likely to automatize their performance to some degree. The more complex items also measure response to novelty, in that the relations subjects have to recognize and reason with will usually be somewhat unfamiliar.

Psychometric Tasks

The psychometric tasks found on ability tests are likely to measure intelligence for the same reasons as the complex laboratory tasks, in that they contain essentially the same kinds of contents. They are apt to be slightly better measures than the laboratory tasks for three reasons. First, the pencil-and-paper psychometric items tend to be harder because laboratory tasks are often simplified in order to reduce error rates. Harder tasks will, on the average, involve greater amounts of novelty. Second, psychometric test items are usually presented en masse (subjects are given a fixed amount of time to solve all of them) rather than individually (subjects are given a fixed or free amount of time to solve each separate item). Presenting the items en masse requires individuals to plan an inter-item as well as an intra-item strategy, and hence requires more "executive" kinds of behaviors. Such behaviors may have been previously automatized in part, but are also necessarily responses to whatever novelty inheres in the particular testing situation confronted (content, difficulty, time limits, etc., for a particular test). Third, the psychometric test items found in most test batteries have been extensively validated, whereas the items used in laboratory experiments almost never have been.

Implications for Task Selection

The proposed theory carries with it certain implications for the selection of tasks used to measure intelligence. In particular, one wishes to select tasks that involve some blend of automatized behaviors and behaviors in response to novelty. This blending is probably best achieved within test items, but may also be achieved by items that specialize in measuring either the one skill or the other. The blending may be achieved by presenting subjects with a novel task, and then giving them enough practice with the task so that performance becomes differentially automatized (across subjects). Such a task will thereby measure both response to novelty and degree of automatization, although at different times during the course of testing.

Resolution of Puzzles in the Literature on Intelligence

The proposed theory suggests resolutions to four of the puzzles that appear in the literature on intelligence.

Why Do So Many Tasks Measure Intelligence?

Almost any task one encounters is unfamiliar in some degree; thus, most tasks involve at least some coping with novelty. Similarly, almost any task that is not totally new has been encountered before, at least in part or in analogue; thus, most tasks involve at least some prior automatization in their performance. The result is that most tasks measure intelligence in greater or lesser degree. It is for this reason that it is so easy to find *some* degree of correlation between task performance and scores on tests specifically designed to measure intelligence. But not many tasks (including the tasks found in IQ tests) are exceptionally well suited to measuring either response to novelty or automatization of task performance. As a result, the number of tasks that provide highly valid measurement of intelligence is probably fairly limited. The present view would suggest selecting tasks that are valid in the sense of measuring skills involved in coping with novelty and automatizing performance.

At What Point in Practice on a Task Does it Best Measure Intelligence?

A lively debate has arisen over the point in practice at which a task best measures intelligence. Noble, Noble, and Alcock (1958) used tests from the Thurstone Primary Mental Abilities battery to predict individual differences in trial-and-error learning. They found that prediction was higher for total correct scores than for initial correct scores, suggesting that the higher correlation came from performance in later trials. Fleishman (1965) and Fleishman and Hempel (1955) also found that the percentage of variance accounted for in motor tasks by traditional psychometric tests increases with practice. Results such as these have led Glaser (1967) to conclude that "the usual psychometric variables are correlated to a lesser degree with initial acquisition performance (p. 12)." These results, however, seem to be inconsistent with the idea that tasks measure intelligence to the extent that they are novel.

The proposed theory, however, can account for these findings, as well as for the more common finding that correlations with intelligence remain about the same at all levels of practice (Guyote & Sternberg, 1981; Sternberg, 1980b). Indeed, psychometric tests are predicated on the idea that they are measuring intelligence to the same degree earlier and later during testing. From the present viewpoint, a given task will tend to measure novelty-coping skills earlier during practice and automatization skills later during practice. As a result, whether the correlation with intelligence as measured by a psychometric test will increase, decrease, or remain the same over practice will depend upon the extent to which the task successfully measures novelty and automatization at the various stages of practice. Thus, the overall correlation with measured intelligence may actually remain the same over practice, even though the skills that contribute to that correlation differ over time.

Can Tests of Intelligence be Culture Fair?

No test of intelligence can be culture *free*: All tests require some degree of acculturation for their successful completion. But there is some question as to whether a test can be culture *fair*. Can a given task measure intelligence to the same degree across cultures or even subcultures? According the present view, a test will be culture fair to the extent that it measures coping with novelty and automatization equally across (or even within) cultures. Unfortunately, people's experiences with tasks and classes of tasks tend to differ widely across cultures (and even, to a fairly large extent, within cultures). I doubt whether tests can be precisely equated in terms of the extent to which they measure each of coping with novelty and automatization across different groups. Consider, for example, the common finding that abstract, nonverbal items, which have often been proposed to be culture fair (Cattell & Cattell, 1963), tend to show greater discrepancies across cultural groups than do verbal tests (Jensen, 1980). From the present view, this is because such tests can measure quite different skills across groups. For individuals who are familiar with these types of items (from taking tests or from everyday experiences with abstract kinds of materials), the nonverbal tests may hardly measure novelty-coping skills at all. For individuals unfamiliar with these types of items, the items may primarily measure the ability to cope with novelty. Thus, although the objective stimulus item is the same, the item measures different skills for the different individuals, and performance could not be compared fairly across those individuals.

Why do Abilities Tend to Cluster into Two Groups, "Fluid" and "Crystallized"?

Research using a variety of approaches has suggested that there are two main groups of abilities, which have been called "fluid" and "crystallized" by Cattell (1971), Horn (1968), and Snow (1980); "practical-mechanical" and "verbal-educational" by Vernon (1971); and problem solving and verbal by Sternberg, Conway, Ketron, and Bernstein (1981). Fluid types of abilities are measured particularly well by reasoning items such as analogies and series completions, whereas crystallized abilities are measured well by tests such as reading comprehension and vocabulary. According to the present view, fluid ability tests tend to stress ability to deal with novelty, whereas crystallized ability tests tend to stress automatization of high level processes. Laboratory tasks stressing response to novel demands measure fluid abilities. In contrast, laboratory tasks that stress automatization of higher level skills such as the letter-comparison task used by Hunt et al. (1975), are probably better understood as measures of precursors of crystallized abilities than of fluid abilities (Hunt, 1978). Because of the extreme number of skills required in such complex verbal tasks as reading, it is necessary to have a large number of operations automatized for their successful completion. If these operations are not automatized, specific disabilities in performance may result (Sternberg & Wagner, 1982).

In sum, it has been proposed that behavior is intelligent when it involves either or both of two sets of skills: adaptation to novelty and automatization of performance. This proposal has been used to explain why so many tasks seem to measure "intelligence" to a greater or lesser degree, as well as to account for other puzzling findings in the literature on human intelligence. The present theory is not a "complete" theory of intelligence. It needs to be supplemented by a theory of the mental mechanisms involved in coping with novelty and automatizing task performance (Sternberg, 1980c) and by a theory of how the context of behavior influences what is intelligent in a given task or situation (Sternberg, in press, a). But the theory does suggest the characteristics to look for in choosing tasks on which performance reflects an individual's intelligence. Most importantly, the theory is an *a priori* specification of what a task or situation must measure in order to assess intelligence. The theory is distinctive in that it is not linked to any arbitrary choice of tasks or situations, which should follow from theory, rather than the other way around.

REFERENCES

Atkinson, J. W. *Motives in fantasy, action, and society.* Princeton, N.J.: Van Nostrand, 1958.

Atkinson, J. W. *An introduction to motivation.* New York: American Book Company, 1964.

Atkinson, J. W., & Raynor, J. O. (Eds.). *Personality, motivation, and achievement.* Washington, D.C.: Hemisphere, 1978.

Baron, J., & Strawson, C. Use of orthographic and word-specific knowledge in reading words. *Journal of Experimental Psychology: Human Perception and Performance,* 1976, *2,* 386–93.

Berger, M. The "scientific approach" to intelligence: An overview of its history with special reference to mental speed. In H. J. Eysenck (Ed.), *A model for intelligence.* Berlin: Springer-Verlag, 1982.

Brown, A. L. Knowing when, where, and how to remember: A problem of metacognition. In R. Glaser (Ed.), *Advances in instructional psychology* (Vol. 1). Hillsdale, N.J.: Lawrence Erlbaum Associates, 1978.

Burt, C. *The factors of the mind.* London: University of London Press, 1940.

Carroll, J. B. Second-language abilities. In R. J. Sternberg (Ed.), *Human abilities: An information-processing approach.* San Francisco: W. H. Freeman, in press.

Cattell, J. M. Mental tests and measurements. *Mind,* 1890, *15,* 373–80.

Cattell, R. B. On the measurement of "perseveration." *British Journal of Educational Psychology,* 1935, *5,* 76–92.

Cattell, R. B. *Personality and motivation: Structure and measurement.* New York: World Publishing, 1957.

Cattell, R. B. *Abilities: Their structure, growth, and action.* Boston: Houghton Mifflin, 1971.

Cattell, R. B., & Cattell, A.K.S. *Test of* g: *Culture fair, Scale 3.* Champaign, Ill.: Institute for Personality and Ability Testing, 1963.

Cronbach, L. J. *Essentials of psychological testing* (3rd. ed.). New York: Harper & Row, 1970.

Cronbach, L. J., & Snow, R. E. *Aptitudes and instructional methods.* New York: Irvington, 1977.

Crowder, R. G. *The psychology of reading: An introduction.* Oxford, England: Oxford University Press, 1982.

Diller, K. C. *The language teaching controversy.* Rowley, Mass.: Newbury House, 1978.

Eysenck, H. J. (Ed.). *A model for intelligence.* Berlin: Springer-Verlag, 1982.

Flavell, J. H. Cognitive monitoring. In W. P. Dickson (Ed.), *Children's oral communication skills.* New York: Academic Press, 1981.

Fleishman, E. A. The prediction of total task performance from prior practice on task components. *Human Factors,* 1965, *7,* 18–27.

Fleishman, E. A., & Hempel, W. E., Jr. The relation between abilities and improvement with practice in a visual discrimination reaction task. *Journal of Experimental Psychology,* 1955, *49,* 301–12.

Galton, F. *Inquiry into human faculty and its development.* London: Macmillan, 1883.

Glaser, R. Some implications of previous work on learning and individual differences. In R. M. Gagne (Ed.), *Learning and individual differences.* Columbus, Ohio: Charles Merrill, 1967.

Greeno, J. G. Natures of problem-solving abilities. In W. K. Estes (Ed.), *Handbook of learning and cognitive processes* (Vol. 5): *Human information processing.* Hillsdale, N.J.: Lawrence Erlbaum Associates, 1978.

Guilford, J. P. *The nature of human intelligence.* New York: McGraw-Hill, 1967.

Guilford, J. P., & Hoepfner, R. *The analysis of intelligence.* New York: McGraw-Hill, 1971.

Guttman, L. A faceted definition of intelligence. In R. R. Eiferman (Ed.), *Scripta Hierosolymitana* (Vol. 14). Jerusalem: Magnes Press, 1965.

Guyote, M. J., & Sternberg, R. J. A transitive-chain theory of syllogistic reasoning. *Cognitive Psychology,* 1981, *13,* 461–525.

Hebb, D. O. *The organization of behavior.* New York: Wiley, 1949.

Hendrickson, A. E. The biological basis of intelligence. Part 1: Theory. In H. J. Eysenck (Ed.), *A model for intelligence.* Berlin: Springer-Verlag, 1982.

Holzinger, K. J. Relationships between three multiple orthogonal factors and four bifactors. *Journal of Educational Psychology,* 1938, *29,* 513–19.

Horn, J. L. Organization of abilities and the development of intelligence. *Psychological Review,* 1968, *75,* 242–59.

Hunt, E. B. Mechanics of verbal ability. *Psychological Review,* 1978, *85,* 109–30.

Hunt, E. B., Lunneborg, C., & Lewis, J. What does it mean to be high verbal? *Cognitive Psychology,* 1975, *7,* 194–227.

"Intelligence and its measurement: A symposium." *Journal of Educational Psychology,* 1921, *12,* 123–147, 195–216, 271–275.

Jackson, M. D., & McClelland, J. L. Processing determinants of reading speed. *Journal of Experimental Psychology: General,* 1979, *108,* 151–81.

Jensen, A. R. *Bias in mental testing.* New York: Free Press, 1980.

Jensen, A. R. Reaction time and psychometric *g.* In H. J. Eysenck (Ed.), *A model for intelligence.* Berlin: Springer-Verlag, 1982.

Just, M. A., & Carpenter, P. A. A theory of reading: From eye fixations to comprehension. *Psychological Review,* 1980, *87,* 329–54.

Kaufman, A. S., & Kaufman, N. L. *Kaufman Assessment Battery for Children.* Circle Pines, Minn.: American Guidance Service, 1982.

Keating, D. P., & Bobbitt, B. L. Individual and developmental differences in cognitive processing components of mental ability. *Child Development,* 1978, *49,* 155–67.

LaBerge, D., & Samuels, J. Toward a theory of automatic information processing in reading. *Cognitive Psychology,* 1974, *6,* 293–323.

Lally, M., & Nettelbeck, T. Intelligence, reaction time, and inspection time. *American Journal of Mental Deficiency,* 1977, *82,* 273–81.

Lemmon, V. W. The relation of reaction time to measures of intelligence, memory, and learning. *Archives of Psychology,* 1927–28, *15,* 5–38.

Lunneborg, C. E. Choice reaction time: What role in ability measurement? *Applied Psychological Measurement*, 1977, *1*, 309–30.

MacLeod, C. M., Hunt, E. B., & Mathews, N. N. Individual differences in the verification of sentence-picture relationships. *Journal of Verbal Learning and Verbal Behavior*, 1978, *17*, 493–507.

Mathews, N. N., Hunt, E. B., & MacLeod, C. M., Strategy choice and strategy training in sentence-picture verification. *Journal of Verbal Learning and Verbal Behavior*, 1980, *19*, 531–548.

McClelland, D. C. *Assessing human motivation*. New York: General Learning Press, 1971.

Newell, A. Production systems: Models of control structures. In W. G. Chase (Ed.), *Visual information processing*. New York: Academic Press, 1973.

Newell, A., & Simon, H. A. *Human problem solving*. Englewood Cliffs, N.J.: Prentice-Hall, 1972.

Noble, C. E., Noble, J. L., & Alcock, W. T. Prediction of individual differences in human trial-and-error learning. *Perceptual and Motor Skills*, 1958, *8*, 151–72.

Pellegrino, J. W., & Glaser, R. Components of inductive reasoning. In R. E. Snow, P. -A. Federico, & W. Montague (Eds.), *Aptitude, learning, and instruction: Cognitive process analyses of aptitude* (Vol. 1). Hillsdale, N.J.: Lawrence Erlbaum Associates, 1980.

Pellegrino, J. W., & Glaser, R. Analyzing aptitudes for learning: Inductive reasoning. In R. Glaser (Ed.), *Advances in instructional psychology* (Vol. 2). Hillsdale, N.J.: Lawrence Erlbaum Associates, 1982.

Piaget, J. *The psychology of intelligence*. Totowa, N.J.: Littlefield, Adams, 1972.

Posner, M. I., & Mitchell, R. F. Chronometric analysis of classification. *Psychological Review*, 1967, *74*, 392–409.

Raaheim, K. *Problem solving and intelligence*. Oslo: Universitetsforlaget, 1974.

Schmidt, F. L., & Hunter, J. E. Development of a general solution to the problem of validity generalization. *Journal of Applied Psychology*, 1977, *62*, 529–40.

Schneider, W., & Shiffrin, R. M. Controlled and automatic human information processing: I. Detection, search, and attention. *Psychological Review*, 1977, *84*, 1–66.

Shiffrin, R. M., & Schneider, W. Controlled and automatic human information processing: II. Perceptual learning, automatic attending, and a general theory. *Psychological Review*, 1977, *84*, 127–90.

Simon, H. A. Identifying basic abilities underlying intelligent performance of complex tasks. In L. B. Resnick (Ed.), *The nature of intelligence*. Hillsdale, N.J.: Lawrence Erlbaum Associates, 1976.

Snow, R. E. Aptitude processes. In R. E. Snow, P. -A. Federico, & W. E. Montague (Eds.), *Aptitude, learning, and instruction: Cognitive process analyses of aptitude* (Vol. 1). Hillsdale, N.J.: Lawrence Erlbaum Associates, 1980.

Snow, R. E. Toward a theory of aptitude for learning: I. Fluid and crystallized abilities and their correlates. In M. Friedman, J. P. Das, & N. O'Connor (Eds.), *Intelligence and learning.* New York: Plenum Press, 1981.
Spache, G. D., & Spache, E. B. *Reading in the elementary school* (3rd ed.). Boston: Allyn & Bacon, 1973.
Spearman, C. *The nature of "intelligence" and the principles of cognition.* London: Macmillan, 1923.
Spearman, C. *The abilities of man.* New York: Macmillan, 1927.
Sternberg, R. J. *Intelligence, information processing, and analogical reasoning: The componential analysis of human abilities.* Hillsdale, N.J.: Lawrence Erlbaum Associates, 1977.
Sternberg, R. J. The nature of mental abilities. *American Psychologist*, 1979, *34*, 214–30.
Sternberg, R. J. Factor theories of intelligence are all right almost. *Educational Researcher*, 1980, *9*, 6–13, 18. (a)
Sternberg, R. J. Representation and process in linear syllogistic reasoning. *Journal of Experimental Psychology: General*, 1980, *109*, 119–59. (b)
Sternberg, R. J. Sketch of a componential subtheory of human intelligence. *Behavioral and Brain Sciences*, 1980, *3*, 573–84. (c)
Sternberg, R. J. Intelligence and nonentrenchment. *Journal of Educational Psychology*, 1981, *73*, 1–16. (b)
Sternberg, R. J. The evolution of theories of intelligence. *Intelligence*, 1981, *5*, 209–30. (a)
Sternberg, R. J. (Ed.). *Handbook of human intelligence.* New York: Cambridge University Press, 1982. (a)
Sternberg, R. J. Lies we live by: Misapplication of tests in the identification of the gifted. *Gifted Child Quarterly*, 1982, *26*, 157–61. (b)
Sternberg, R. J. Natural, unnatural, and supernatural concepts. *Cognitive Psychology*, 1982, *14*, 451–58. (c)
Sternberg, R. J. A contextualist view of the nature of intelligence. *International Journal of Psychology*, in press. (a)
Sternberg, R. J. Mechanisms of cognitive development: A componential approach. In R. J. Sternberg (Ed.), *Mechanisms of cognitive development.* San Francisco: W. H. Freeman, in press. (b)
Sternberg, R. J., Conway, B. E., Ketron, J. L., & Bernstein, M. People's conceptions of intelligence. *Journal of Personality and Social Psychology*, 1981, *41*, 37–55.
Sternberg, R. J., & Davidson, J. E. The mind of the puzzler. *Psychology Today*, 1982, *16*, June, 37–44.
Sternberg, R. J., & Davidson, J. E. Insight in the gifted. *Educational Psychologist*, 1983, *18*, 52–8.
Sternberg, R. J., & Gardner, M. K. Unities in inductive reasoning. *Journal of Experimental Psychology: General*, 1983, *12*, 80–116.
Sternberg, R. J., & Wagner, R. K. Automatization failure in learning disabilities. *Topics in Learning and Learning Disabilities*, 1982, *2*, July, 1–11.
Sternberg, R. J., & Weil, E. M. An aptitude-strategy interaction in linear syllogistic reasoning. *Journal of Educational Psychology*, 1980, *72*, 226–34.

Sternberg, S. Memory-scanning: Mental processes revealed by reaction-time experiments. *American Scientist*, 1969, *4*, 539–56.
Thurstone, L. L. *Primary mental abilities*. Chicago: University of Chicago Press, 1938.
Vernon, P. E. *The structure of human abilities*. London: Methuen, 1971.
Whitely, S. E. Latent trait models in the study of intelligence. *Intelligence*, 1980, *4*, 97–132.
Wissler, C. The correlation of mental and physical tests. *Psychological Review Monograph Supplement*, 1901, *3*, 6, (Whole No. 16).

7

APPLICATIONS OF SCHEMA THEORY IN COGNITIVE RESEARCH

Perry W. Thorndyke
Perceptronics, Inc.
Menlo Park, California

AN OVERVIEW OF SCHEMA THEORY

The cognitive research community has recently witnessed a surge of interest in developing a set of ideas about memory structures that can be collectively referred to as schema theory. A *schema* comprises a cluster of knowledge representing a particular generic procedure, object, percept, event, sequence of events, or social situation. This cluster provides a skeleton structure for a concept that can be "instantiated," or filled out, with the detailed properties of the particular instance being represented. For example, a schema for the American Psychological Association (APA) annual meetings would encode the standard properties of a scientific conference, such as its location, date, attendees, session types, and the length of presentations. In psychology and artificial intelligence (AI) literature, knowledge structures encoding prototypical properties of concepts have been variously referred to as frames, scripts, units, objects, as well as schemata (Bobrow & Norman, 1975; Minsky, 1975; Rumelhart & Ortony, 1977; Schank & Abelson, 1977; Winograd, 1975). Hereafter, I use the term *schema* to refer to the set of ideas and assumptions common to all of these variants.

Schema theory refers to the collection of models that presume that humans encode such knowledge clusters in memory and use them to comprehend and store new instances of the concept. In particular, a schema guides comprehension of new instances of the concept by providing expectations for and constraints on the set of related properties associated with that concept. Thus, one could infer several facts about the 1983 APA meeting, based on knowledge of the "generic" APA meeting without knowing any of the details about the 1983 meetings. For example, the person could specify the approximate dates (the last half of August, beginning on Monday and ending on Friday), type of location (a large U.S. city in a state that has ratified the Equal Rights Amendment), and the nature of the program (a mixture of paper sessions, symposia, and invited addresses) without actually knowing the detailed arrangements.

Numerous papers have recently appeared in the psychological literature interpreting observations or experimental results in terms of the schema theoretic framework. In fact, there has been something of a stampede toward the adoption and development of this notion to explain a broad range of psychological phenomena. In general, most schema-based research has attempted to explain people's ability to comprehend, encode in memory, and recall complex yet familiar aggregations of facts or percepts. Schema theory explains these phenomena by assuming that schemata, or organized collections of facts and relations, are matched against the incoming information and provide a structure in which to encode this information.

This research has generally taken one of two approaches. One major group of models has focused on input processes associated with the use of schemata. These models address (1) how memory schemata are activated and used to guide the organization of incoming information and (2) how that information is represented in memory. Essentially, these *comprehension*-oriented models show how schemata contain the knowledge necessary to interpret and encode complex world events (Brewer & Treyens, 1981; Chi, Feltovich, & Glaser, 1981; Minsky, 1975; Rumelhart & Ortony, 1977; Schank & Abelson, 1977; Schmidt, 1976; Stein & Nezworski, 1978; Thorndyke & Hayes-Roth, 1979).

Consider the concept of a desk. In schema theory, the representation of a desk would include the important defining features of a generic desk, such as:

DESK	
Specialization of:	furniture
Parts:	top, body, drawers, legs
Number of legs:	4
Composition of top:	wood, formica, particle board
Composition of body:	wood, metal, particle board
Function:	work space, storage
Typical location:	office

This knowledge can be used to recognize and encode information about a particular instance of a desk that one might see. Thus, we might represent in memory our knowledge of Gordon's desk as:

GORDON'S DESK	
Specialization of:	desk
Parts:	top, body, drawers, legs
Number of legs:	4
Composition of top:	simulated walnut (formica)
Composition of body:	walnut
Function:	work space, storage
Location:	Gordon's office

The existence of a generic schema can aid recognition and the encoding of features for a new instance by indicating which characteristics to notice and what their values are likely to be. By providing such information, the schema allows learners to have expectations for what they are likely to encounter and how to interpret it. For example, when one walks into an office one is not surprised to see a desk, since that is a desk's typical location. Furthermore, one expects the desk to have four legs and drawers. Similarly, the fact that the schema provides descriptions of the concepts they represent helps people interpret novel occurrences in terms of known concepts. Consider, for example, an office containing a pair of two-drawer file cabinets, about 4 feet apart, with a piece of plywood lying across them. One might guess that the plywood and file cabinets were being used as a desk, with the plywood serving as the desk top and the file cabinets serving as drawers. The attempt to match this contraption to the desk schema is motivated by its location in an office and the desire to view the makeshift equipment as an instance of a "typical" office furnishing.

A related approach to schema research has emphasized the importance of people's "perspective" in comprehension, demonstrating that frequently a single text permits different interpretations based on alternative schemata (Anderson, 1977, 1978; Anderson, Reynolds, Schallert, & Goetz, 1977; Bower, 1978; Pichert & Anderson, 1977). For example, Pichert and Anderson found that subjects' memory of particular details from a story about a house depended on whether they read the story from the point of view of a burglar or a potential home-buyer. They interpreted these results as evidence for high-level schemata that guided the storage in memory of different types of information. In the "burglar" schema, the presence of a color television would be of interest, whereas in the "home-buyer" schema, a leaking roof would be more salient.

A second category of schema models has focused on output functions associated with the use of schemata. These models describe how schemata influence recall of information from memory (Bower, Black, & Turner, 1979; Kintsch & Greene, 1978; Mandler, 1978; Mandler & Johnson, 1977; Rumelhart, 1975; Thorndyke, 1977, 1978); and how they affect summarization of texts from memory (Kintsch & Greene, 1978; Kintsch, Mandel, & Kozminsky, 1977; Rumelhart, 1975, 1977; Thorndyke, 1977, 1978). For instance, Bower, Black, and Turner (1979) found that subjects recalling a text they previously read include both actions stated in the text and unstated actions implied by schema. People also preferred to recall actions in a familiar, "schematic" order, even when actions were scrambled in the original text. However, Thorndyke (1977) has shown that people remember more events from the original passage if actions are presented in their normal order rather than a scrambled order.

Admittedly, the distinction between comprehension models and recall models is somewhat arbitrary. Indeed, a few models have attempted more general and comprehensive formulations of memory schemata (Bobrow & Norman, 1975; Kintsch & van Dijk, 1978; Rumelhart & Ortony, 1977; Winograd, 1977). Nevertheless, these categories do reflect the two primary types of memory phenomena addressed by most schema theorists.

The "schema" concept is not a new one. As an explanatory concept, the schema has existed in psychology for well over 50 years. The term "schema" itself dates at least from Kant (1787/1963), who developed the idea that a person's experiences are collected together in memory and that these collections are defined by certain common elements. Since these common elements identify categories of experiences, they permit the synthesis of abstract knowledge that represents the category. This higher-order concept can be understood without reference to any particular occurrence within the category. In addition, one identifies experiences in a category by referring to the general schema that describes that category. This view of schemata was adopted by the neurologist Head (1920), who stated that anything entering consciousness is "charged with its relation to something that has gone before." In his classic text on experimental psychology, Woodworth (1938) remarked in a similar vein that the process of remembering involves the "revival of one's own experiences."

The schema concept rapidly spread to many branches of psychology; it took on similar but slightly different meanings in each. Gestalt psychologists found the concept of abstract schemata useful in describing memory for perceptual information (e.g., Woodworth, 1938). Piaget's (1926) early work with children used schemata to describe both the creation of and developmental change in cognitive structures. Early researchers in problem solving (e.g., Betz, 1932; Flach, 1925; Selz, 1913, 1922) viewed schemata as solution methods or as plans of operations guiding the problem solver's behavior.

This latter variant on schemata (as problem-solving method) is most similar to that adopted by Frederick Bartlett, the acknowledged originator of the use of schemata to describe story recall. Bartlett (1932) assumed that abstract knowledge structures aided recall of past events. His "War of the Ghosts" experiments demonstrated that prose recall involved both *reconstructive* and *reproductive* memory processes. Bartlett's subjects consistently produced idiosyncratic elaborations of some of the original facts in the story. Bartlett interpreted these data as evidence that subjects reconstruct the events of a story using a few of the original details plus an abstract cognitive schema as an elaboration plan.

The significant advance of recent research over previous work lies in the detailed specification of the data structures that encode schematic knowledge. This advance was made possible by the development during the past 20 years of syntactic grammars in linguistics and list-processing data structures in computer science. In artificial intelligence, researchers have been developing representations for knowledge of complex situations, events, and concepts. The data structures that have emerged consistently utilize knowledge clusters that encode typical cases of the concepts they represent. This research is typified by notions such as "frames" (Bobrow & Winograd, 1977; Kuipers, 1975; Minsky, 1975; Winograd, 1975); "scripts" (Schank & Abelson, 1975, 1977), or some other form of schemata (Moore & Newell, 1974; Schmidt, 1976; Stefik, 1981).

A second domain of research in which detailed memory structures have appeared is that of psychological studies of memory for prose. Principally inspired by the work of Bartlett (1932), researchers have begun to extend and formalize his ideas by modeling the text "grammars" underlying memory for story information (Kintsch & van Dijk, 1975, 1978; Mandler, 1978; Mandler & Johnson, 1977; Rumelhart, 1975, 1977; Rumelhart & Ortony, 1977; Stein & Glenn, 1978). This research has focused on demonstrating that text comprehension, encoding, and memory retrieval rely heavily on the activation and on the use of well-learned memory schemata. These schemata encode knowledge of how events are structured, how event sequences combine and form episodes, and how entire stories are constructed from sequences of episodes.

For example, a simple plot sequence might involve a problem facing the main character, a sequence of episodes in which the main character attempts to solve the problem, and some eventual resolution of the problem. The representational schema formalizes these relationships in the form of a grammar describing the narrative elements and the dependencies governing their occurrence in combination. The grammar thus provides a framework for encoding, or *parsing*, the organization of text information according to its narrative structure.

The grammar consists of a set of rules of narrative syntax and is independent of the linguistic content of any particular story. Each rule specifies a pattern of situation and event occurrences that characterizes some critical element in a story, such as the motivation and intention of a character. These patterns are hierarchically organized: combinations of patterns can organize into higher-order, more inclusive patterns. The successive application of the rules that formalize the schema results in a hierarchical representation of a story that includes the semantic content of individual propositions, as well as the organization of these propositions into abstract narrative patterns. Intermediate nodes in the structure represent patterns encoding narrative relationships among propositions. Terminal nodes represent actual propositions from the story. For example, consider the following simply story:

1 Gordon wanted to have the best pizza available in San Francisco for dinner.

2 So he looked in his restaurant guide for Italian restaurants.

3 Finally, he found one with a four-star recommendation.

4 He visited the restaurant and declared their sausage pizza a success.

This story may be viewed as a single episode, and the narrative relations among the four events may be represented by the following rule:

5 Episode ◊ Goal + Attempt* + Outcome.

The *goal*, or desired state, can be matched to statement 1, Gordon's desire for a pizza. Statements 2 and 3 represent *attempts*, that is, events initiated by Gordon, to attain the goal. (The "*" in statement 5 indicates that the element may be repeated.) The *outcome* is an event or state that indicates either success or failure in attaining the goal.

In more complex stories, simple episodes are embedded in a narrative that has a setting, a plot, and some resolution of the plot. The plot is some number of individual episodes comprising attempts to achieve the goal or some subgoal created by the main character. These episodes may be successively embedded as attempts to resolve subgoals produced during efforts to satisfy higher-order goals.

This approach to the analysis of text structure presumes a stereotype in the organization of knowledge in this class of narratives. It further presumes that the schema forms an integral part of the story representation. While the schema provides some constraints on the combination of events in a story, it can be modified to fit the unique properties of a particular story, just as the "desk" schema can be modified to represent the detailed features of a particular desk.

In spite of differing orientations of the researchers utilizing schemata as computer data structures or psychological constructs, several common assumptions underlie the various formulations of current schema models. These commonalities include five properties of schemata: concept abstraction, hierarchical organization, instantiation, prediction, and induction (Thorndyke & Yekovich, 1980). Briefly, these properties may be described as follows.

A schema represents a prototypical *abstraction* of the concept it represents, encoding the constituent properties that define a typical instance of its referent. The constituent properties may consist of perceptual features, semantic primitives, states or events in the world, or other schemata.

Schemata are *hierarchically organized* in memory. The hierarchy relates concepts of different degrees of specificity. For example, the schema for APA conventions presumably specifies and elaborates a more general "professional-convention" schema.

While both have many of the same properties, the properties of APA conventions are more constrained and precisely specified than those for a generic professional convention. The properties that characterize a schema are represented as variables that can be filled, or *instantiated*, whenever the schema is used to organize incoming information. Such instantiation is similar to the creation of a "token" node in semantic network models (Anderson & Bower, 1973) to represent the specific occurrence of a general concept.

The use of general schemata to organize new, incoming data permits reasoning from incomplete information. This reasoning takes the form of *predictions* about information the processor expects to obtain to fill the slots in the currently active schema. Such predictions can guide the interpretation of incoming information and support inferential processes that match input to expectations.

Finally, schemata are formed by *induction* from numerous previous experiences with various exemplars of the generic concept. Presumably, schemata develop through a process of successive refinement—as one accumulates additional experiences with a concept, expectations for the expected properties of the concept become more clearly defined.

The recent developments in the theoretical refinement of schemata and its application to psychological data highlight both the opportunities for and pitfalls of much current research in psychology. On the one hand, experimental psychology has always had a commitment to developing and testing theories of the knowledge structures and mechanisms that support learning, memory, and reasoning. The current work on schema theory certainly fits well in that tradition. However, as the next section argues, these efforts have only partially succeeded in producing scientifically acceptable explanatory theories. On the other hand, experimental and educational psychologists have an opportunity to translate the theoretical and empirical results obtained from schema theory research into prescriptions for human behavior in classroom or everyday situations.

The remainder of this paper defends this prescriptive role of schema theory in cognitive research. However, to do so, I must place the recent trends in schema theory within a larger context of cognitive research and its current directions. Thus, I must address two goals: The first is to argue in behalf of a particular role that I believe psychological research should play and for a research emphasis that reflects that role. The second goal is to discuss in detail the particular strengths and weaknesses of schema theory as a research perspective in educational and cognitive psychology.

THE CURRENT PSYCHOLOGICAL RESEARCH ENVIRONMENT

A major influence on the style and content of recent psychological research has been the evolution of *cognitive science*, an intellectual Zeitgeist within which a new style of psychological research flourishes. Cognitive science refers to interdisciplinary study of intelligent behavior in human and/or computer systems; it draws on the fields of cognitive and social psychology, artificial intelligence (the branch of computer science concerned with intelligent or expert systems), linguistics, education, and philosophy. Under the general heading of intelligent behavior, a number of specific problem areas receive considerable attention in the cognitive science community. These areas include representations for knowledge, language understanding, reasoning, planning, problem solving, and image understanding.

Two criteria distinguish the research that qualifies as cognitive science from more traditional discipline-specific work. First, cognitive science seeks to develop theories of complex processing and intelligent behavior, with implications for both the modeling of human performance and the construction of intelligent computer systems. Theories must be broad in scope, consider multiple cognitive operations, and transcend particular paradigms, even if this is achieved at the expense of analytic granularity. For example, a model describing the serial position effect in list-learning experiments would not be regarded as cognitive science because the model would be an extremely focused, fine-grain analysis of a single phenomenon observed in a particular experimental paradigm. However, a model for the more general phenomenon of how people answer questions could be considered cognitive science. Second, there is an explicit emphasis on real (versus artificial) tasks. A model of human learning of nonsense syllables would not be considered cognitive science, whereas a model of human learning of narrative texts might be.

These criteria challenge many of the traditional concerns and methods of investigation in experimental psychology and create a tension between the desire to investigate complex cognitive tasks and the ability to obtain logical validity of empirical results. Frequently, psychologists design experiments with control and treatment groups using simple, artificial laboratory tasks. The conclusions drawn from such experiments may often be valid according to the laws of deductive inference (i.e., the conclusions may follow logically from the assumptions and the observed data), but the generalizability of the results to normal processing situations is often suspect. For example, psychologists often test models of memory in experiments requiring subjects to memorize sets of arbitrary, meaningless sentences. Such experimental stimuli allow the researcher to control for possible biases in subjects' performance due to pre-experimental knowledge of the material. However, since people rarely memorize lists of meaningless sentences, the task from which the conclusions were drawn is extremely artificial. A skeptic might argue that subjects' means of processing information in this artificial experiment bears little resemblance to the way they process information in natural situations.

On the other hand, tests of more global theories of natural behavior often involve informal methods, such as protocol analyses or demonstrations of working computer programs. "Protocol analysis" involves the recording of subjects' comments about their own behavior, thoughts, and introspections as they perform an experimental task. The researcher then examines these protocols to extract the set and sequence of cognitive operations the subject used, and then uses this analysis to either construct or verify a theory of performance. Alternatively, the researcher might develop a computer program whose behavior on the task was similar to that of the human subject. The data structures and processes the computer program used might then be claimed to be a cognitive theory for how people perform the task. These methods permit the investigation of more complex processes but do not resolve the uncertain status of the theories as psychologically "valid".

One may reasonably question whether people's reports of their mental activities are, in fact, an accurate reflection of the actual internal events. Similarly, a computer program that behaves as a human does not necessarily use the same knowledge and internal actions as the human. This trade-off between problem granularity and theory testability has created an intellectual rift between some psychologists, who view builders of intelligent computer systems as contributing little to psychological modeling, and computer scientists, who view many psychological models as contributing little to the understanding of human behavior.

A second influence shaping cognitive research during the 1970s and 1980s has been a growing tendency for psychologists to investigate behavior on tasks that naturally occur outside the laboratory setting—tasks that may be thought of as more "real" or "applied." One applied area demanding considerable attention recently is instruction and training. During the past several years, for instance, the basic skills of young adults have been slowly declining (as evidenced by Scholastic Aptitude Test scores), while the current electronics revolution has created a demand to train new skills and retrain adults with obsolete skills. Skill deficiencies have been particularly acute in the military, where voluntary enlistment and low wages have reduced personnel quality at a time when the complexity of equipment operations and maintenance is increasing rapidly. Thus, there is need to devise new, high-technology methods for training and instruction. More generally, however, there is a need for cognitive research to play a visible role in maintaining an educated and skilled society.

To fill this need, some cognitive scientists have begun to consider how to represent what a student is learning, what he or she needs to know, and how to tutor the student in the acquisition of new skills. To attack such problems, researchers must develop robust and general models and then apply these models to devise prescriptive methods for learning and thinking. However, because of aforementioned difficulty of operationalizing theories with broad scope, cognitive researchers often fail to provide the stringent tests required to refine a general theory. These tests are necessary to provide constraint for the theory—that is, qualifications on the conditions under which the theory is valid or useful. In addition, unlike educational or human factors psychologists, cognitive psychologists often do not venture beyond descriptive theory-building (i.e., how the subject is performing the task) to the specification of prescriptive methods that may follow from the theory (i.e., how the subject *should* perform the task). The first approach attempts to explain errors and deficiencies; the second attempts to eliminate them.

As an illustration of these points, Figure 7-1 presents a rough sketch of the 8-year renaissance of schema theory in artificial intelligence and psychology. The starting point is taken to be the publica-

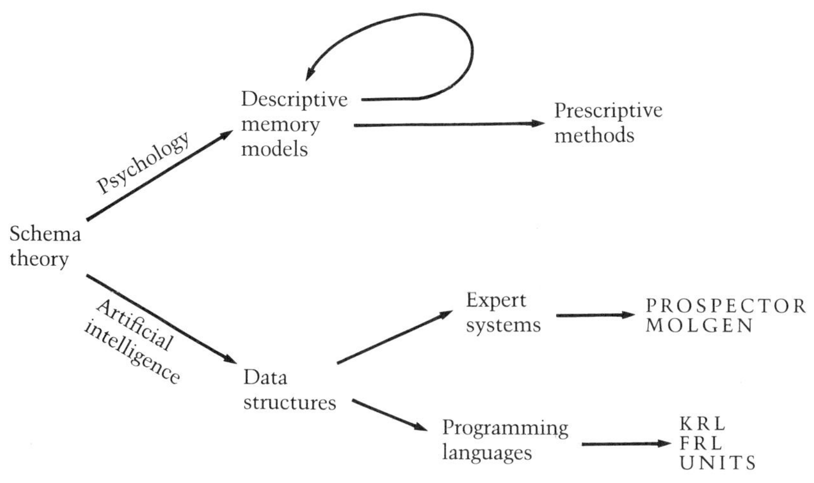

FIGURE 7-1 The recent evolution of schema theory.

tion in 1975 of Minsky's paper on *frames* (a type of schema), and the publication of Bobrow and Collins' collection of papers presenting schemata both as computer data structures and psychological constructs (Minsky, 1975; Bobrow & Collins, 1975).

In artificial intelligence research, the concept of memory schemata led to the development of specific data structures to encode schematic knowledge. These data structures provided memory representations that could be used to model skilled performance on difficult cognitive tasks. The memory representations, in turn, led to the development of expert systems that exhibit cognitive skills in a particular domain as good as (or better than) the best human experts. For example, the PROSPECTOR system can determine the mineral composition of soil samples (Duda, Hart, Nilsson, & Sutherland, 1978). Similarly, another expert system, MOLGEN, can design and predict the outcome of complex genetics experiments (Stefik, 1981). Concurrent with expert system development, the theoretical development of schemata as data structures have led to the further development of a variety of advanced programming languages. These languages, such as KRL (Knowledge Representation Language; Bobrow & Winograd, 1977), FRL (Frame Representation Language; Goldstein & Roberts, 1977), and UNITS (Stefik, 1981), have been used to support the development of other expert systems. The "proof" of schema theory as a viable formalism for representing knowledge was in the demonstration of working systems—that is, by adding sufficient constraint and detailed specification to the theoretical framework to demonstrate its utility in systems whose performance matched or surpassed that of skilled experts.

When the researcher's goal is to model human memory, adding constraint to the model entails different scientific activities. In this case, the researcher must postulate theoretical assumptions, develop empirical predictions, and qualify the applicability of the model. In cognitive psychology, this process typically requires experiments that help refine the theory (hence, the looping arrow in Figure 7-1 suggests a process of theory test and revision). However, additional benefits may be obtained, as in the AI domain, from the development of "useful systems." For psychologists, such systems are the pedagogical applications of theory to the improvement of human cognitive skills. Clearly, the development of these applications must follow progress on the basic issues of memory representation and cognitive processes that constitute the descriptive models. Despite the considerable effort in the development of descriptive models based on memory schemata, however, relatively little attention has focused on the development of a "cognitive technology" based on principles of schema theory.

In the remainder of my chapter, I argue two points regarding the value of schema theory as a descriptive and prescriptive model in cognitive science. First, schema theory is relatively underdeveloped as a descriptive psychological theory. In particular, it lacks the constraint necessary to test its viability or to specify the parameters governing its utility in pedagogical situations. Such constrained theory development and testing is critical to the derivation of prescriptive methods based on the theory. Second, schema theory provides numerous possibilities for the development of useful techniques for learning, problem solving, and reasoning. If these techniques can be developed and widely adopted, schema theory may provide a powerful vehicle for the application of principles from cognitive psychology to prescriptive methods for processing information in everyday situations.

DESCRIPTIVE MODELING AND SCHEMA THEORY

Since publication of Rumelhart's (1975) application of schema theory to the analysis of the structural dependencies in folk fables, psychologists have proposed a variety of extensions or variations to the basic notion of schemata as prototypical memory structures. Following Rumelhart's lead, some of these efforts have focused on human learning of narrative texts (e.g., Mandler & Johnson, 1977; Stein & Glenn, 1978; Thorndyke, 1977). Others have developed Schank and Abelson's (1977) notion of scripts as familiar, prototypical event sequences, such as a trip to a restaurant (Bower, Black, & Turner, 1979).

A considerable number of studies have appeared in the literature that purport to support the general, often vague notion of schemata. Typically, this support derives from experimental demonstrations of the validity of schemata as models of memory structures. For example, consider the following sketch of a version of schema theory that might appear in the introduction of a paper:

SCHEMA THEORY, VERSION A

People comprehend and represent narrative texts in memory according to a schema.

The schema guides the hierarchical encoding of knowledge.

Important elements of the overall plot structure appear near the top of the hierarchy.

Less important details, encoding instrumental actions and consequences, appear near the bottom of the hierarchy.

Important information receives more attention at comprehension time and thus has a stronger representation in memory.

PREDICTION B

Therefore, people should recall more high-level information than low-level information.

Experiments typically support the predictions of such a schema theory and thus are taken as evidence for the validity of the theory. However, note the fallacious logic of this approach. The argument takes the form:

If A then B.

B.

Therefore, A.

That is, since the prediction is confirmed, the theory is presumably confirmed. In fact, observing B to be true implies nothing about A. If B is false, however (i.e., the prediction is disconfirmed), then one can conclude that A (the theory) is false. That is, this approach makes it possible only to disconfirm, but not confirm, the theory. Admittedly, this problem applies not just to schema theory, but to all theories that are tested according to the scientific method. However, when the theory in question is carefully constrained, the number of predictions is large, and the predictions are very specific, one tends to worry less about faulty logic than when few predictions are made and a multitude of other theories make the same prediction. Typically, however, the latter situation characterizes many of the predictions based on schema theory. The theory is so general that it is a simple matter to generate other models that might produce the same data.

This situation (of too much generality) presents something of a dilemma, however, since researchers prefer to develop and defend their favored theories, rather than propose and reject alternatives. In practice, researchers sidestep this dilemma in one of two ways. Both result in the addition of constraint to the theory of interest. The first method involves a process of elimination, by which the researcher designs a set of diagnostic comparisons among alternative theories. The tests are designed so that the competitors make different predictions about a set of observations. A theory whose predictions are confirmed on these observations then receives implicit support relative to the several rejected alternatives, whose predictions are disconfirmed.

The second method of adducing support for a theory involves subjecting the theory to a series of independent tests to which it is vulnerable. These tests, or experiments, take the form:

If A then B1.

If A then B2.

If A then B3.

While none of the confirmed predictions actually confirms A, the repeated accuracy of A's predictions increases its credibility because it becomes increasingly difficult for any arbitrary theory to survive by chance. That is, the more such tests A passes satisfactorily, the lower the probability that any randomly selected theory would correctly predict the outcome of all these tests. In general, the more such predictions A can make, the more constrained A is, and the more vulnerable A is to disconfirmation.

Such systematic refinement through elimination and constraint building has been somewhat slow to occur in applications of schema theory to psychological modeling. Several factors have contributed to the dearth of these activities. First, most schema theorists have focused primarily on memory structures and relatively little on the processes that utilize these schemata. Thus, there is relatively little constraint on the types of models that could account for observed results. For example, the hierarchical "levels" effect in recall (described above, at the beginning of this section) might occur either because of differential processing of information at storage time (as was suggested by Theory A) or because of differential retrieval of information at recall time.

The relative emphasis on structure versus process reflects the Zeitgeist of cognitive science in which this theory has developed. Structural models provide the rudiments of a *competence* model of understanding—that is, one that accounts for error-free, "perfect" performance. Such a model can be used either for the construction of automated understanding systems or human processing models. These models thus achieve the interdisciplinary applicability sought by the cognitive science approach. In contrast, the development of *process* models in psychology entails concern for particularly human activities, such as forgetting, retrieval failures and errors, attentional lapses, and so on—in short, a *performance* model. While mechanisms to account for these phenomena are crucial to a human processing model, they are less interesting to the designers of intelligent systems, and hence, are less in the mainstream of cognitive science.

A second deterrent to the critical evaluation of schema theory is that an alternative is difficult to formulate. The fundamental concept in schema theory is that people have memory and predictions about familiar concepts—that is, they have *knowledge*. The assumption that knowledge is organized into clusters of facts amounts to a prediction about associative strength of related concepts in memory. However, without a definitive statement about what knowledge is or is not part of a schema (or for what concepts schemata do or do not exist), it is impossible to test these strength assumptions.

Finally, schema theory embodies both a popular and a powerful set of ideas, and researchers are understandably more interested in developing their own version of schema theory than in seeking alternatives. Researchers have a tendency to avoid seeking alternative models because (1) it is easier to revise an existing theory than to propose a radical alternative, and (2) it is easier to obtain peer support for ideas in a popular area and paradigm than in a radical alternative.

In this regard, the debate over the theoretical adequacy of story schemata published recently in *Cognitive Science* is undoubtedly healthy for schema theory. Black and Wilensky (1979) argued that existing grammars are far too restrictive in the number and type of stories they could represent to be an adequate psychological theory. Rumelhart (1980) and Mandler and Johnson (1980) defended the story grammar approach and qualified its applicability. Such debates force schema theorists to defend and refine their models, or even their entire approach, to accommodate criticism and parry attacks. As Kuhn points out in *The Structure of Scientific Revolutions* (1962), science progresses through a cyclical process of theory proposal and refinement. A newly proposed theory typically accommodates some set of prior data. Over time, researchers generate new data, both consistent and inconsistent with the theory. The proponents of the theory must patch their theory, by adding constraint, to accommodate the new data. This process continues until the theory is so laden with special cases and qualifications that it is discarded and replaced by an entirely new theory.

For a theory to be subject to this type of evolution, it must possess four properties: it must be descriptive, plausible, predictive, and testable (Thorndyke & Yekovich, 1980). The first criterion requires the theory to accommodate available empirical data, so that it is able to provide an explanation for observed behaviors. The second criterion—plausibility—requires the theory to provide a parsimonious yet complete account for the data, and to provide opportunities for extending its scope of applicability. Third, the theory should be sufficiently constrained and precise to be able to make predictions about the outcome of potential future experiments. Finally, the criterion of testability requires that the theory be *vulnerable* to the results of experiments. That is, the theory cannot be consistent with all possible results obtained in these experiments. Rather, it should be confirmed by some potential outcomes and disconfirmed by others. According to these criteria, then, psychoanalytic theory is not a true theory, since no data are in principle inconsistent with the treatment framework. By the same token, the majority of the work in schema theory to date has treated schemata in a rather general, somewhat vague and imprecise manner, so that it is often difficult to isolate precise predictions of the theory and test its assumptions.

In response to this deficiency in the tractability of schema theory as psychologically valid, some psychologists have conducted studies that sought to impose constraints on memory models for schemata (Chiesi, Spilich, & Voss, 1979; Cirilo & Foss, 1980; Kintsch & van Dijk, 1978; Yekovich & Thorndyke, 1981). For example, Yekovich and Thorndyke evaluated several schema models of how people encode and retrieve narrative texts. The models differed on assumptions regarding (1) whether or not text information is encoded differently as a function of its importance in a narrative structure, (2) whether or not the representation is hierarchical, and (3) how information is retrieved from memory for recall. Of the six models tested, only one correctly predicted all of the experimental results. This study thus placed some constraints on the possible roles of memory schemata in guiding comprehension, encoding, and retrieval. However, studies such as these represent a minority compared with studies that either extend the purely theoretical assumptions about schemata or test isolated predictions of a particular version of the theory.

The addition of constraint to a theory is pivotal because constraints suggest a theory's practical utility. For example, to develop prescriptive methods for the use of schemata in real-world cognition, we require answers to questions such as:

In what types of cognitive activities are schemata useful?

Under what conditions can learned schemata improve performance?

In the next section, I propose some tentative answers to these questions and suggest promising directions for the development of prescriptive cognitive methods that utilize schemata.

PRESCRIPTIVE METHODS AND SCHEMA THEORY

I turn now to what I consider to be a more fruitful area for research in schema theory: the development of *prescriptive* methods for the use of schemata in educational and real-world settings. Schemata may perform at least three functions in organizing different types of knowledge to support and streamline cognitive processing. They may provide (1) structures for acquiring new knowledge, (2) representations for problem-solving strategies, and (3) multi-dimensional data structures to support situation assessment. Let us consider each of these functions in more detail.

Structures for Acquiring Knowledge

As suggested by the research on human story memory, schemata may provide a framework for the organization and encoding of incoming information. When used in this way, schemata provide a sophisticated type of advanced organizer that an individual uses to make sense of and efficiently encode new facts. Unlike some of the psychological research on advanced organizers and contextual cues, however, such a framework provides more than a text title, an explanation of key concepts, or an orienting point of view. Rather, a schema should provide a structural syntax or skeleton on which to "hang" new facts and assertions.

In a study of this application of schemata, Thorndyke and Hayes-Roth (1979) investigated the utility of previously learned structural schemata for acquiring new facts. The schemata comprised fairly simple sets of concepts and associations that could be instantiated with different specific facts, as shown in Figure 7-2. A model developed within the schema theoretic framework assumed both costs and benefits for the repeated use of such schemata for the acquisition of new sets of facts. The use of a familiar encoding structure facilitated memory access at storage and retrieval time. However, multiple uses of the shared structure within a short time interval produced interference among concepts from the various contexts. The combination of these two factors produced a non-monotonic effect on the "learnability" of new information as a function of the number of prior uses of the schema. To produce an unqualified positive effect of the schema on learnability, it was necessary to space the presentation of fact sets that utilized the

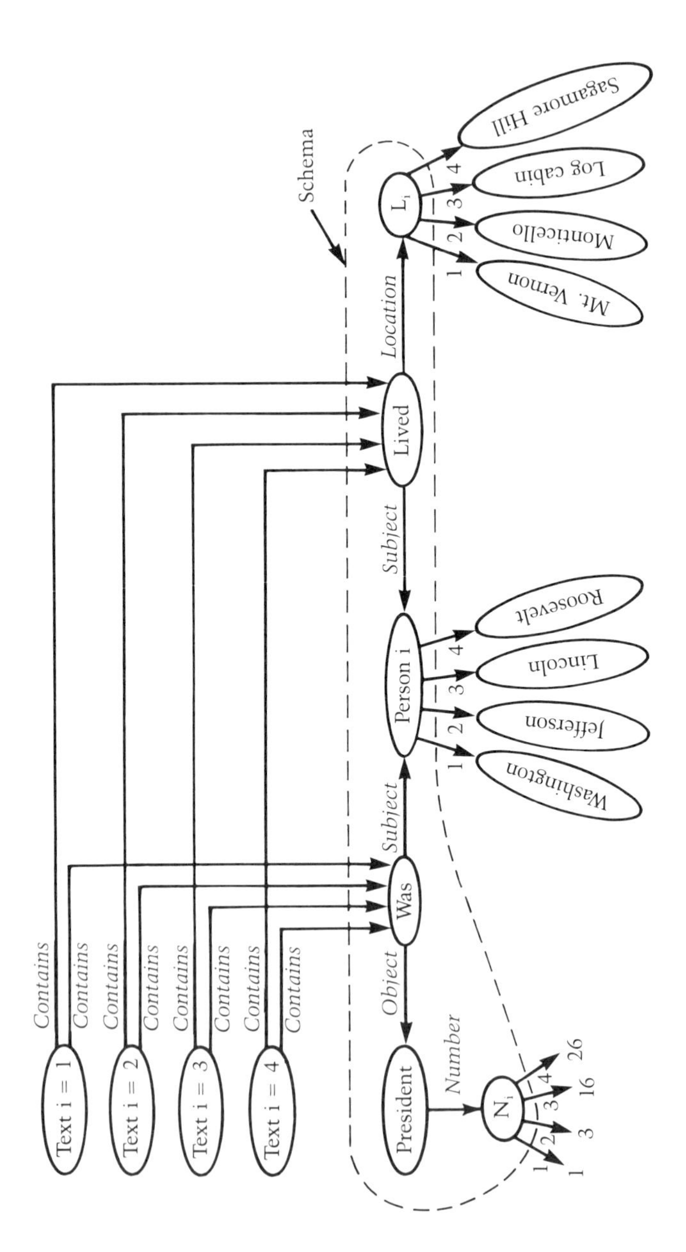

FIGURE 7-2 A representation of multiple facts from a text. The dotted lines enclose the abstract schema encoding the information that is common across multiple sentences in the text.

schema. This increased the discriminability among the various fact sets and thus eliminated the interference effect. The net result was an unqualified facilitation in learning of new facts that increased with increasing usage of the general schema.

The Thorndyke and Hayes-Roth study illustrates two points germane to the prescriptive use of schemata in natural learning situations. First, while we normally think of schemata as representing very familiar concepts or situations from everyday life, they may also be artificially constructed and taught in order to facilitate the acquisition of new information. Second, the use of familiar memory schemata does not facilitate performance in all situations. Any normative statements about the use of schemata for learning new information must be qualified by the conditions under which they either facilitate or inhibit memory retrieval.

Strategies for Problem Solving

The concept of the schema has a long history of use in the literature of problem solving. Some of the earliest problem-solving researchers, working between 1910 and 1920, viewed schemata as solution methods or plans of operation guiding the problem solver's behavior (for a review, see Woodworth, 1938).

Newell and Simon (1972) refined this rather vague notion, though without reference to the term "schema," suggesting a problem-solving method whereby many details of the problem are initially ignored and the problem is solved at a suitably high level of abstraction. The solution may then be refined by considering the problem details. Such high-level solutions may be thought of as problem-solving schemata because they are general methods that may be instantiated with the details of the particular problem being considered.

I will illustrate this point using the real-world problem-solving domain of air traffic control (Thorndyke, McArthur, & Cammarata, 1981). Frequently, an air traffic controller must make a rapid decision about what flight path an aircraft must take through the airspace to avoid collisions with other aircraft in the same area. For example, in Figure 7-3, the symbol T5 indicates the current location and altitude (5000 feet) of aircraft T, and the "1" in the lower left side of the figure indicates its desired exit point from the airspace. The dashed lines indicate the flight paths resulting from the application of three "strategies" for moving T to position 1. Similarly, the symbols "A5" and "U4" indicate the positions and altitudes of two other aircraft, and the arrows indicate their desired flight paths and destinations (airport "%" for U, airspace exit point "2" for A).

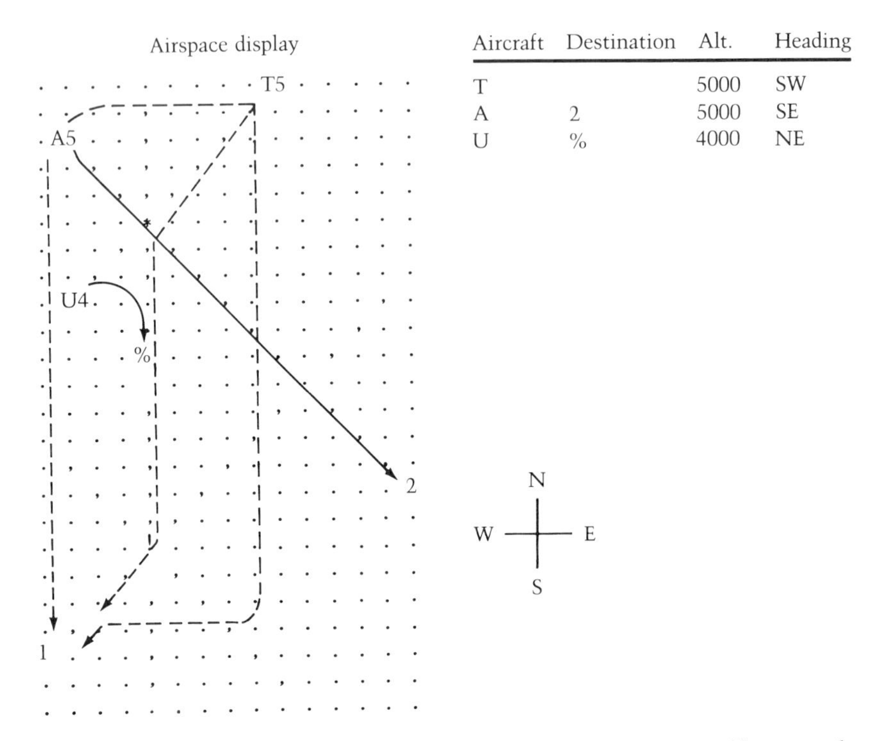

Aircraft	Destination	Alt.	Heading
T		5000	SW
A	2	5000	SE
U	%	4000	NE

FIGURE 7-3 Alternative flight paths for aircraft T in an air traffic control sector.

The precise commands required to navigate aircraft T along these paths may not be explicitly stored in the controller's memory; indeed, these flight paths may only represent alternative "types" of paths T could take: a westerly routing, a direct routing along the standard airways (the center route), or an easterly routing. Because of the necessity of attending immediately to aircraft U, an aircraft that wants to be cleared for approach and landing and nearby airport "%," the controller may not have time to generate a complete and detailed plan for T. On the other hand, a decision must also be made immediately about aircraft T, since it is destined for a conflict and possible collision with A, flying southeast. Thus, the controller may select the westerly route as the one that will avoid the conflict with A, and radio T to turn right and head west. Then, making a mental note that he must later transmit a complete plan to T, the controller may then turn his attention to guiding U in to a landing.

The point of this example is that schematized strategies may streamline problem-solving efforts and reduce processing time. In fact, in simulations of highly time-stressed control situations, we find that experts outperform novices in avoiding aircraft collisions precisely because experts have a mental library of such high-level strategies from which to develop detailed plans. A major component of acquiring expertise through practice on such a control task amounts to learning a set of high-level route descriptions for various combinations of airspace entry and exit points. Obviously, such schematic problem-solving methods could be useful in a variety of task domains.

Data Structures for Situation Assessment

People frequently collect data from many diverse sources to analyze and build a mental model of the current situation. For example, to decide if it will rain in the morning, one might (1) read the weather forecast in the newspaper, (2) look at the sky, and (3) check an arthritic joint for stiffness. This process has been called *situation assessment* (Hayes-Roth, 1980).

To decide on the appropriate "model" for the world in such situations, one often relies on a conjunction of conditions. If, for example, the weather forecast predicts rain, the sky is clear, and my arthritic joint hurts, then I conclude that rain is imminent. Over time, it may be possible to build a relatively accurate method for situation assessment based on a large data base of these *situation-event* pairs. The "situation" part of the pair corresponds to a multidimensional description of conditions, events, and states of the world that occurred at some point in time. The "event" part of the pair corresponds to the outcome of interest in the situation (in this example, whether or not it rained and how much).

Such multidimensional descriptions may be thought of as schemata because they represent aggregations and abstractions of states and events gleaned from a large number of instances. In an attempt to select the appropriate model of the situation, an individual can match or instantiate, these descriptions with actual observations in a particular new situation. (In many cases, the current situation will partially match a number of these schemata; some weighted evaluation function must select the "best" match.)

Such schemata have practical value for both people and systems builders, insofar as they provide accurate situation assessments. Two real-world applications of the use of such schemata will serve to illustrate their utility. The first application—"analog" weather modeling—seeks to predict weather by matching a collection of observations of atmospheric and meteorological data against a large data base of previous situation-event pairs (Miller, 1966). For many years, this method was the primary technique for weather prediction, although it is recently been superseded by a more "dynamic," inferential method that relies heavily on the use of thermodynamic and energy exchange equations.

A second application, developed recently at The Rand Corporation, assesses intentions and likely behaviors of the Soviet Union in a variety of world situations. The data base comprises a catalog of descriptions of various world situations and Soviet responses, including both actual historical data and hypothetical situation-response sets based on Soviet doctrine. Situations are described according to 15 attributes, thus defining a 15-dimensional space of potential world situations. Each new situation represents a point somewhere in this space. Likely Soviet responses to a new situation may be assessed by determining the distance from its point in the space to the actions associated with nearby points (i.e., other similar situations). For example, the situation representation surrounding the civil unrest in Afghanistan closely matched the description of Czechoslovakia in 1968, suggesting (1 week before the fact) that a Soviet invasion would be their most likely response. This system provides a realistic tool for foreign policy assessment and strategic analysis, and has promise as a general method for situation assessment.

CONCLUSIONS

I have ranged over a large number of issues and examples in this chapter in an attempt to defend two somewhat controversial points: (1) the enterprise of cognitive and educational psychology should be the development of cognitive technologies for use in applied settings; (2) schema theory currently promises more as a prescriptive theory than it delivers as a descriptive theory. To tie these points together, I have argued that we should craft our theories carefully and begin to apply them to the development of "thinking tools." The decade of the 1980s is a particularly critical time to shift our emphasis. We are currently facing a revolution in the amount of knowledge available, literally at the fingertips of each person in our society. New advances in computer networking, on-line encyclopedic data bases, sophisticated graphics, and video technologies present tremendous opportunities to train a new generation and a new set of skills. One need only observe the highly skilled, highly motivated teenage aces in videoarcades to appreciate the training and instructional potential of high-technology systems. Educators and cognitive researchers should be the leaders in exploiting these tools to guarantee a skilled and knowledge-rich society.

REFERENCES

Anderson, J., & Bower, G. *Human associative memory*. Washington, D.C.: J. H. Winston, 1973.

Anderson, R. C. The notion of schemata and the educational enterprise. In R. C. Anderson, R. J. Spiro, & W. E. Montague (Eds.), *Schooling and the acquisition of knowledge*. Hillsdale, N.J.: Lawrence Erlbaum Associates, 1977.

Anderson, R. C. Schema-directed processes in language comprehension. In A. Lesgold, J. Pellegrino, S. Fokkema, & R. Glaser (Eds.), *Cognitive psychology and instruction*. New York: Plenum Press, 1978.

Anderson, R. C., Reynolds, R. E., Schallert, D. L., & Goetz, E. T. Frameworks for comprehending discourse. *American Educational Research Journal*, 1977, *14*, 367–81.

Bartlett, F. *Remembering*. Cambridge: Cambridge University Press, 1932.

Betz, W. *Zeitschrift fur Angewandte Psychologie*, 1932, *41*, 166–78.

Black, J., & Wilensky, R. An evaluation of story grammars. *Cognitive Science*, 1979, *3*, 213–30.

Bobrow, D., & Collins, A. (Eds.). *Representation and understanding*. New York: Academic Press, 1975.

Bobrow, D., & Norman, D. Some principles of memory schemata. In D. G. Bobrow & A. Collins (Eds.), *Representation and understanding*. New York: Academic Press, 1975.

Bobrow, D., & Winograd, T. An overview of KRL, a knowledge representation language. *Cognitive Science*, 1977, *1*, 3–46.

Bower, G. H. Experiments on story comprehension and recall. *Discourse Processes*, 1978, *3*, 211–32.

Bower, G. H., Black, J. B., & Turner, T. J. Scripts in memory for text. *Cognitive Psychology*, 1979, *11*, 177–220.

Brewer, W., & Treyens, J. Role of schemata in memory for places. *Cognitive Psychology*, 1981, *13*, 207–30.

Chi, M., Feltovich, P., & Glaser, R. Categorization and representation of physics problems by experts and novices. *Cognitive Science*, 1981, *5*, 121–52.

Chiesi, H., Spilich, G., & Voss, J. Acquisition of domain-related information in relation to high and low domain knowledge. *Journal of Verbal Learning and Verbal Behavior*, 1979, *18*, 257–74.

Cirilo, R., & Foss, D. Text structure and reading time for sentences. *Journal of Verbal Learning and Verbal Behavior*, 1980, *19*, 96–109.

Duda, R., Hart, P., Nilsson, N., & Sutherland, G. Semantic network representations in rule-based inference systems. In D. Waterman & F. Hayes-Roth (Eds.), *Pattern-directed inference systems*. New York: Academic Press, 1978.

Flach, A. *Archive fur die Gesamte Psychologie*, 1925, *52*, 369–440.

Goldstein, I., & Roberts, R. NUDGE: A knowledge-based scheduling program. *Proceedings of the International Joint Conference in Artificial Intelligence*, 1977, 257–63.

Hayes-Roth, F. Artificial intelligence for systems management. In J. Prewitt (Ed.), *Machine intelligence 1980*. Washington, D.C.: American Association for the Advancement of Science, 1980.

Head, H. *Studies in neurology*. New York: Oxford University Press, 1920.
Kant, I. [*Critique of pure reason*. (2nd ed.)] (N. K. Smith , trans.). London: Macmillan, 1963. (Originally published, 1787.)
Kintsch, W., & Greene, E. The role of culture-specific schemata in the comprehension and recall of stories. *Discourse Processes*, 1978, *1*, 1–13.
Kintsch, W., Mandel, T., & Kozminsky, E. Summarizing scrambled stories. *Memory and Cognition*, 1977, *5*, 547–52.
Kintsch, W., & van Dijk, T. Recalling and summarizing stories. *Languages*, 1975, *40*, 98–116.
Kintsch, W., & van Dijk, T. Toward a model of text comprehension and production. *Psychological Review*, 1978, *85*, 363–94.
Kuhn, T. *The structure of scientific revolutions*. Chicago: University of Chicago Press, 1962.
Kuipers, B. J. A frame for frames: Representing knowledge for recognition. In D. G. Bobrow & A. Collins (Eds.), *Representation and understanding*. New York: Academic Press, 1975.
Mandler, J. A code in the node: The use of a story schema in retrieval. *Discourse Processes*, 1978, *1*, 14–35.
Mandler, J., & Johnson, N. Remembrance of things parsed: Story structure and recall. *Cognitive Psychology*, 1977, *9*, 111–51.
Mandler, J., & Johnson, N. On throwing out the baby with the bathwater: A reply to Black and Wilensky's evaluation of story grammars. *Cognitive Science*, 1980, *4*, 305–12.
Miller, A. *Meteorology*. Columbus, Ohio: Merrill Books, 1966.
Minsky, M. A framework for the representation of knowledge. In P. Winston (Ed.), *The psychology of computer vision*. New York: McGraw-Hill, 1975.
Moore, J., & Newell, A. How can MERLIN understand? In L. W. Gregg (Ed.), *Knowledge and cognition*. Potomac, Md.: Lawrence Erlbaum Associates, 1974.
Newell, A., & Simon, H. *Human problem solving*. Englewood Cliffs, N.J.: Prentice-Hall, 1972.
Piaget, J. *The language and thought of the child*. New York: Harcourt, Brace, 1926.
Pichert, J. W., & Anderson, R. C. Taking different perspectives on a story. *Journal of Educational Psychology*, 1977, *69*, 309–15.
Rumelhart, D. Notes on a schema for stories. In D. Bobrow & A. Collins (Eds.), *Representation and understanding*. New York: Academic Press, 1975.
Rumelhart, D. Understanding and summarizing brief stories. In D. LaBerge & J. Samuels (Eds.), *Basic processes in reading: Perception and comprehension*. Hillsdale, N.J.: Lawrence Erlbaum Associates, 1977.
Rumelhart, D. On evaluating story grammars. *Cognitive Science*, 1980, *4*, 313–16.
Rumelhart, D., & Ortony, A. The representation of knowledge in memory. In R. C. Anderson, R. J. Spiro, & W. E. Montague (Eds.), *Schooling and the acquisition of knowledge*. Hillsdale, N.J.: Lawrence Erlbaum Associates, 1977.

Schank, R., & Abelson, R. Scripts, plans, and knowledge. In *Proceedings of the Fourth International Joint Conference on Artificial Intelligence.* Tblisi, Georgia, USSR, 1975.

Schank, R., & Abelson, R. *Scripts, plans, goals, and understanding.* Hillsdale, N.J.: Lawrence Erlbaum Associates, 1977.

Schmidt, C. Understanding human actions: Recognizing the plans and motives of other persons. In J. Carroll & J. Payne (Eds.), *Cognition and social behavior.* Hillsdale, N.J.: Lawrence Erlbaum Associates, 1976.

Selz, O. *Uber die gesitze des geordneten denkverlaufs,* 1913.

Selz, O. *Zur psychologie des produktiven denkens und des irrtums,* 1922.

Stefik, M. Planning with constraints (MOLGEN: Part 1). *Artificial Intelligence,* 1981, *16,* 111–40.

Stein, N., & Glenn, C. An analysis of story comprehension in elementary school children. In R. Freedle (Ed.), *Multidisciplinary perspectives in discourse comprehension.* Norwood, N.J.: Ablex Publishers, 1978.

Stein, N., & Nezworski, T. The effects of organization and instructional set on story memory. *Discourse Processes,* 1978, *1,* 177–94.

Thorndyke, P. Cognitive structures in comprehension and memory of narrative discourse. *Cognitive Psychology,* 1977, *9,* 77–110.

Thorndyke, P. Pattern-directed processing of knowledge from texts. In D. A. Waterman & F. Hayes-Roth (Eds.), *Pattern-directed inference systems.* New York: Academic Press, 1978.

Thorndyke, P., & Hayes-Roth, F. The use of schemata in the acquisition and transfer of knowledge. *Cognitive Psychology,* 1979, *11,* 82–106.

Thorndyke, P., McArthur, D., & Cammarata, S. AUTOPILOT: A distributed planner for air fleet control. *Proceedings of the International Joint Conference in Artificial Intelligence,* 1981, 171–77.

Thorndyke, P., & Yekovich, F. A critique of schema-based theories of human story memory. *Poetics,* 1980, *9,* 23–49.

Winograd, T. Frame representations and the declarative-procedural controversy. In D. G. Bobrow & A. Collins (Eds.), *Representation and understanding.* New York: Academic Press, 1975.

Winograd, T. A framework for understanding discourse. In M. A. Just & P. A. Carpenter (Eds.), *Cognitive processes in comprehension.* Hillsdale, N.J.: Lawrence Erlbaum Associates, 1977.

Woodworth, R. *Experimental psychology.* New York: Henry Holt, 1938.

Yekovich, F., & Thorndyke, P. An evaluation of alternative functional models of narrative schemata. *Journal of Verbal Learning and Verbal Behavior,* 1981, *20,* 454–69.

8

MENTAL MODELS IN PROBLEM SOLVING

Keith J. Holyoak
University of Michigan

People often feel that a great gulf separates memory from imagination. Memory seems relatively mundane, a passive storehouse of facts and past events. Imagination is endowed with more mystical qualities, somehow generating new ideas in a manner roughly comparable to immaculate conception. Memory preserves old knowledge; imagination creates new. What does the one have to do with the other?

My goal in this essay is to show how the gulf between memory and imagination can be bridged. Memory is not so mundane, nor imagination so mystical, as naïve opinion would have it. New ideas do not arise out of nothing; rather, they are typically the product of intelligent, goal-directed transformations of existing knowledge. The general notion that new ideas are derived from old ones has a long history; but recent work in cognitive science lends substance to a more concrete framework for understanding the genesis of ideas. The core of this theoretical framework is the concept of a *mental model*—a psychological representation of the environment and its expected behavior. I will present both an intuitive and a more systematic account of what mental models are, emphasizing their role in the process of solving problems. I will focus especially on the

This chapter was prepared while the author held an NIMH Research Scientist Development Award, 1-K02-MH00342-02. Many of the ideas discussed here originated in collaborative work with my colleagues John Holland, Richard Nisbett, and Paul Thagard.

processes by which problem models can be constructed—on how new knowledge structures are developed from old ones.

At first it appears that a discussion of problem solving would necessarily avoid the issue of how memory and imagination are linked, since solving problems so often involves the use of "cut-and-dried" procedures, rather than any kind of creativity. Consider the task of solving a quadratic equation, a clear example of a "well-defined" problem (Reitman, 1964). Well-defined problems are those for which the *initial situation* (e.g., an equation to be solved), the *actions* that can be taken in seeking a solution (e.g., algebraic operations), and the desired state of affairs, or *goal* (e.g., values for certain variables in the equation), are all clearly specified. The landmark work on the theory of human problem solving by Newell and Simon (1972) focussed on well-defined problems; largely as a consequence, empirical studies have also tended to use such problems. For example, several studies (Greeno, 1974; Jeffries, Polson, Razran, & Atwood, 1977; Simon & Reed, 1976) examined the procedures by which people solve the "missionaries and cannibals" problem:

> Three missionaries and three cannibals are on one side of a river. They have a boat capable of carrying two people at a time across the river. If the cannibals ever outnumber the missionaries on one side of the river, the missionaries will be eaten. How can all six people be transported safely across to the other side of the river?

Note how the initial situation, allowable actions, and goal are clearly specified.

However, many of the problems people deal with are much less well defined. Such activities as composing a song, designing a reusable spacecraft, or developing a theory of human memory, can also be viewed as problems to be solved. Such "ill-defined" problems (Reitman, 1964) are relatively vague, in that the initial situation, allowable actions, and even the goal may not be very clear when the problem is posed. As a result, it is often difficult to decide even how to begin working on solving the problem. In contrast to well-defined problems, ill-defined problems seem more closely linked to our intuitive sense of creativity.

Theorists such as Newell (1969) and Simon (1973) have suggested some ways in which ill-defined problems can be made sufficiently well-defined to be tackled with appropriate solution methods. However, the process of transforming ill-defined problems has only recently begun to be examined in detail. This more recent work has led to a broader definition of problem solving than was generally applied in the past.

Problem solving, as I will use the term, involves recognizing that a problem exists, forming some initial mental representation (model) of it, transforming an initially vague model into one that is better specified, and eventually, if all goes well, using the model to plan and execute a concrete solution. This extended process of problem finding, defining, and refining, which I call *model construction*, provides ample opportunity for the exercise of imagination. Later, I intend to discuss in some detail how the development of new theories can be understood as an example of solving problems by construction of mental models.

MENTAL MODELS AS PROBLEM REPRESENTATIONS

What is a Model?

In order to gain an intuitive grasp of what a mental model is, let us first examine a physical example. Perhaps the most familiar models are children's toys, such as a model airplane. This example serves to illustrate a critical property of models in general: some components of the model correspond to components of what is being modelled. For example, the wings and fuselage of the toy will correspond to those of the airplane that it represents. Certain relations among components, such as the angle at which the wings are attached to the body of the plane, are also preserved in the model. Notice, however, that the correspondence between the model and the "real thing" is far from complete. The model will be enormously smaller, of course; in addition, it will preserve very little of the internal structure of the airplane, such as its engines and electrical system. In a sense, then, the toy model is an *abstraction*, representing not one particular real airplane, but a category of airplanes. This implicit category will include not only the "real" aircraft on which the model is based (e.g., a Boeing 747), but also all the possible aircraft that have the same external shape and markings. Differences in size or details of internal structure, which the model does not attempt to capture, are unimportant in defining the category. As we shall see, models of problems are also abstractions in a similar sense.

Not surprisingly, a toy airplane will carry us only a little way toward an understanding of mental models. The most critical shortcoming is that the toy is essentially a static representation, providing little help, for instance, in the prediction of how the corresponding aircraft being modelled would actually fly. In contrast, we will see that problem models are used to predict the results of hypothetical changes in the external situation. The correspondences preserved by the model are intimately tied to its function in attempting to achieve the goal of the problem.

We can find more illuminating physical examples simply by moving from toy airplanes to models used by grown-ups. If we were to take a tour of Boeing headquarters in Seattle, we would encounter a variety of different types of airplane models. One would be a cockpit simulator for the 747, which is used to train pilots. The simulator is designed to mimic the experience of handling the real aircraft with maximum realism. The pilot enters a room that contains an exact replica of the cockpit of a 747. The voices of air traffic controllers are heard on the radio, giving instructions for takeoff. Images of movement along a runway appear in the window, and the bumps of the wheels are reproduced. The pilot can experience a takeoff from Seattle, hours of routine flying, an emergency situation, and a landing in New York, all without leaving the ground.

At first glance such a detailed simulation hardly seems like an abstraction. But if the simulator is viewed as a model of a 747, the correspondence is actually far from complete. The model does not preserve the exterior appearance of the aircraft, nor indeed any part except the cockpit. Nevertheless, the model is entirely adequate for its purpose, to mimic the experience of a pilot making a flight. The correspondences preserved by the model are thus those that are causally relevant to its intended function. This principle of *causal relevance* governs the construction of problem models.

The simulator also illustrates another critical aspect of problem models—the correspondences between the model and what is being modelled are preserved under state changes. For example, as the mimicked takeoff proceeds, the visual display and other sensations produced by the model change accordingly. However, the correspondences between state transitions and reality, like those involving static components of the model, are only approximate. Most notably, if the pilot bumbles a landing and brings the plane down nose-first, the simulator will mercifully refrain from providing an accurate model of the expected change of state. As we will see shortly, the approximate preservation of state transitions allows a more formal characterization of problem models.

We can find additional illustrations of the dependency between essential correspondences and the function of the model by continuing our Boeing tour. In the development of new types of aircraft, as well as in prediction of the long-term performance of existing ones, precise scale models are subjected to simulated flight conditions in wind tunnels. The behavior of the model may be used, for example, to predict the capacity of the actual aircraft to withstand various types of stress. In this case, the scale model must correspond to the modelled aircraft in terms of properties known to be causally relevant to susceptibility to stress. Properties of the aircraft's interior, such as design of the seats, need not be preserved, since they are irrelevant to the function of the model.

To take one further example, early stages of aircraft design involve even more abstract models, often involving computer graphics, which can be manipulated to simulate expected consequences of design variations. Such models will consist not only of a visual representation, but also mathematical statements of relevant laws of aerodynamics. Once again, the essential correspondences are determined by the function of the model.

These examples of physical models thus illustrate several critical features of models in general. Models preserve correspondences between both static elements and state transitions. However, only correspondences between components causally relevant to the model's predictive function need be preserved. A model thus "abstracts away" nonessential elements of the modelled domain.

It should be added that problem models need not be as visual as the above physical examples might suggest. Although visual imagery may sometimes play an important role in human problem solving (Clement, 1982), some form of propositional representation is essential. (See the essay by Stephen Kosslyn in this volume for a discussion of mental representation.)

Components of Problem Models

A problem arises with the perception of a "problematic situation" (Schon, 1979). This essential perception has two aspects: (1) awareness that something is amiss and (2) awareness of one's inability to directly resolve the difficulty by immediate action. The range of circumstances in which something can be perceived as being "amiss" is, of course, enormous. At the most primitive level, a problematic situation can be based on an unsatisfied biological need (e.g., hunger in the absence of food). Humans must also deal with more sophisticated difficulties, such as a perceived threat to one's self-esteem.

In the context of scientific discovery, problems seem to arise most generally out of the recognition of some sort of contradiction within a domain of interest. Such contradictions can take many forms: a phenomenon that seems to defy common sense or an established scientific model (e.g., evidence for "subliminal" perception); two apparently incompatible accounts of the same phenomenon (e.g., wave versus particle models of light); two fields that seem related but have not yet been integrated (e.g., the fields of genetics and cytology earlier this century); or simply an interesting phenomenon (e.g., human problem solving) that lacks a satisfactory scientific explanation. A perceived contradiction flouts the scientist's need to achieve order and hence creates a problematic situation.

As the term is meant to suggest, a problematic situation is not yet a problem; rather it is the precursor of a problem. The problem solver must now begin to analyze the circumstances of the situation in order to form an *initial* problem model—a symbolic internal description of the problematic situation that can then be manipulated by problem-solving methods. A problem model can be described in terms of four central components, which are closely related to the problem components identified by Newell and Simon (1972).

The first and most basic problem component is a *goal*—a description of a state (or type of state) that the problem solver wishes to achieve in order to resolve the perceived difficulty. The goal description, like all the other components of a problem model, may be initially characterized at any level of abstraction. Minimally, the initial goal is simply to lessen the problematic aspects of the situation. However, even vague initial goals can exert powerful influences on the course of a solution attempt. Two scientists may both recognize that Theory A and Theory B seem incompatible; if one sets the goal of reconciling the two theories, while the other sets the goal of disconfirming Theory B, two very different research programs will likely ensue.

A second representational component entails a description of the various entities, or *objects*, that may be involved in solution attempts and the relations among them. Relevant objects will include resources at the problem solver's disposal (i.e., objects that may be used to construct a solution), the problem solver himself, and any opponents or allies of the problem solver.

A third component describes actions, or *operators*, that can potentially transform the object component. As I use the term here, operators do not have to correspond to concrete actions; they can also represent abstract action categories. Minimally, the problem solver can simply posit an abstract operator that defines goal achievement. For example, even the extremely ill-defined problem of transmuting lead into gold provides an initial operator equivalent to "transform X into Y." The immediate difficulty, of course, is that "transforming" is too abstract an operator to realize at a useful level of action. Nonetheless, the operator "transform" makes it possible to at least conceive of lead somehow turning into gold.

Finally, the fourth component specifies *constraints* that an adequate solution may not violate (Carbonell, 1982). Constraints may limit or prohibit the use of certain classes of objects or operators. In naturally occurring problems, constraints are imposed to prevent forseeable negative side effects of certain types of solution attempts. Given the goal of becoming wealthy and knowledge of the combination to a bank vault, a constraint of avoiding jail may nonetheless preclude a robbery attempt. Puzzle problems often specify constraints that block "obvious" solutions simply in order to make the puzzle more challenging.

It may be helpful to provide an informal example of a possible initial problem model. I will use the "radiation problem," made famous by the Gestalt psychologist Duncker (1945), which has figured prominently in more recent work on the process of modelling problems (Gick & Holyoak, 1980, 1983). The problem can be stated as follows:

> Suppose you are a doctor faced with a patient who has a malignant stomach tumor. It is impossible to operate on the patient, but unless the tumor is destroyed the patient will die. There is a kind of ray that at a sufficiently high intensity can destroy the tumor. Unfortunately, at this high intensity the healthy tissue that the rays pass through on the way to the tumor will also be destroyed. At lower intensities the rays are harmless to healthy tissues, but will not affect the tumor either. How can the rays be used to destroy the tumor without injuring the healthy tissue?

This problem is reasonably realistic, since it describes a situation similar to that which actually rises in radiation therapy. Our first step in solving the problem is to outline an initial problem model in terms of the four central components described above:

1 *Goal*: Use rays to destroy tumor.

2 *Objects*: Tumor is in patient's stomach. Doctor has rays. High-intensity rays can destroy both tumor and healthy tissue. Low-intensity rays can destroy neither tumor nor healthy tissue.

3 *Operators*: Alter effects of rays. Avoid contact between rays and healthy tissue.

4 *Constraints*: Avoid damaging healthy tissue. Operation is not possible.

Most of the problem components are reasonably well specified; however, the operators are extremely vague. The problem solver might imagine the possibilities of altering the effects of the rays, or of avoiding contact between the rays and the healthy tissue. However, none of these operators immediately specify realizable actions; they remain at the level of "wishful thinking." As a result, the problem is seriously ill-defined. A more specific model will be required before a potential solution can possibly be developed. (The process of transforming an initially vague model into one that is well specified will be discussed below.)

Models as Morphisms

Having outlined some general properties of models, and also the basic components of mental models of problems, it is now possible to describe problem models somewhat more formally by extending certain concepts of modelling theory (Zeigler, 1976). A model can be represented by a type of mathematical structure known as a morphism, but to understand what this term means, we first must define two other concepts: mapping and transition function.

In terms of mathematical set theory, a *mapping* is a system of correspondences between the elements of two sets. For example, suppose all the students in a class take a midterm exam, and the scores are used to rank order the students. Then there will be a one-to-one mapping between the set of students and the set of ranks. However, not all mappings are one-to-one. For example, suppose the test scores were used to define letter grades, A through D. Then there would likely be several students mapped onto the same letter grade—a "many-to-one" mapping. Furthermore, not all mappings are complete, in the sense that all elements in each set enter into the system of correspondences. Suppose one student was excused from the midterm because of illness, and hence has no score. That student would not enter into a mapping either in terms of ranks or grades, making the mapping incomplete. (My use of such terms as "one-to-one" to describe mappings differs from technical mathematical usage. For a concise discussion of the technical use of such terms, see Wickelgren, 1974, pp. 204–208.)

A mapping generally defines the static, relatively fixed relationships among sets of objects. In contrast, the concept of a *transition function* captures dynamic relationships. The external world is continually changing from one state to another in accord with lawful regularities. For example, suppose a raw egg is held 10 feet above concrete. Let us call that $State_i$, or S_i, for short. Now suppose the egg is released: $Action_j$, or A_j. Then the state of the world will change to one in which the egg is broken, which we may term S_k. In other words, the world is in part governed by a transition function, which we can write as (S_i, A_j) ——> S_k; that is, a particular initial state, coupled with a particular action, leads to a particular subsequent state. Of course, the complete transition function for the real world is enormously complex; in fact, it cannot be known, since we often cannot predict changes with certainty. However, we have at least imperfect knowledge of small parts of the transition function (e.g., a part dealing with the physics of dropping eggs), and this information can be used to solve problems.

Now we are ready to define the concept of a morphism and describe its relevance to problem models. A *morphism* is a mapping between two sets, each consisting of states and actions, such that the mapping is preserved under corresponding state changes described by the respective transition functions. In particular, the relationship between the external world and a *valid* problem model is a *homomorphism*—a morphism in which the mapping is many-to-one.

A homomorphic problem model is shown as a schematic in Figure 8–1. The top of the diagram depicts transitions between states in the external world. The symbol S_I is the problematic initial state; S_G is the state (or states) that would satisfy the goal; and T is the transition function that describes potential sequences of state changes that could transform S_I into S_G (if the problem is solvable). The bottom of the diagram, depicts corresponding elements of the problem solver's mental representation of the world. The mapping h relates states in the world to elements of the model. The symbol S'_I is the initial object description; S'_G is the goal description; and T' is the transition function for the model (T' corresponds to potential operator sequences that satisfy the constraints).

To make our discussion more concrete, imagine that a problem model is being used to answer the simple question: "What would happen if a raw egg were dropped on concrete from a height of 10 feet?" In this case, S'_I would be a description of the initial state of the egg. The mapping from the initial state of the world (S_I) to S'_I would be many-to-one because not all properties of the "real" egg

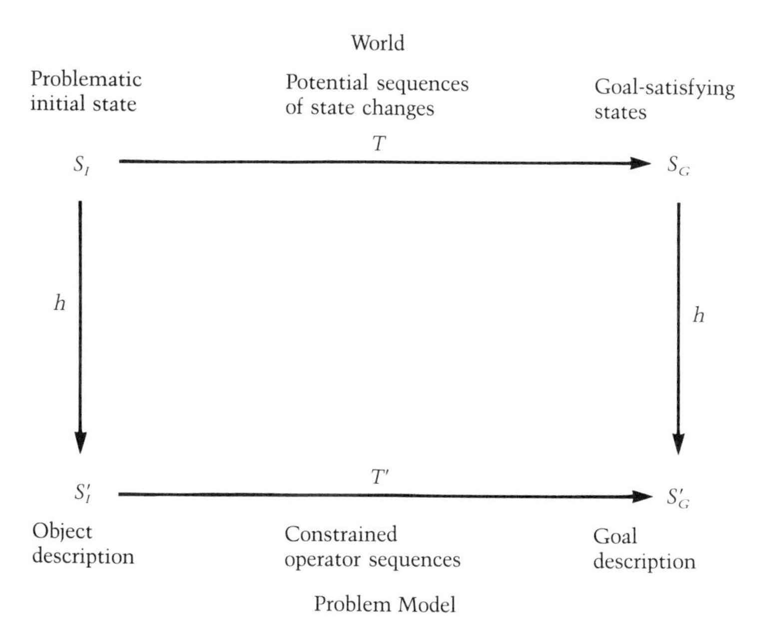

FIGURE 8–1 A problem model as a homomorphism.

would need to be included in the object description. For example, it would not matter whether the egg is white or brown. For the purpose of answering this particular question, many different types of eggs could be mapped into an identical description. In general, only aspects of the world causally relevant to attainment of a goal-satisfying state need be represented in a problem model. This observation is the reason problem models involve many-to-one mappings, and hence are homomorphisms.

Now, if we have an accurate mental representation of the consequences of egg-dropping behavior, the transition function T' will generate a description of a broken egg. Mapping back from this S'_G in the model to the world, we can predict that performing a corresponding overt action will in fact produce a "real" broken egg.

More technically, a homomorphism implies *commutativity*; i.e., alternative paths through the relational diagram depicted in Figure 8–1 will yield the same result. In particular, the result of applying T to S_I should correspond to the result of mapping S_I to S'_I by way of h, applying T', and then performing the inverse mapping h^{-1}. It follows that if $h^{-1}T'h(S_I) = S_G$, then $T(S_I) = S_G$. In other words, a valid model can be applied to develop a solution plan that describes a sequence of changes in the world that would achieve a goal-satisfying state.

Because the mapping from the world to a problem model is many-to-one, the inverse mapping from the model back to the world will be one-to-many. This feature leads to some degree of vagueness in a model's predictions. In the egg example, the model predicts that the result of the specified action will be a broken egg, but (as it stands) it does not predict the color of the pieces of egg shell that will result from the fall. The resulting broken egg may have brown or white pieces of shell, a large or small yolk, and so on; all these possibilities are consistent with the model.

In this simple case the vagueness of the prediction is quite minor. However, in more complex examples the model may be so abstract that the "solution" it suggests is too vague to actually be realized. For example, the initial model for the radiation problem presented previously contains abstract operators, such as "alter effects of rays," which are generalizations of more specific operators that could in fact be used to achieve the goal state. As it stands, the model is inadequate because the homomorphism is too abstract to generate a realizable solution plan. Operators such as "alter effects of rays" can at best yield a "solution in principle"; it remains to be discovered exactly how to alter the effects of the rays.

An "ideal" problem model is one that describes all those elements of the world that are necessary and sufficient for the concrete realization of a successful solution plan. As we have seen, even a valid homomorphic model may fall short of this ideal if the mapping relations are too abstract. In fact, most problem models are not even entirely valid. The homomorphism may be incomplete, either because some causally relevant aspects of the world are not mapped into the model or because the transition function in the model does not accurately mirror the relevant parts of the transition function of the world. Such problem models constitute incomplete, or quasi, homomorphisms (more generally, *quasimorphisms*). Even though a quasimorphism is, strictly speaking, an invalid model (because relevant aspects of the world are excluded or modelled erroneously), it may nevertheless be useful. As we will see, an initially inadequate problem model may be gradually improved by continuing the process of model construction until it generates an acceptable solution plan.

CONSTRUCTION OF PROBLEM MODELS

Figure 8–2 presents a schematic outline of the process of solving problems by means of a mental model. The process is divided into four major steps. The first step is to form an initial problem model. Next the model is *applied* to construct a potential solution plan.[1] Problem-solving methods are used to select operators to apply to the objects in an attempt to reach the goal state. If this can be done at a realizable level of action (as opposed to an abstract "solution in principle"), an attempt can be made to execute the solution plan (Step 4 in Figure 8–2). If the attempt works, the problem is solved; if it fails, the process cycles back to Step 2 and the application process will be repeated in an attempt to generate a new plan of action.

The main focus of the rest of this essay will be the remaining step depicted in Figure 8–2—Step 3, in which an attempt is made to *transform* the problem model. This step will be taken whenever the application step (Step 2) fails to yield a concrete solution plan. If the model can be transformed, another attempt can be made to apply it; if not, the problem-solving process is "stuck." The process of model construction, then, refers to the formation of an initial problem model (Step 1) and any subsequent attempts to transform it (Step 3).

What methods can be used to transform a problem model? At a global level, virtually all model transformations involve the addition of information not available in the current problem model (e.g., a more specific goal description). It follows that the operators used in

[1]A great deal could be said about the different types of problem-solving methods that can be used to apply a problem model (Newell & Simon, 1972), but space does not permit a detailed discussion here.

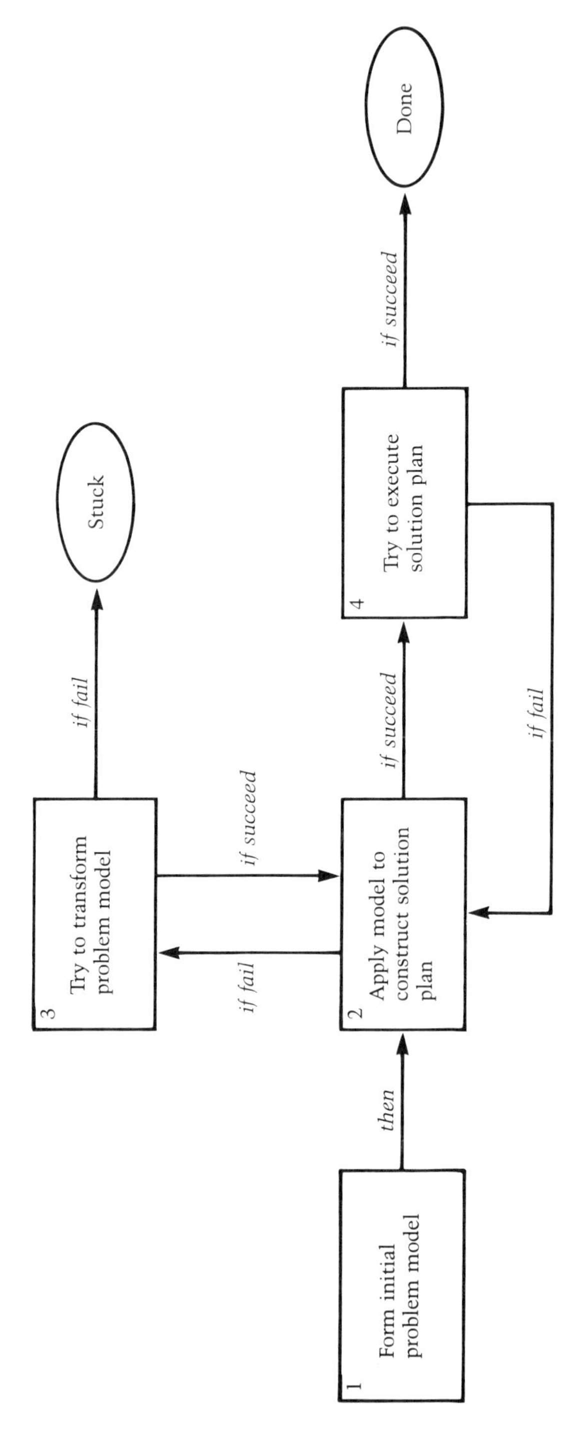

FIGURE 8–2 A schematic outline of the process of using a mental model to solve a problem.

model construction primarily involve seeking information. The search for information may be directed either externally, toward the problem-solver's world, or internally, toward the problem-solver's store of knowledge. An external search can involve additional analysis of the problematic situation or a broader search for relevant information (e.g., consulting with an expert in the problem area). Our concern here will be with operators that are directed internally, to recruit knowledge that the problem solver already had stored in memory when first confronted with the problem. How can an autonomous problem solver, using information from memory, transform an ill-defined problem into one that is solvable?

Perhaps the most basic procedure (which is perhaps better described as model *retrieval* as opposed to construction) is to classify the problem as an instance of a known *category* of problems. The mental representation of a complex category is often called a *schema* (see the essay by Perry Thorndyke in this volume). A problem schema contains a variety of information, such as a description of the features that can be used to identify problem situations of the relevant type (e.g., algebra problems involving quadratic equations; see Hinsley, Hayes, & Simon, 1977). The schema also specifies those features of the situation that are critical to achieving a solution, and it provides information about specialized solution methods that may be useful. In essence, a problem schema is a prestored mental model for a category of problems.

There is now abundant evidence that a major factor differentiating expert problem solvers from novices involves quantitative and qualitative differences in their respective stores of relevant problem schemas (Chase & Simon, 1973; Larkin, McDermott, Simon, & Simon, 1980; also, see the essay by Alan Lesgold in this volume). A study of experts and novices in the domain of physics problems by Chi, Feltovich and Glaser (1981) is especially illuminating in this regard. Advanced graduate students (experts) and undergraduates (novices) were presented with a set of physics problems and were asked to sort the problems into clusters according to similarity. Chi et al. then analyzed the kinds of features the subjects used to divide the problems into categories. Novices tended to form categories on the basis of relatively "surface" features of the problem statements (e.g., "inclined plane" problems). In contrast, experts sorted the problems with respect to applicable physical laws (e.g., "problems solvable by the second law of thermodynamics"). Further differences were apparent in protocols that the subjects used to describe their problem categories. The experts were able to articulate the equivalent of rules for realizable actions, that is, explicit solution procedures for problems of a given type. The novices' protocols, on the other hand, even when they mentioned abstract problem features, usually did not reveal such rules for action. Rather, their rules seemed to set further abstract subgoals that lacked specific solution procedures.

The richer problem schemas of the experts in the Chi et al. study can account for the observation that the degree to which a problem is ill-defined depends on the knowledge of the problem solver. To use an example discussed by Simon (1973), most of us would find the problem of designing a house quite ill-defined. An architect, however, can quickly call up a hierarchy of relevant schemas that effectively decompose the problem (e.g., a "house" can be viewed as a "floor plan" plus a "structure"). At specific levels the resulting subproblems may be tied to realizable solution procedures, often involving a choice among a small set of alternatives (e.g., gas versus electricity for heating). If the process of problem transformation proceeds rapidly enough, the expert problem solver may scarcely notice that the original problem statement was left vague.

Difficulties arise, of course, when the problem solver lacks a suitable schema for the problem. This is not only the situation of a novice, but also of an expert pressed to the limits of his or her expertise. There is a sense in which anyone working at the frontiers of their knowledge—including the creative scientist—faces some of the same difficulties as a novice. What modelling tools are available when no adequate problem schema is forthcoming?

Modelling with Intradomain Analogies

An important heuristic method for dealing with a novel type of problem is to find a similar, better understood problem in the same domain; solve it by some method (or retrieve its solution from memory); and then try to transform the method and/or solution into one appropriate to the original problem. (Since the concept of problem domain is intrinsically hierarchical, by "same" domain I really mean "relatively similar".) For example, Polya (1954) suggests that a three-dimensional geometry problem can be approached by relating it to a corresponding two-dimensional problem. Following the suggestion of Gentner (1982), I will refer to the original problem as the *target* and to an analogous problem as a *base*. In Polya's example, and many others, the base is simpler than the target, in the sense of having fewer elements. Most generally, a useful base will be one that (1) can itself be successfully modelled and (2) preserves the critical causal features relevant to an adequate solution to the target problem. A simpler problem is quite likely to satisfy condition 1; however, it may well fail to meet condition 2. The additional complexity of the target problem may directly determine the solution required, in which case the solution to a simpler problem may be unhelpful or even misleading. (Many three-dimensional geometry problems, for example, have solutions quite different from those of their two-dimensional counterparts.)

An account of modelling with intradomain analogies (or, as we shall see shortly, with interdomain analogies) must address two basic issues. First, how can a promising base analog be found? Second, how can a solution to a base be transformed into a potential solution to the target? Some hypotheses regarding both issues are suggested by the work of Clement (1982), who analyzed the protocols of two experienced problem solvers dealing with physics problems and found clear evidence of the spontaneous use of analogies. In his "spring coils" problem, subjects were told that a weight has been hung on a spring. Then, they were told, the original spring was replaced with one made of the same kind of wire, with the same number of coils, but with coils twice as wide in diameter. The subjects were asked to decide whether the spring would now stretch more, less, or the same amount under the same weight, and to explain why. (It will in fact stretch more.)

The protocols Clement obtained suggested that useful analogous variants of this problem were sometimes obtained by transforming the original problem, that is, by altering one of its features. An important type of problem transformation was the generation of an extreme case by transforming a relevant quantitative dimension to its minimal or maximal value. For example, one subject imagined a very narrow spring, and decided that a spring with minimal material could not stretch very far. Extreme cases were typically created by varying a dimension, such as spring width, that was presented as being directly relevant to the problem solution. But both of Clement's subjects also varied other qualitative features of the problem, which the statement had *not* suggested as variables. Both considered a problem variant in which the spring was reduced to a single coil (extreme case), and then unwound into a bending rod. It seemed that stating the original problem in terms of "stretching" triggered retrieval of the similar (and presumably better understood) relation of "bending," which is conventionally a property of rods. Such a chain of associations would motivate construction of a "bending rod" analogy. One subject went on to consider a coil as a square, and then as a hexagon, in the process discovering the possibility that a torsion force (in addition to bending) might operate on the spring. The hexagon coil, which is "intermediate" between ones that are square or circular, seemed to serve as a kind of "bridge," increasing the subject's confidence that a square coil indeed preserves the relevant properties of the original circular one.

Modelling with Interdomain Analogies

Sometimes the search for a useful analogy leads yet farther afield, into a different domain of knowledge. An *interdomain* analogy is in effect a kind of metaphor, based on the perception of structural similarities hidden beneath a veneer of surface differences. As we will see, there is reason to believe that interdomain analogies play an important role in the generation and initial justification of scientific hypotheses. Clement (1982) observed several spontaneous references to interdomain analogies in the protocols produced by his subjects. For example, one subject working on the spring problem made a deliberate effort to consider situations involving rubber bands, molecules, and polyesters. What the objects in this disparate collection seem to have in common are links to the key relation of "stretching," which is central to the goal of the target problem. The subject seemed to be searching memory for other, better understood systems in which something like stretching occurs. This kind of focusing on critical relations as retrieval cues may be central to the generation of interdomain analogies.

Gick and Holyoak (1980, 1983) conducted an extensive investigation of the use of interdomain analogies in problem solving, using the radiation problem discussed earlier as the target. Our initial study demonstrated that variations in the solution to an available base analog can lead subjects to generate qualitatively different solutions to the target. Subjects were given various stories (base analogs) about the predicament of a general who wished to capture a fortress located in the center of a country. Many roads radiated outward from the fortress, but these were mined so that although small groups could pass over them safely, any large group would detonate the mines. Yet the general needed to get his entire army to the fortress in order to launch a successful attack. The general's situation was thus substantially parallel to that of the doctor in the radiation problem.

Different versions of the story described different solutions to the military problem. For example, in one version the general discovered an unguarded road to the fortress and sent his entire army along it; in another version the general divided his men into small groups and dispatched them simultaneously down multiple roads to converge on the fortress. All subjects were then asked to suggest solutions to the radiation problem, using the military story to help them. Those who read the first version of the analogy were especially likely to suggest sending the rays down an "open passage" such as the esophagus, so as to reach the tumor while avoiding contact with healthy tissue. Some subjects developed a more detailed version of this solution, in which a "ray-proof tube" was first inserted down the esophagus to ensure avoidance of contact, since the esophagus is of course not straight. (As this example illustrates, the solution provided by a base analog may need to be adapted and specialized to take account of important aspects of the target that are not analogous; see the discussion of "patches" below.) In contrast, subjects who received the second story version were especially likely to suggest a "convergence" solution, which involved directing multiple weak rays at the tumor from different directions.

Our results suggest that an interdomain analogy can provide a model that guides the process of transforming the representation of the target problem. The base analog may influence even high-level descriptions of the goal in the target problem (e.g., "avoid contact with the healthy tissue" versus "alter the effects of the rays"). In a real sense, the base analog may not only suggest a solution to the target problem, but also determine what the problem solver takes the problem to be. Schon (1979) has cogently argued that complex social problems, which initially present themselves as poorly understood problematic situations, often come to be defined by goals suggested by a metaphorical interpretation. Within the domain of urban housing, for example, slums have been characterized by the alternative metaphors of "blight" and "natural communities." The former characterization leads to the goal of sweeping reconstruction ("urban renewal"), whereas the latter leads to the goal of selectively aiding the existing social arrangement. In such cases the target problem is to a large extent defined in the process of modelling it by analogy.

The Process of Analogical Transfer

Analogical problem solving can be viewed as "second-order" modelling, in that a model of the target problem is constructed by modelling the model after that used for the base problem. As shown in the schematic diagram in Figure 8–3, the model of the base problem is used as a model of the target problem, generating a new model that can be applied to the novel problematic situation. In an ideal case, the mapping between the resulting target model and the base model (h') will be one-to-one, producing an *isomorphism*. That is, goals, objects and constraints will be mapped in a one-to-one fashion so that corresponding operators preserve the transition function of the base. Note that even in the ideal case not all elements of the base situation need be mapped, only those included in the *model* of the base (i.e., those causally relevant to the achieved solution). The modelling framework thus provides a principled basis for delimiting the information transferred from base to target. (Hesse, 1966, was the

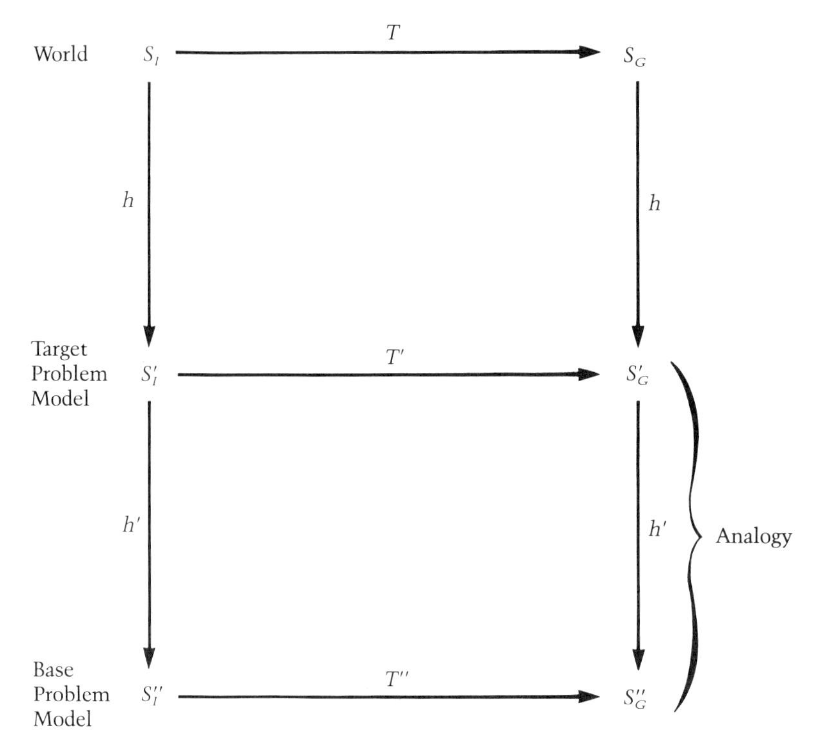

FIGURE 8–3 An analogy with the model for a base problem can be used to construct a model for a target problem.

first to stress the central importance of causal elements in analogical transfer.)

In actuality, however, the initial target model derived by analogy will be less than isomorphic to the base, and even an eventual, adequate target model will typically fall short of this ideal. Since the target problem will not be adequately modelled prior to the mapping process (otherwise the analogy would be superfluous), the initial mapping with the base will inevitably be partial. Initiation of the mapping process will depend on the problem solver having first identified some element of the target problem that is similar to an element of the base model (i.e., an element included in either the base model or some generalization thereof). In most cases the initial mapping will involve detection of a high-level similarity between corresponding goals, constraints, object descriptions, or operators. Gick and Holyoak (1983) refer to the basis of an analogical mapping as the "implicit schema" common to the two analogs.

Elements of the implicit schema that are identified in the target can serve as retrieval cues to access relevant base analogs, as well as to initiate the mapping process when a base analog is made available. Once the relevance of the base is considered and an initial partial mapping has been established, the analogical model of the target can be developed by extending the mapping. Since models are hierarchically structured, and the mapping will usually be initiated at an abstract level, the extension process will typically proceed from the top downward. As the base model is "unpacked," the problem solver will attempt to construct a parallel structure in the target model using elements appropriate to the new domain. For example, a subject in a study such as those of Gick and Holyoak (1980, 1983) might first establish a mapping between the doctor's goal of "using rays to destroy a tumor" and the general's goal of "using an army to capture a fortress," since both are instances of the implicit schema of "using a force to overcome a target." The rays are now (tentatively) mapped with the army; accordingly, the problem solver will attempt to construct operators for acting on the rays which match those that act on the army in the base model. For example, since the army could be divided into small groups, it follows that the rays could be "divided into little rays."

This process of model development will continue until an adequate target model is created, or until a point is reached at which the analogy begins to "break down." What does it mean for an analogy to break down? I distinguish among four types of mapping relations (Holyoak, in press). (1) *Identities* are those elements that are the same in both analogs (e.g., the generalized goal of "using a force to overcome a target"). The identities are equivalent to the implicit schema. (2) *Indeterminate correspondences* are elements that the problem solver has yet to map. The other two types of mappings involve known differences between the two analogs. For example, the mapped objects of "rays" and "army" obviously will generate a host of differences when the concepts are analyzed. However, differences do not necessarily impair the morphism (after all, the problems are only supposed to be analogous, not identical). (3) *Structure-preserving differences* are those that allow construction of corresponding operators and hence maintain the causal structure of the base model. For example, an army is visible, whereas radiation is not; however, since no necessary operators are blocked simply because the rays are invisible, this difference is structure preserving. (4) Other differences, however, will be *structure violating* because they prevent the construction of corresponding operators. For example, an army, unlike rays, consists of sentient beings. Accordingly, the general can simply tell his men to "divide up," and the army can be expected to regroup appropriately without further intervention. Rays, of course, do not respond to such "orders." Although they can indeed be divided, the requisite operator will be of a very different type. Subjects often introduce multiple "ray machines" (with no counterparts in the base analog) to achieve the desired result.

An analogy "breaks down," then, roughly at the level of specificity at which differences prove to be predominantly of the structure-violating sort. Analogies vary in their *completeness*, that is, in their degree of approximation to a morphism in which all differences are structure preserving. If analogies are typically incomplete quasimorphisms, one might ask, how can they be of any use at all? Essentially, an analogy is useful if the quasimorphism can be "patched" by other problem-solving methods to create an adequate target model. The "ray machines" mentioned above represent such a patch. If a needed operator cannot be constructed by analogy, a different, viable operator with a comparable effect may be constructed by other means; if not, the analogy fails. The process of patching a quasi-morphic target model to achieve a criterion of adequacy can itself be treated as a problem-solving task (Carbonell, 1982). Analogical problem solving must be viewed as an integral part of the overall process of model construction.

Analogies and Problem Schemas

An interdomain analogy, by definition, is one in which the commonalities are relatively abstract, whereas the differences are blatantly obvious. As a result, it may be difficult for a problem solver to spontaneously retrieve or notice the relevance of a base analog. Gick and Holyoak (1980) found direct evidence that subjects' ability to spontaneously notice an interdomain analogy can fall far short of their ability to make use of it once it is pointed out. After reading the "multiple approach routes" version of the military story, about 30 percent of subjects proceeded to generate the "converging rays" solution to the radiation problem without any hint to apply the story. Although this figure was significantly higher than the mere 10 percent of subjects who generated this solution in the absence of a prior story analog, it was much less than the 75 percent who gave the solution if they were told to consider the story.

Sometimes people are explicitly taught to think about one domain in terms of a very different one. For example, students are often told that electricity behaves like an hydraulic system. Electricity is analogous to water flowing through a pipe; batteries act like reservoirs and resistors act like constrictions in a pipe. Gentner and Gentner (1982) have demonstrated that the ease with which high-school and college students solve particular types of electricity problems depends on the degree to which the interdomain analogy they have been taught in fact generates correct inferences about the relevant electrical concepts. Some students used the hydraulic analogy, whereas others used an alternative "moving objects" analogy (batteries are like a force pushing the objects, and resistors are like gates). Each of the two possible analogies provides a model that is more valid for some aspects of electricity than for others. In particular, the hydraulic analogy proved superior for questions about batteries, whereas the moving-objects analogy was superior for questions about resistors.

In addition to using specific base analogs to build models for novel problems, analogies may also be used to construct more general models—problem schemas of the sort discussed earlier—that can be applied to a broader range of problems. The basic mechanism for such schema induction is to identify the causally relevant aspects common to the various individual models (Winston, 1980). This type of induction may often be an important incidental byproduct of performing an analogical mapping.

Gick and Holyoak's (1983) study of the use of analogies in solving the radiation problem provides support for this claim. In some of our experiments subjects initially received two stories, each of which illustrated a "convergence" solution to a problem in some domain (e.g., two military stories involving an attack from multiple directions). The subjects were asked to describe ways in which the stories were similar, thus encouraging them to map the two stories and hence to potentially induce a "convergence schema." When such subjects subsequently attempted to solve the radiation problem, they were much more likely to generate the parallel solution (either with or without a hint to use the stories) than were subjects who received only one story analog.

Furthermore, more detailed analyses revealed that the more closely a subject's description of story similarities approximated a statement of the solution principle, the more likely it was that the subject would transfer the solution to the medical problem. Thus a subject who said that both stories illustrated the use of "many small forces applied together to add up to one large force necessary to destroy the object" was almost certain to give the convergence solution to the ray problem, without requiring any kind of hint; in contrast, one who said that "in both stories a hero was rewarded for his efforts" was unlikely to do so.

As Gick and Holyoak (1983) argued, there are theoretical reasons to expect an abstract problem schema to yield greater interdomain transfer than would a single base analog. The schema renders explicit the identities common to the base analog and the target, while effectively deleting their differences. A target problem will therefore be more similar to a schema than to a corresponding base analog (Tversky, 1977). Accordingly, a similarity-based retrieval mechanism will be more likely to access a schema than a specific analog.

MODEL CONSTRUCTION AND SCIENTIFIC DISCOVERY

Scientific discovery might serve as an example *par excellence* of the process of model construction. Problematic situations arise out of apparent contradictions; initially vague problem representations undergo a series of transformations, largely effected by operators for information seeking, which generate more specific representations that include new subgoals. Of course, scientific discovery differs from everyday problem solving in important ways. The interrelations among scientific problems can be extremely complex, and the discovery process is a social enterprise that may span generations of scientists. The criteria for adequacy of models (a term that in this context includes the conventional meaning of "theory") are far more demanding than is the case in other problem-solving situations. In particular, model development is driven by perpetual striving for increased generality, that is, for new theoretical representations that tie together phenomena previously treated by unrelated models. No scientific model, however much it is accepted as today's "received view," ever gains immunity from eventual revision or replacement. (For an extended analysis of science as a problem-solving activity, see Laudan, 1977.)

As many have observed (e.g., Oppenheimer, 1956), analogies often play a major role in the development of scientific models. Furthermore, the ways in which analogies appear to be generated and used in the scientific context can be readily related to our discussion of model construction. Darden's (1976, 1980) analysis of Charles Darwin's development of an early genetic theory is a case in point. Darwin listed a number of basic "facts" (some of which, like the assumed inheritance of acquired characteristics, were later to be rejected) that he wished his theory to explain. His theory was based on the postulation of material units, called "gemmules," which were responsible for the transmission of traits. (Gemmules were thus an intellectual precursor of the modern concept of germ cells.) Among the facts he wished to explain was the phenomenon of *reversion*: the resemblance of offspring to ancestors more remote than the parents. Darden suggests that Darwin may have first generalized this problem. Reversion can be viewed as an instance of a more general category of phenomena in which something is present, then disappears, and then reappears again. Within the broad domain of biology, Darwin found other situations of the same schematic form, that is, examples of "dormancy." Seeds lie quiescent in the earth through the winter, as do buds in the bark of a tree. Darwin then used such analogs to develop an explanation of reversion: gemmules can be dormant, remaining inactive over one or more generations, until they are reactivated in a remote descendant.

As one might well expect, the dormancy analogy was by no means sufficient to generate a theory to account for the full range of phenomena that Darwin considered relevant. The case study in fact provides a nice illustration of ways in which the use of analogy can be coordinated within a broader process of model construction. To begin with, the analogy with seeds and buds failed to explain why gemmules remain dormant and are subsequently reactivated. The cyclic progression of the seasons has no apparent parallel with successive generations of organisms. Accordingly, Darwin "patched" the analogy to explain the dormancy of gemmules: various types of gemmules are effectively in competition; one type will be dormant through generations in which other types are more numerous or vigorous and then be reactivated when it regains the advantage. Gemmules thus acquired certain properties via the analogy with seeds, and others from different sources. These sources included additional analogies. For example, Darwin also needed to explain how an adequate number of gemmules could be maintained. To do so he attributed to them the property of self-division, apparently on the basis of an analogy with cells.

Darwin's initial problem representation, then, included the goals of explaining a wide range of phenomena. These explanations were to be unified by common theoretical concepts, most notably gemmules. The task of theory construction thus established a hierarchy of subgoals, the solutions of which demanded elaboration of the theoretical concepts. In attacking his various subgoals, Darwin's procedures for model construction called upon a number of different analogies. Each analogy, as well as other knowledge sources, generated some properties of the theoretical concepts. The resulting genetic theory was thus a hybrid, based on the coordinated transmission of ideas from multiple conceptual parents. (A similar description seems to apply to the development of Darwin's more notable theory, that of evolution by natural selection; Gruber, 1980; Ruse, 1980).

Although Darwin's pattern of model construction is not atypical, other cases illustrate important variations. For example, the analogies Darwin used were based on "real" base analogs, such as the dormancy of seeds. Sometimes, however, an analogy (even an interdomain analogy) is drawn with a base analog that is itself an idealized construction. An example is James Maxwell's analogy between a system of electrical and magnetic poles and that of a field of "incompressible fluid" (North, 1981). In such cases, the base analog is not simply retrieved, but rather is itself the product of an ongoing process of model construction.

Another important distinction is that Darwin's use of analogies has the flavor of a "shotgun approach," in that a variety of more or less unrelated analogies were brought to bear on different parts of the model under construction. In other cases a single, multifaceted analogy can be used to develop a new model. Because they impose a unified set of constraints on the target model, such extended analogies can potentially yield a relatively complete and conceptually coherent product. The development of the wave theory of light from that of sound is a case of the latter sort.

A current example from psychology is provided by recent systematic attempts to develop a model of operant conditioning in animals by analogy to classical economics (Rachlin, Green, Kagel & Battalio, 1976). The core of the latter analogy is the idea that an animal's choice of a response to be made (or to make no response at all) can be viewed as a problem in the allocation of scarce resources. In fact, many very different problems seem to plausibly fit the "scarce resource" schema. Another example from psychology is the application of microeconomic theory to develop a model of the allocation of attention among cognitive tasks (Navon & Gopher, 1979).

Other forms of model construction, even more constraining than extended interdomain analogies, involve the construction of *interfield theories* (Darden & Maull, 1977). These are cases in which theories emerge from the integration of ideas from diverse scientific fields that share an interest in a common set of phenomena. Direct links, such as causal relations, may be developed between concepts in the contributing fields. An illustrative example of an interfield theory is provided by the development of chromosome theory as a bridge between genetics and cytology. Darden (1980) argues that attempts to develop interfield theories can be especially fruitful sources of new scientific ideas. Perhaps theories of problem solving, designed to explain the goal-directed behavior of both people (cognitive psychology) and some computer programs (artificial intelligence) will provide support for Darden's claim.

CONCLUSION

Where do new ideas come from? An important source, I have tried to argue, lies in the process of constructing mental models to solve problems. The genesis of ideas is not haphazard, but rather is goal-directed. Memory and imagination merge as stored knowledge, sometimes drawn from disparate domains, is retrieved and transformed to serve the functions dictated by a novel problem. Newly constructed models can be stored in memory, providing potential schemas and analogies from which other models may eventually be built. The modelling framework highlights the continuity between everyday problem solving and the complex mechanisms involved in scientific discovery. The process of model construction reveals how human memory, rather than merely storing the past, helps to create the future.

REFERENCES

Carbonell, J. G. Learning by analogy: Formulating and generalizing plans from past experience. In R. Michalski, J. G. Carbonell, & T. M. Mitchell (Eds.), *Machine learning: An artificial intelligence approach.* Palo Alto, Calif.: Tioga Press, 1982.

Chase, W. G., & Simon, H. A. The mind's eye in chess. In W. G. Chase (Ed.), *Visual information processing.* New York: Academic Press, 1973.

Chi, M. T. H., Feltovich, P. J., & Glaser, R. Categorization and representation of physics problems by experts and novices. *Cognitive Science,* 1981, *5,* 121–52.

Clement, J. Spontaneous analogies in problem solving: The progressive construction of mental models. Paper presented at the meeting of the American Educational Research Association, New York, 1982.

Darden, L. Reasoning in scientific change: Charles Darwin, Hugo de Vries, and the discovery of segregation. *Studies in the History and Philosophy of Science,* 1976, *7,* 127–69.

Darden, L. Theory construction in genetics. In T. Nickles (Ed.), *Scientific discovery: Case studies.* Dordrecht, Holland: Reidel, 1980.

Darden, L., & Maull, N. Interfield theories. *Philosophy of Science,* 1977, *44,* 43–64.

Duncker, K. On problem solving. *Psychological Monographs,* 1945, *58* (Whole No. 270).

Gentner, D. Are scientific analogies metaphors? In D. S. Miall (Ed.), *Metaphor: Problems and perspectives.* Brighton, England: Harvester Press, 1982.

Gentner, D., & Gentner, D. R. Flowing waters or teeming crowds: Mental models of electricity. In D. Gentner & A. Stevens (Eds.), *Mental models.* Hillsdale, N.J.: Lawrence Erlbaum Associates, 1982.

Gick, M. L., & Holyoak, K. J. Analogical problem solving. *Cognitive Psychology,* 1980, *12,* 306–55.

Gick, M. L., & Holyoak, K. J. Schema induction and analogical transfer. *Cognitive Psychology,* 1983, *15,* 1–38.

Greeno, J. G. Hobbits and orcs: Acquisition of a sequential concept. *Cognitive Psychology,* 1974, *6,* 270–92.

Gruber, H. E. The evolving systems approach to creative scientific work: Charles Darwin's early thought. In T. Nickles (Ed.), *Scientific discovery: Case studies.* Dordrecht, Holland: Reidel, 1980.

Hesse, M. B. *Models and analogies in science.* Notre Dame, Ind.: University of Notre Dame Press, 1966.

Hinsley, D., Hayes, J. R., & Simon, H. A. From words to equations. In P. Carpenter & M. Just (Eds.), *Cognitive processes in comprehension.* Hillsdale, N.J.: Lawrence Erlbaum Associates, 1977.

Holyoak, K. J. Analogical thinking and human intelligence. In R. J. Sternberg (Ed.), *Advances in the psychology of human intelligence*, Vol. 2. Hillsdale, N.J.: Lawrence Erlbaum Associates, in press.

Jeffries, R., Polson, P. G., Razran, L., & Atwood, M. E. A process model for missionaries-cannibals and other river-crossing problems. *Cognitive Psychology*, 1977, *4*, 412–40.

Larkin, J. H., McDermott, J., Simon, D., & Simon, H. A. Expert and novice performance in solving physics problems. *Science*, 1980, *208*, 1335–42.

Laudan, L. *Progress and its problems*. Berkeley: University of California Press, 1977.

Navon, D., & Gopher, D. On the economy of the human-processing system. *Psychological Review*, 1979, *86*, 214–55.

Newell, A. Heuristic programming: Ill-structured problems. In J. S. Aronofsky (Ed.), *Progress in operations research* (Vol. 3). New York: Wiley, 1969.

Newell, A., & Simon, H. A. *Human problem solving*. Englewood Cliffs, N.J.: Prentice-Hall, 1972.

North, J. D. Science and analogy. In M. D. Grmek, R. S. Cohen, & G. Cimino (Eds.), *On scientific discovery*. Dordrecht, Holland: Reidel, 1981.

Oppenheimer, J. R. Analogy in science. *American Psychologist*, 1956, *11*, 127–35.

Polya, G. *Mathematics and plausible reasoning* (2 Vols.). Princeton, N.J.: Princeton University Press, 1954.

Rachlin, H., Green, L. , Kagel, J. H., & Battalio, R. C. Economic demand theory and psychological studies of choice. In G. H. Bower (Ed.), *The Psychology of Learning and Motivation* (Vol. 10). New York: Academic Press, 1976.

Reitman, W. Heuristic decision procedures, open constraints, and the structure of ill-defined problems. In M. W. Shelley & G. L. Bryan (Eds.), *Human judgments and optimality*. New York: Wiley, 1964.

Ruse, M. Ought philosophers consider scientific discovery? A Darwinian case-study. In T. Nickles (Ed.), *Scientific discovery: Case studies*. Dordrecht, Holland: Reidel, 1980.

Schon, D. A. Generative metaphor: A perspective on problem-setting in social policy. In A. Ortony (Ed.), *Metaphor and thought*. Cambridge, England: Cambridge University Press, 1979.

Simon, H. A. The structure of ill-structured problems. *Artificial Intelligence*, 1973, *4*, 181–201.

Simon, H. A., & Reed, S. Modeling strategy shifts in a problem-solving task. *Cognitive Psychology*, 1976, *8*, 86–97.

Tversky, A. Features of similarity. *Psychological Review*, 1977, *84*, 327–52.

Wickelgren, W. A. *How to Solve Problems*. San Francisco: W. H. Freeman, 1974.

Winston, P. H. Learning and reasoning by analogy. *Communications of the ACM*, 1980, *23*, 689–703.

Zeigler, W. P. *Theory of modelling and simulation*. New York: Wiley, 1976.

9

THE PLANNING AND CONTROL OF MOVEMENTS

David A. Rosenbaum
Hampshire College

This chapter is concerned with a neglected topic in cognitive psychology—the planning and control of bodily movements. Without movements of the body, cognitive activity would be useless: perceiving, remembering, problem solving, and decision making would be futile if the results of these activities could not be translated into physical action. To appreciate this point, one need only consider what it would be like to be totally paralyzed.

Despite the obvious importance of movement to cognition, psychologists have done relatively little research on the cognitive control of movement. Indeed, when I entered graduate school in 1973, few if any books on psychology made mention of the importance of movement. Nevertheless, when I asked Gordon Bower, in my second year at Stanford, to supervise me in a project on the planning and control of aimed hand movements, he was quite encouraging. He was willing to tolerate my excursion into this area of research because he recognized that a complete account of the human information-processing system would require a picture of information *output* as well as information *intake* (Bower, 1975).

Preparation of this chapter was supported in part by grant BNS-8120104 from the National Science Foundation, and benefited from comments by Judith Kroll, Saul Sternberg, and Neal Stillings. Gordon Bower, too, took it upon himself to offer extensive comments on an early draft of this chapter. As always, his comments were both trenchant and constructive. For his input on this chapter and for all the other guidance he has provided me, I am most grateful.

Moreover, Gordon believed that existing analyses of the traditionally studied areas of cognitive psychology—perception, attention, memory, and decision making—might augment the analysis of motor control in ways that had not been achieved before and that a better understanding of motor control in turn might shed light on these topics.

Whether Gordon's optimism was justified remains to be seen. Nevertheless, the similarity of questions in movement control research and other cognitive research areas suggests that the simultaneous pursuit of both lines of investigation will be fruitful. The following questions are central in cognitively oriented research on movement control:

1 How are movements internally represented before, during, and after their production?

2 Are the representations decomposable into basic units, and if so, how are those basic units integrated?

3 How are movement representations accessed?

4 Are special memory stores associated with the maintenance of movement representations?

5 What are the major stages in the planning and preparation of movements?

For anyone engaged in cognitive psychological research today, these questions should sound familiar. Questions concerning fundamental units of storage (Johnson, 1970; Simon, 1974), the nature of representation (Anderson, 1978; Kosslyn, 1980), the organization of memory storage (Cermak & Craik, 1979), access to memory representations (Shoben, 1982), and the time course of information processing (McClelland, 1979; Miller, 1982) are at the heart of contemporary cognitive psychological research. The commonality of questions in the cognitive analysis of motor control and in cognitive psychology more generally suggests that a comparison of the findings in the two areas could cross-fertilize developments in each of them.

This point has not gone unnoticed. In the past decade, an increasing number of investigators have undertaken detailed psychological studies of movement control, as evidenced by books published by Stelmach (1976, 1978), Stelmach and Requin (1980), Gallistel (1980), Holding (1981), Kelso (1982), Schmidt (1982), and Magill (1983). I have been fortunate to be involved in this growing field of research, and I believe that the contributions I have made to it derive in large part from Gordon Bower's continual support and encouragement.

In this chapter I will review some of the main lines of research in the cognitive psychology of movement control that have heavily influenced my own work. The discussion will follow a theoretical framework that helps to organize much of the data that have been reported in the movement control literature and serves to point out important similarities between information processing on the motor and sensory sides.

Before beginning the review, I should emphasize that the research summarized here is not explicitly concerned with the *acquisition* of motor skills, the topic that many people associate with the phrase "movement control." Rather, the work I will outline comprises a relatively microscopic analysis of the structures and processes involved in the *performance* of single acts or classes of acts. The research is not aimed directly at improving how people teach or learn motor skills, although it potentially could have that effect.

PLANS RATHER THAN LINEAR CHAINS

What form should a cognitive theory of movement control take? To begin with, it is useful to say what form it should *not* take. It should not take the form of a reflex chaining mechanism, where each movement is triggered by sensory feedback from the movement that took place before it. As Lashley (1951) pointed out over thirty years ago, there are important reasons to reject a reflex chain theory and there are equally important reasons to favor a theory which holds that movement sequences are governed by hierarchically organized central plans.

Lashley's evidence against reflex chain theory came from two main sources. One pertained to timing: times between successive movements in sequences such as piano playing, typing, or talking are often too short for execution of each movement to be triggered by feedback from the immediately preceding movement. (For more recent discussions of this point, see Adams, 1976; Rosenbaum and Patashnik, 1980a, 1980b; and Rosenbaum, 1983a.) Lashley's second source of evidence against reflex chain theory was the occurrence of anticipatory errors, primarily in speech production. Saying "the queer old dean," when "the dear old queen" was intended, demonstrates that information about the entire statement was available in some form before the statement began. (For more recent discussions of speech and related errors, see Fromkin, 1973, 1980; Garrett, 1975, 1982; and Norman, 1981).

In recent years, additional evidence has accumulated for anticipatory effects in movement performance. Studies of changes in spinal reflexes prior to voluntary movements (Requin, Bonnet, & Semjen, 1977; Turvey, 1977), changes in neuronal discharge patterns within the brain prior to manual and other responses (Deecke, Grozinger, & Kornhuber, 1976; Evarts, 1973), modification of speech production patterns prior to forthcoming utterances (Kent & Minifie, 1977; MacNeilage & Ladefoged, 1976), and changes in the time to begin speaking or typing depending on the amount to be said or typed (Sternberg, Monsell, Knoll, & Wright, 1978) all support the hypothesis that a representation of an entire act is established in the central nervous system before the act begins.

HIERARCHICAL DECODING

Given the convergent evidence for central representations of forthcoming movement sequences, we can ask what form the representations take: Are they hierarchical, as Lashley thought, or are they simply linear? A study conducted by Rosenbaum, Kenny, and Derr, (1983) attempted to answer this question. Subjects were required to produce memorized sequences of keyboard responses as quickly as possible. A representative sequence was MmMmIiIi, where M denotes the right middle finger, m denotes the left middle finger, I denotes the right index finger, and i denotes the left index finger. Subjects performed this sequence six times consecutively, and the times between successive component responses were recorded by a computer.

Figure 9–1 shows the mean latency to perform each response after the response that immediately preceded it. The figure shows that the mean latency for any given response depended systematically on its serial position within the sequence.

How can these results be explained? Suppose the memory representation for the sequence MmMmIiIi is hierarchically organized, so that MmMm and IiIi constitute two major units, each of which can be further decomposed into smaller units. The MmMm unit is decomposed into two Mm units, each of which is decomposed into an M unit and an m unit; the IiIi unit is likewise decomposed into two Ii units, each of which is decomposed into an I unit and an i unit.

Suppose, moreover, that this hierarchically organized representation is used to control production of the physical sequence through an orderly decoding process such as that shown in Figure 9–2. It is seen here that the decoding of units into their constituents

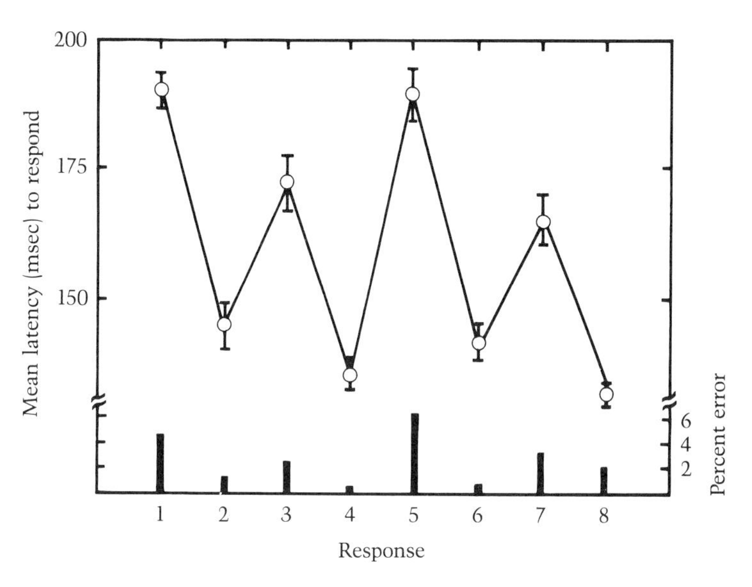

FIGURE 9–1 Mean latency to produce one response after the other in the experiment of Rosenbaum, Kenny, and Derr (1983). The data come from the sequence MmMmIiIi, as well as seven other sequences that differed with respect to starting hand (left or right), starting finger (middle or index), and whether the predominant type of transition between responses used homologous or nonhomologous fingers; besides MmMmIiIi, the other sequences were MiMiImIm, IiIiMmMm, ImImMiMi, mMmMiIiI, mImIiMiM, iIiImMmM, and iMiMmImI. The mean latency for the first response does not include the time to initiate the six consecutive renditions of the sequence. Estimates of ±SE were based on between-subject differences. The bars at the bottom indicate the percentage of errors at each serial position.

can be depicted as a "tree-traversal" process. All the units within a larger unit are successively decoded in a left-to-right fashion, and physical production of a response occurs whenever a terminal unit is encountered. If it is assumed that each decoding operation takes a finite, measurable amount of time, the timing data of Figure 9–1 can be explained by observing that more time would be needed as more decoding operations are necessary. Indeed, if we plot response time against number of hypothesized decoding operations, as shown in Figure 9–3, we see that each decoding operation may reasonably be assumed to have taken a constant amount of time (on average). (For further discussion and elaboration of the hierarchical decoding model, see Collard & Povel, 1982; Cooper & Paccia-Cooper, 1980; Inhoff, Rosenbaum, Gordon, & Campbell, 1983; Klein, 1983; Rosenbaum, 1983b; Rosenbaum, Inhoff, & Gordon, 1983; Rosenbaum, Saltzman, & Kingman, 1984.)

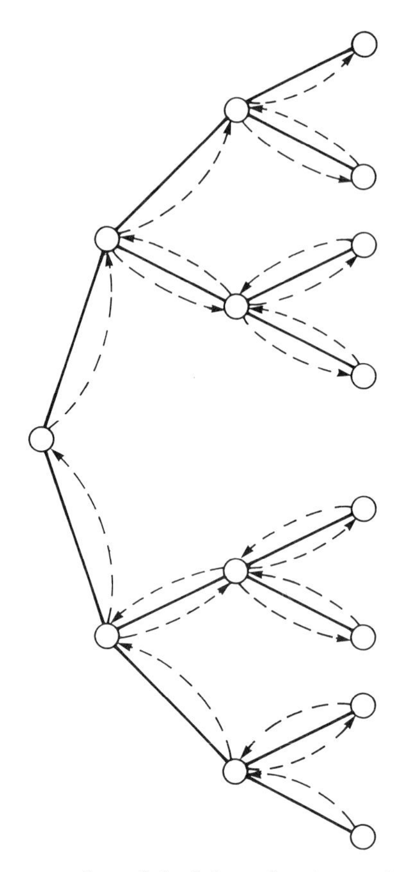

FIGURE 9–2 Tree-traversal model of the selection and production of motor responses. Production of a response occurs when its corresponding terminal node is activated (after Rosenbaum, Kenny, & Derr, 1983).

The success of the hierarchical decoding model supports Lashley's original conjecture about the structure of central plans for movement. Furthermore, it provides a mechanism for the implementation of such plans. An appealing aspect of the proposed mechanism is that it has been proposed before. Yngve (1960), Bower and Winzenz (1969), Johnson (1970), Restle (1970), Reitman and Rueter (1980), and others have suggested that serial recall of verbal information is governed by a hierarchical decoding, or "unpacking," system. Finding that the same sort of system is used in the performance of finger sequences suggests that the representation and retrieval of serially ordered information may be fundamentally similar (if not identical) for symbolic and motoric activities.

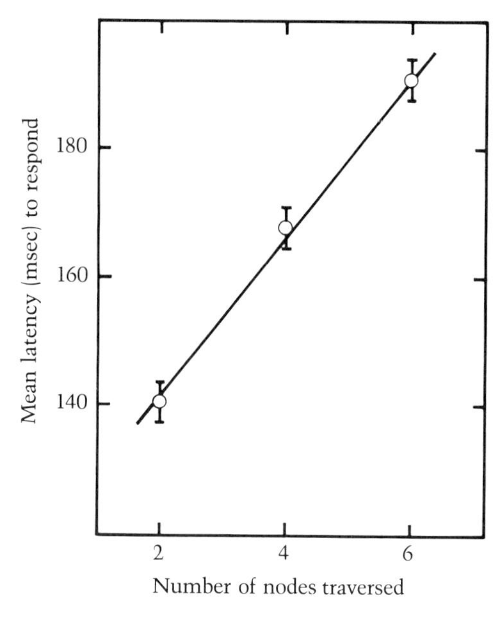

FIGURE 9–3 Mean latency when two nodes had to be traversed in the hypothesized tree-traversal process (responses 2, 4, 6, and 8); when four nodes had to be traversed (responses 3 and 7); and when six nodes had to be traversed (responses 1 and 5). Based on the data shown in Figure 9–1; after Rosenbaum, Kenny, & Derr, 1983.

CONSTRUCTION OF MOVEMENT PLANS

If plans for sequences of movement are hierarchically organized, does that organization influence the way the plan is initially put together? A study by Miller (1982) suggests that the construction of movement plans follows a hierarchical course. Miller's subjects performed a reaction-time experiment in which one of four possible responses (button-presses made with the left or right index or middle finger) were required. On each trial, a signal appeared on a screen to indicate which of the responses should be performed. Before the signal, advance information was given about the hand to be used (left or right), about the finger to be used (index or middle), about both the hand and finger to be used, or about neither. Miller found that advance information about hand resulted in reduced reaction time (RT). However, advance information about finger did not reduce RTs relative to the control condition in which no advance information was provided. Finally, advance information about both hand and finger reduced RTs the most.

The most natural way to interpret these results is in hierarchical terms. Suppose that there are superordinate nodes in memory corresponding to the two hands and subordinate nodes corresponding to the fingers of each hand. Miller's results suggest that hand nodes can be readied for subsequent activation before finger nodes can be, but that the reverse is not true. The suggestion, in other words, is that the selection of a motor plan runs strictly from the top down. Elements at one level cannot be selected unless elements at a higher level have already been selected.

Unfortunately, such a simple model is not always supported. Rosenbaum (1980) sought evidence for an ordered construction process in the preparation of plans for aimed hand movements. In the main experiment, subjects moved either the left or right hand toward or away from the frontal plane of the body over a long or short distance. Prior to the appearance of the signal that indicated which movement was required, advance information was given about the hand, direction, or distance of the upcoming movement. (Actually, advance information was given about all possible combinations of the three features, including none of them in the control condition.)

From a hierarchical standpoint, it is reasonable to expect that choice of hand should take priority over choice of direction, and that choice of direction should take priority over choice of distance (Megaw, 1972). Thus, one might expect to find that advance information about direction is only useful if information about hand is also supplied, and that advance information about distance is only useful if information about hand and direction is also supplied. The actual result was that advance information reduced RTs and errors regardless of the type of feature divulged. Therefore, a strict top–down model need not be adopted to account for the data in this task.

Nevertheless, a hierarchical planning model for aimed hand movements need not be *rejected* on the basis of these results. Advance information about direction alone could have reduced later decision times if direction decisions were made in advance under each hand node. Likewise, advance information about distance alone could have reduced later decision times if distance decisions were made in advance under each direction node. The data in fact are consistent with such an interpretation. Advance information about distance reduced RTs less than advance information about direction, which in turn reduced RTs less than advance information about hand. Thus, for those types of advance information that would have required decisions under more nodes, RTs were reduced less, perhaps because of capacity limitations. (For an alternative account see Goodman & Kelso, 1980, and for a reply see Rosenbaum, 1983c.)

Another result from the Rosenbaum (1980) study that supports a hierarchical planning hypothesis was that the time to reach the target (in contrast to the oice time to leave the home position) was strongly affected by distance uncertainty, but was less affected by direction uncertainty, and was completely unaffected by hand uncertainty. This result fits with the idea that distance tended to be the last-determined feature, that direction tended to be the second-determined feature, and that hand tended to be the first-determined feature. (The error data also supported this interpretation.)

In sum, the study by Rosenbaum (1980) supports the hierarchical planning hypothesis even though it does not support a strict top–down model, as Miller's (1982) study did. Both studies, nevertheless, add weight to the widely discussed hypothesis that movement planning is a hierarchical process (Garrett, 1975, 1982; Keele, 1981; MacKay, 1982; Pew, 1974). (For a review of studies using advance information, or *precuing*, to investigate motor planning, see Rosenbaum, 1983c.)

MOTOR SCHEMAS

We have seen that evidence has been adduced for the hypothesis that movement plans are hierarchically organized when they are ready to be implemented and that movement plans are constructed for implementation via a hierarchical decision process. The question that now arises is why the construction process is hierarchical. The answer, I believe, is to be found in the construct of the motor schema (Bartlett, 1932; Pew, 1974; Schmidt, 1975, 1982).

Consider the observation that motor skills can transfer between tasks. An expert violinist is likely to be a credible violist. An effective baseball batter is likely to be a competent batsman in cricket. An accomplished ice skater is bound to be a proficient roller skater. These examples demonstrate that the memory representations guiding performance in highly practiced skills are not so specific that they permit only particular sets of muscle movements. Rather, the memory representations are schematic and can be instantiated differently depending on the needs of the moment.

The ability to transfer between similar motor tasks implies that some aspects of motor schemas are modifiable. However, other aspects are presumably fixed. The fixed aspects distinguish motor schemas from one another. The search for fixed aspects of motor schemas has culminated in the discovery of invariances in the way motor tasks are performed. Perhaps the most widely cited example of such an invariance is found in handwriting. According to Merton (1972) and Raibert (1977), regardless of whether one signs one's name on a bank check, across the expanse of a blackboard, or with one's toes or teeth, the individual's writing style is preserved. This phenomenon (which to my knowledge has not been rigorously evaluated through a procedure involving visual matching or some other experimental technique) has been taken to suggest that people possess extremely abstract programs for handwriting behavior. This claim has been strengthened by the discovery that the relative timing of writing strokes remains constant over changes in writing size (Viviani & Terzuolo, 1980). (For a review of demonstrated invariances in motor performance, see Kelso, 1981.)

In some of my work I have taken a somewhat different approach to the search for motor schemas. Subjects in one study (Rosenbaum, 1977) were required to perform such tasks as turning a crank in a forward or backward direction with one hand as quickly as possible for 30 sec followed by turning the crank in either the forward or backward direction with the other hand as quickly as possible for 30 sec. The rate of cranking in the second bout was lower if the direction of cranking was the same as in the first bout. This result, and others from the study, can be taken to suggest that neural representations subserving the control of motor tasks are susceptible to selective adaptation or fatigue, much as neural representations activated by particular types of stimuli show reduced sensitivity following prolonged exposure to those stimuli. The neural representations in this case can be viewed as physiological substrates of motor schemas for complex motor patterns such as cranking, with one of their adjustable parameters being the hand that is called upon to act. (For evidence against the hypothesis that such motor adaptation effects were due to sensory fatigue, see Rosenbaum and Radford, 1977, and for further applications of the motor adaptation procedure, see Heuer, 1980.)

On the basis of results such as these, we can return to the question with which this section began: Why does the construction of movement plans appear to proceed hierarchically? A likely answer is that motor schemas are used for different classes of movement, and that after the appropriate motor schema has been selected, lower level parameters are supplied to it to produce movements appropriate to the particular task required (see Glencross, 1980, for further discussion of this position).

CONCLUSIONS

This chapter has reviewed some findings of cognitive psychological research on human movement control. The research has pointed to the hierarchical organization of plans for movement. Evidently, movements are planned by selecting appropriate motor schemas and then instantiating the selected schemas by setting variable parameters within them depending on the task to be completed. After all the necessary parameters have been set, the fully determined program is implemented by successively decoding the program into its constituents.

One of the intriguing aspects of this theoretical framework is that the maximum rate of motor output is assumed to be limited by the need for continual decoding and decision making. Contrary to what one might expect, especially after watching the extremely rapid performance of a skilled typist or concert pianist, the evidence obtained so far does not suggest that movement instructions are simply "reeled off" from a linear string representation. Rather, movement instructions appear to be executed via a continual process of selecting or decoding motor programs into their component parts.

Why is such a process used? The answer may be found in George Miller's (1956) well-known concept of "chunking." Miller argued that the storage capacity of peripheral or low-level memory stores involved in perceptual processing is severely limited, and that this limitation is compensated for by fast access to high-level codes in long-term memory. The data reviewed here suggest that the same limitations and compensations characterize the output system. Rather than loading up peripheral buffers with extended sequences of low-level movement instructions to be read out *seriatum*, the motor system appears to alternate between translating information within symbolic memory stores and executing low-level information as it is encountered in the translation process. That similar methods of information processing seem to be used by the motor and perceptual systems suggests that the dialogue between cognitive psychologists concerned with these two kinds of systems will become increasingly important in the future.

REFERENCES

Adams, J. A. Issues for a closed-loop theory of motor learning. In G. E. Stelmach (Ed.), *Motor control: Issues and trends*. New York: Academic Press, 1976.

Anderson, J. R. Arguments concerning representations for mental imagery. *Psychological Review*, 1978, *85*, 249–77.

Bartlett, F. C., *Remembering: A study in experimental and social psychology*. Cambridge: Cambridge University Press, 1932.

Bower, G. H. Cognitive psychology: An introduction. In W. K. Estes (Ed.), *Handbook of learning and cognitive processes*, (Vol. 1). Hillsdale, N.J.: Lawrence Erlbaum Associates, 1975.

Bower, G. H., & Winzenz, D. Group structure, coding, and memory for digit series. *Journal of Experimental Psychology*, 1969, *80* (2, Pt.2).

Cermak, L. S., & Craik, F.I.M. (Eds.). *Levels of processing in human memory*. Hillsdale, N.J.: Lawrence Erlbaum Associates, 1979.

Collard, R., & Povel, D-J. Theory of serial pattern production: Tree traversals. *Psychological Review*, 1982, *85*, 693–707.

Cooper, W. E., & Paccia-Cooper, J. *Syntax and speech*. Cambridge, Mass.: Harvard University Press, 1980.

Deecke, L., Grozinger, B., & Kornhuber, H. H. Voluntary finger movements in man: Cerebral potentials and theory. *Biological Cybernetics*, 1976, *23*, 99–119.

Evarts, E. V. Brain mechanisms in movement. *Scientific American*, 1973, *229*(6), 96–103.

Fromkin, V. A. (Ed.). *Speech errors as linguistic evidence*. The Hague, Netherlands: Mouton, 1973.

Fromkin, V. A. (Ed.). *Errors in linguistic performance: Slips of the tongue, ear, pen, and hand*. New York: Academic Press, 1980.

Gallistel, C. R. *The organization of action: A new synthesis*. Hillsdale, N.J.: Lawrence Erlbaum Associates, 1980.

Garrett, M. F. The analysis of sentence production. In G. H. Bower (Ed.), *Psychology of learning and motivation* (Vol. 9). New York: Academic Press, 1975.

Garrett, M. F. Production of speech: Observations from normal and pathological language use. In A. Ellis (Ed.), *Normality and pathology in cognitive functions*. London: Academic Press, 1982.

Glencross, D. J. Response organization and levels of control. In G. E. Stelmach & J. Requin (Eds.), *Tutorials in motor behavior*. Amsterdam: North-Holland, 1980.

Goodman, D., & Kelso, J. A. S. Are movements prepared in parts? Not under compatible (naturalized) conditions. *Journal of Experimental Psychology*, 1980, *109*, 475–495.

Greene, P. H. Problems of organization of motor systems. In R. Rosen & F. M. Snell (Eds.), *Progress in theoretical biology* (Vol. 2). New York: Academic Press, 1972.

Heuer, H. Selective fatigue in the human motor system. *Psychological Research*, 1980, *41*, 345–54.

Holding, D. H. (Ed.). *Human skills*. Chister: Wiley, 1981.

Inhoff, A. W., Rosenbaum, D. A., Gordon, A. M., & Campbell, J. A. *Stimulus-response compatibility and motor programming of manual response sequences.* Manuscript submitted for publication, 1983.

Jeannerod, M. Intersegmental coordination during reaching at natural visual objects. In J. Long & A. D. Baddeley (Eds.), *Attention and performance* (Vol. IX). Hillsdale, N.J.: Lawrence Erlbaum Associates, 1981.

Johnson, N. F. The role of chunking and organization in the process of recall. In G. H. Bower (Ed.), *Psychology of learning and motivation* (Vol. 4). New York: Academic Press, 1970.

Keele, S. W. Behavioral analysis of movement. In V. B. Brooks (Ed.), *Handbook of physiology*. Baltimore: American Physiological Society, 1981.

Kelso, J. A. S. Contrasting perspectives on order and regulation in movement. In A. Baddeley & J. Long (Eds.), *Attention and performance* (Vol. 9). Hillsdale, N.J.: Lawrence Erlbaum Associates, 1981.

Kelso, J. A. S. (Ed.). *Human motor behavior: An introduction*. Hillsdale, N.J.: Lawrence Erlbaum Associates, 1982.

Kent, R. D., & Minifie, F. D. Coarticulation in recent speech production models. *Journal of Phonetics*, 1977, *5*, 115–33.

Klein, R. Nonhierarchical control of rapid movement sequences. *Journal of Experimental Psychology: Human Perception and Performance*, 1983, *9*, 834–836.

Kosslyn, S. M. *Image and mind*. Cambridge, Mass.: Harvard University Press, 1980.

Lashley, K. S. The problem of serial order in behavior. In L. A. Jeffress (Ed.), *Cerebral mechanisms in behavior*. New York: Wiley, 1951.

MacKay, D. G. The problems of flexibility, fluency, and speed-accuracy trade-off in skilled behavior. *Psychological Review*, 1982, *89*, 483–506.

MacNeilage, P., & Ladefoged, P. The production of speech and language. In E. C. Carterette & M. P. Friedman (Eds.), *Handbook of perception* (Vol. 7). New York: Academic Press, 1976.

Magill, R. A. (Ed.). *Memory and control of action*. Amsterdam: North-Holland, 1983.

McClelland, J. L. On the time relations of mental processes: An examination of systems of processes in cascade. *Psychological Review*, 1979, *86*, 287–330.

Megaw, E. D. Direction and extent uncertainty in step-input tracking. *Journal of Motor Behavior*, 1972, *4*, 171–86.

Merton, P. A. How we control the contraction of our muscles. *Scientific American*, 1972, *226*(5), 30–37.

Miller, G. A. The magical number seven, plus or minus two: Some limits on our capacity for processing information. *Psychological Review*, 1956, *63*, 81–97.

Miller, J. Discrete versus continuous stage models of human information processing: In search of partial output. *Journal of Experimental Psychology: Human Perception and Performance*, 1982, *8*, 273–96.

Norman, D. A. Categorization of action slips. *Psychological Review*, 1981, *88*, 1–15.

Pew, R. W. Human perceptual-motor performance. In B. H. Kantowitz (Ed.), *Human information processing: Tutorials in performance and cognition*. Hillsdale, N.J.: Lawrence Erlbaum Associates, 1974.

Raibert, M. H. *Motor control and learning by the state-space model*, Technical Report AI-TR-439, Artificial Intelligence Laboratory, Massachusetts Institute of Technology, 1977.

Reitman, J. S., & Rueter, H. H. Organization revealed by recall orders and confirmed by pauses. *Cognitive Psychology*, 1980, *12*, 554–81.

Requin, J., Bonnet, M., & Semjen, A. Is there a specificity in the supraspinal control of motor structures during preparation? In S. Dornic (Ed.), *Attention and performance* (Vol. 6). Hillsdale, N.J.: Lawrence Erlbaum Associates, 1977.

Restle, F. Theory of serial pattern learning: Structural trees. *Psychological Review*, 1970, *77*, 481–95.

Rosenbaum, D. A. Selective adaptation of "command neurons" in the human motor system. *Neuropsychologia*, 1977, *15*, 81–91.

Rosenbaum, D. A. Human movement initiation: Specification of arm, direction, and extent. *Journal of Experimental Psychology: General*, 1980, *109*, 444–74.

Rosenbaum, D. A. Central control of movement timing. *Bell System Technical Journal (Special Issue on Human Factors and Behavioral Science)*, July/August 1983, *62*, 1674–1657. (a)

Rosenbaum, D. A. Hierarchical versus nonhierarchical control of rapid movement sequences: A reply to Klein. *Journal of Experimental Psychology: Human Perception and Performance*, 1983, *9*, 837–839. (b)

Rosenbaum, D. A. The movement precuing technique: Assumptions, applications, and extensions. In R. A. Magill (Ed.), *Memory and control of action*. Amsterdam: North-Holland, 1983. (c)

Rosenbaum, D. A., Inhoff, A. W., & Gordon, A. M. *Choosing between movement sequences: A hierarchical editor model*. Manuscript submitted for publication, 1983.

Rosenbaum, D. A., Kenny, S., & Derr, M. A. Hierarchical control of rapid movement sequences. *Journal of Experimental Psychology: Human Perception and Performance*, 1983, *9*, 86–102.

Rosenbaum, D. A., & Patashnik, O. A mental clock-setting process revealed by reaction times. In G. E. Stelmach & J. Requin (Eds.), *Tutorials in motor behavior*. Amsterdam: North-Holland, 1980. (a)

Rosenbaum, D. A., & Patashnik, O. Time to time in the human motor system. In R. S. Nickerson (Ed.), *Attention and performance* (Vol. 8). Hillsdale, N.J.: Lawrence Erlbaum Associates, 1980. (b)

Rosenbaum, D. A., & Radford, M. Sensory feedback does not cause selective adaptation of human "command neurons." *Perceptual and Motor Skills*, 1977, *44*, 447–51.

Rosenbaum, D. A., Saltzman, E., & Kingman, A. Choosing between movement sequences. In S. Kornblum & J. Requin (Eds.), *Preparatory states and processes*. Hillsdale, N.J.: Lawrence Erlbaum Associates, 1984.

Schmidt, R. A. A schema theory of discrete motor skill learning. *Psychological Review*, 1975, *82*, 225–60.

Schmidt, R. A. *Motor control and learning*. Champaign, Ill.: Human Kinetics, 1982.

Shoben, E. J. Semantic and lexical decisions. In C. R. Puff (Ed.), *Handbook of research methods in human memory and cognition*. New York: Academic Press, 1982.

Simon, H. A. How big is a chunk? *Science*, 1974, *183*, 482–88.

Stelmach, G. E. (Ed.). *Motor control: Issues and trends*. New York: Academic Press, 1976.

Stelmach, G. E. (Ed.). *Information processing in motor control and learning*. New York: Academic Press, 1978.

Stelmach, G. E., & Requin, J. (Eds.). *Tutorials in motor behavior*. Amsterdam: North-Holland, 1980.

Sternberg, S., Monsell, S., Knoll, R. L., & Wright, C. E. The latency and duration of rapid movement sequences: Comparisons of speech and typewriting. In G. E. Stelmach (Ed.), *Information processing in motor control and learning*. New York: Academic Press, 1978.

Turvey, M. T. Preliminaries to a theory of action with reference to vision. In R. Shaw & J. Bransford (Eds.), *Perceiving, acting, and comprehending: Towards an ecological psychology*. Hillsdale, N.J.: Lawrence Erlbaum Associates, 1977.

Viviani, P., & Terzuolo, V. Space-time invariance in learned motor skills. In G. E. Stelmach & J. Requin (Eds.), *Tutorials in motor behavior*. Amsterdam: North-Holland, 1980.

Yngve, V. H. A model and an hypothesis for language structure. *Proceedings of the American Philosophical Society*, 1960, *104*, 444–66.

10

UNDERSTANDING AND REMEMBERING STORIES

John B. Black
Yale University

Stories describe a slice of a fictional world that is similar in most respects to the real world. When understanding and remembering stories, readers utilize the same kinds of comprehension processes that they use to understand and remember the real world. For example, Lichtenstein and Brewer (1980) have shown that memory for an event is much the same regardless of whether it is portrayed in a videotape or in a written narrative description. Stories thus provide psychologists with a convenient way to study comprehension and memory in a controlled manner because it is easier to write stories that vary only in certain ways than it is to exert similar control over the real world.

The two main tasks for a psychological study of how people understand and remember stories are to determine how the various pieces of information in the story are connected in the reader's memory and to determine what kinds of knowledge are used to make the connections. Accomplishing these tasks is complicated by the fact that these connections are frequently implicit rather than explicitly stated in the story text, and the knowledge used is tacit rather than apparent. For example, if we read

> The nurse took blood and urine samples then John went in to see the doctor.

The writing of this paper was supported by a grant from the System Development Foundation.

we "know" that the nurse took the samples in order to provide information the doctor needs for diagnosis and that many unstated actions also occurred (e.g., John went from his home to the doctor's office; entered the office; checked in with a receptionist or nurse; etc.). Here our knowledge of the standard set of actions that are conventionally part of visiting a doctor's office allows us to fill in the information not explicitly stated in the text. Similarly, if we read

> John borrowed Jim's stereo and broke it, so Jim took John's personal computer and stepped on it.

then we understand that these two objectively unrelated actions (breaking the stereo and stepping on the computer) are connected here because Jim is taking revenge for his stereo being broken. These two examples illustrate the various kinds of connections between statements in stories and the various kinds of knowledge used to infer these connections when they are implicit.

I have divided my discussion of connections and knowledge into three major parts. First, I discuss the major coherence relations that connect pairs of story statements at a local level in stories. In particular, I describe referential, setting, causal, and motivational relations, and I present the psychological evidence for each of them. Second, I discuss how story statements become tightly connected so as to form cognitive units at a higher level than individual statements. In particular, I describe and present the evidence for the cognitive units of episode, plot, and schema-plus-correction. In the final section, I describe the various overall frameworks (superstructures) that provide ways to access the information in memory that was contained in the story. In particular, I describe reference hierarchies, episode hierarchies, and plot unit networks, and I present evidence for their role as memory retrieval structures.

COHERENCE RELATIONS

Referential

The minimal criterion for textual coherence is that the statements in the text refer to common objects, people, and/or concepts (Kintsch, 1974; Kintsch & van Dijk, 1978). When such common referents do not exist, they must be established by inferences if the text is to be coherent. Thus we expect that competent readers would make such inferences; there are several kinds of evidence that they do. Three kinds of memory evidence have been found for referential inferencing in text understanding: (1) erroneously recognizing items on a later memory test that were implied but not stated; (2) demonstrating better memory for texts that are connected by many coherence inferences than for those that are connected by few or none, and (3) showing that recognition of one statement from a story speeds up recognition of another connected to it by a coherence inference.

The argument behind the erroneous-memory evidence is that if people mistakenly recall or recognize an inference during a later memory test, then they must have made the inference during comprehension and stored it in memory in a form that is later indistinguishable from information that was stated explicitly. For example, Anderson and Bower (1973) found that after reading the statements

> George Washington has good health.
> The first president of the United States was a bad husband.

people would misrecognize

> The first president of the United States had good health.

as having been stated, even though they only inferred it. Here the readers know that "George Washington" and "the first president" refer to the same person, so they make the referential inference connecting the property of good health with the first president.

The second kind of memory evidence for referential inferences is that the more inferential relations that connect text statements, the better the text will be remembered. In particular, de Villiers (1974) found that subjects recalled texts like

> The store contained a row of wood cages.
> The man bought a dog.
> The child wanted the animal.
> The father drove to the house.

better than if they read the same texts with each *the* replaced by an *a*. This result indicates that when reading the original version, the subjects made the linking referential inferences that "the man" and "the father" refer to the same person and that the "a dog" and "the animal" refer to the same creature.

The third type of evidence for referential links in memory is that having just thought of a statement will speed up memory retrieval of other statements referentially linked to it. For example, McKoon and Ratcliff (1980) had subjects read stories that contained sequences like

> The businessman gestured to a waiter.
> The waiter brought coffee.
> The coffee stained the napkins.
> The napkins protected the tablecloth.
> The businessman flourished the documents.

then tested how fast the subjects were at recognizing statements from the stories. The results showed that the subjects were faster at recognizing a statement as part of a story when it was preceded during the test by an item that was referentially linked to it, even when the referentially linked item had been separated from it in the original text. For example, recognizing the "businessman gestured" statement during a test would speed up recognition of the "businessman flourished" statement, even though they are separated by three other sentences in the story text. In fact, merely recognizing one word from the first statement (e.g., waiter) would speed up recognition of a word from the last statement (e.g., documents).

One problem with using memory evidence for inferencing is that the evidence is indirect—the memory measures are made long after the supposed inferencing has taken place. A more direct kind of evidence is provided by measuring the reading times of statements in texts. Haviland and Clark (1974) found that reading times increased when subjects had to infer referential connections between sentences. For example, subjects took longer to read

> The beer was warm.

when it was preceded by

> Horace got some picnic supplies out of the car.

than when it was preceded by

> Horace got some beer out of the car.

The longer reading time in the first case reflects the extra time needed to make the referential inference that the picnic supplies included beer.

Setting

Readers construct a fictional story-world in their minds when they are attempting to understand a story. An essential part of this story-world is the setting in which the plot can take place. The story text provides some of this setting information and the readers make the inferences needed to fill out this skeletal description. For example, Bransford, Barclay, and Franks (1972) found that subjects made appropriate spatial inferences that they later erroneously remembered. They found, for example, that subjects would later misrecognize

> Three turtles rested on a floating log and a fish swam beneath it.

when they originally read the sentence with "them" in place of the word "it." Here the inference was that if the turtles were on the log, then the spatial layout of the scene implied that when a fish swam beneath the turtles, it must have also swum beneath the log. Similarly Bransford et al. found that when subjects read

> There is a tree with a box beneath it.
> A chair is on top of the box.
> The box is to the right of the tree.

they would falsely recognize

> The tree is to the left of the chair.

which is a spatial inference from the stated information.

The memory representation of a story also maintains a consistent point of view within the setting. The point of view is determined by who the main character is and by the perspective in the fictional story-world from which the story is told. This perspective corresponds to where we would place a movie camera if we were filming the scene. Thus, the statement

> Bill was sitting in the living room reading the paper, when John came into the living room.

maintains a consistent point of view because Bill is the initial focus of the sentence and the action is described from the perspective of his location. Thus the movie camera is placed with Bill in the living room so we can film John coming into the room. If the second half of the sentence had said "went" instead of "came," then the point of view would change as one progressed from the first part to the second, and the sequence would be less coherent. Now the movie camera is in the wrong place; it has to be shifted when the reader hits "went" in the second half of the sentence. Black, Turner, & Bower (1979) found that such changes in point of view resulted in sentences that took longer to read, were rated as less comprehensible, were misremembered as having a consistent point of view, and were rewritten to be consistent by subjects asked to edit the story.

Causal

Although reference and setting relations affect the coherence of a story, they are not sufficient to make a story coherent. For example,

> John got a computer from his sister for Christmas.
> Susan gave her sister an ET doll for Christmas.
> Rita went to visit her sister at Christmas.

is rather incoherent, even though the concepts of *sister* and *Christmas* are common referents in all the statements. In fact, explicit repetition of such concepts is not necessary for coherence. For example,

The road became icy.
The truck swerved out of control.
Several cars were smashed.

is quite coherent, even though there is no explicit repetition of common referents. What makes this sequence of statements coherent? Clearly, the reader can link the statements by making causal inferences, such as, the icy road *caused* the truck to swerve and smash the cars. Making such inferences links the statements with implictly common concepts (e.g., truck is implicit in the last statement), but more importantly there are implicit causal links between the statements. Thus, an important criterion for coherence in stories is establishing causal links between the sentences.

Schank (1975) argued that story episodes are stored in the memories of readers as networks of story statements interconnected by causal links. The examples I have just described support this idea, as do the empirical results that I describe next. For example, Mandler and Johnson (1977) found that episodes in children's stories that were interconnected by causal relations were remembered better than episodes that were not causally connected. Similarly, Black and Bern (1981) wrote versions of stories that varied in whether a causal inference could be made linking pairs of statements. For example,

The child was pulling at a bottle.
It fell to the floor and broke.

The causal inference here is that pulling at the bottle caused it to fall and break. The noncausal form of this pair merely replaced "pulling" with "looking." These statements were remembered much better when they were causally related than when they were not. Further evidence for causal relations in memory for stories is provided by the finding that story statements on the main causal path through the story (i.e., the shortest path of actions that connects the beginning and end of the story) are remembered better than those on side paths (Black & Bower, 1980; Trabasso, Seco, & van den Broek, in press).

If the linking inferences become an intimate part of the representation of a story in memory, then readers should frequently be unaware later that they did not explicitly read the implicit causal statements. One source of evidence for this assumption is found in the study of script-based stories. A *script* is a knowledge structure that contains causally related conceptualizations, which represent what we know about the standard actions, objects, and actors in common conventional situations (Schank & Abelson, 1977). For example, if we read

John went to a movie theater.
The movie soon started.

we know that he probably bought a ticket, entered the theater, and found a seat before the movie started. It is our prior knowledge of movie theaters, embodied in the theater script, that allows us to make such causal inferences. Bower, Black, and Turner (1979) found that subjects who had read such script-based stories would soon thereafter be fairly certain that they had read about buying a ticket, entering the theater, finding a seat, and so on. When taking a recognition memory test, the subjects would erroneously recognize (as having been stated) standard script actions that had not been part of the story.

Since understanding a story involves establishing causal links between statements, then the harder it is to establish such links, the longer it should take to read the story. Reading-time studies have shown this to be true. In particular, Haberlandt and Bingham (1978) found that subjects took longer to read sentence triplets when there were no causal relations between them than when there were. Apparently the readers paused and searched in vain for causal relations in the noncausal case, only to finally give up and move on. Similarly, Bower, Black, and Turner (1979) and Abbott, Black, and Smith found that statements took longer to read when standard script actions were skipped in script-based stories.

The causal inferences made when reading a story are also affected by the point of view from which the story is told. Social psychologists have frequently observed that the way people perceive the causes of behavior depends on the point of view from which they view social situations. This bias results in a tendency to attribute the causes of behavior to the actor, when one is an observer, and to the situation if one is the actor (Jones & Nesbitt, 1971). This same bias affects the causal inferences made in attempting to understand a story (Black, 1982; Bower, 1978). In these story studies, all the subjects read a several-page story about three characters going water skiing. However, half the subjects read an introduction to the story designed to identify the boat driver as the main character, whereas the other half read an introduction that identified the skier as the main character. Later, all the subjects took a recognition memory test that included various items corresponding to potential causal inferences not explicitly stated in the story. Which inferences the readers made depended on their point of view (i.e., who they saw as the main character). Readers who had read the skier introduction made inferences identifying causes of unfavorable actions by the skier as being situational (e.g., the tall waves caused the skier to fall down) or due to the other character (e.g., the driver turned the boat too sharply so the skier fell down). On the other hand, readers who read the driver introduction made inferences identifying the skier as the cause of his own troubles (e.g., the skier was clumsy and fell down).

Motivational

Motivational, or goal-based, relations are another way of linking story statements to make stories coherent. Such links connect the source of goals (e.g., we expect certain goals if it is snowing or other goals if a story character is a spy), the goals themselves, and plans for attaining the goals. As with causal relations, when there are implicit motivational links between the statements, we can construct a sequence of statements that is quite coherent without any explicit repetition of common referents. For example,

> Suddenly it started snowing.
> Jim got his shovel out of the basement.
> The sidewalk was clear an hour later.

This sequence is coherent because motivational inferences tell us that the snow storm (source of goal) motivated Jim to get his shovel (plan) in order to clear the sidewalk (goal).

Abbott and Black (1982) provided memory evidence for linking story statements with motivational inferences. In particular, subjects' recall of story statements that were linked by repetition of several common concepts was compared to the recall of statements linked by motivational inferences. If one statement was recalled from a group of statements that were linked by motivational inferences, then other statements in the group were also likely to be recalled, whereas statements recalled from a concept-repetition group were basically independent of one another. Furthermore, the time to recognize a statement as having been in the story was shorter when it was preceded by another story statement from a motivational group, but no such enhancement was observed when it was preceded by a statement from a concept-repetition group.

As with causal links, the harder it is for the reader to construct the motivational links in a story, the longer the story takes to read. If a goal or a plan statement is left to be inferred, the next statement in the story takes longer to read than when the goal or plan statement is stated explicitly (Seifert, Robertson, & Black, 1982). For example, the last statement in the sequence

> Mary and Kate were out to lunch.
> Mary needed to get some money.
> Her pocketbook was empty.
> She told Kate that she had no cash.

takes longer to read in this version than in a version in which the plan is stated explictly (e.g., "She decided to ask Kate for a loan." is inserted as the next-to-last statement). Also, the more goal-related inferences that need to be made to connect two story statements, the longer the statements take to read (Smith & Collins, 1981). For example, a sequence like

> Rita was having stomach pains.
> John got out the telephone book.

takes longer to read than

> Rita needed a doctor fast.
> John got out the telephone book.

because there are more intervening goals to be inferred. That is, in the first version, "having stomach pains" and "got out the telephone book" are separated by more intervening goals (including realizing a doctor is needed) than "needed a doctor" and "got out the telephone book." Thus, the more motivational inferences (whether they be source, goal, or plan) that need be made when reading a story, the longer the story takes to read.

COGNITIVE UNITS

In the previous section, I discussed the four major kinds of coherence relations that connect statements in the memory representation of a story. However, these interconnected story statements do not form a uniform network. Instead they cluster statements into subgroups that form memory units at a higher level of abstraction. These higher level memory units allow people to know a lot without being overwhelmed by information. In particular, the more unintegrated facts one knows about a topic, the longer it takes to retrieve any one of these facts from memory (Anderson, 1974). However, if these facts can be integrated into higher level memory units either through practice (Hayes-Roth, 1977) or through the application of well-learned knowledge (Smith, Adams, & Schorr, 1978), then these higher level units can be used to judge whether or not a given fact is probably true without having to retrieve the specific facts (Reder, 1982; Reder & Anderson, 1980). Thus, higher level memory units keep us from getting bogged down by an inordinate number of details.

Since these higher level cognitive units play such an essential role in keeping our memories organized, it is important that the various types of units be determined for different areas of interest, including story comprehension and memory. (Anderson, 1980, discussed the usefulness of cognitive units for organizing memory and argued for three kinds—concepts, propositions, and schemata. The cognitive units I discuss here are schemata.) The higher level memory unit that has been most fully researched with stories is the goal-based episode, but units corresponding to standard goal-outcome patterns (plot units) have also begun to be investigated. I first discuss the evidence for these higher level cognitive units, then describe how new cognitive units are formed by making corrections to existing ones.

Episodes

The major constituent of stories is the goal-based episode (Rumelhart, 1977; Thorndyke, 1977), which contains a goal (or subgoal if subordinate to other goals), the plan of actions to attain it, and the outcome of trying that plan. If goal-based episodes are truly separate memory units, then we would expect them to exhibit some independence in memory. Black and Bower (1979) found that these episodes showed independence in recall. Specifically, they varied the length of the episodes and found that the length of an episode affected the proportion of the actions recalled from that episode but not the proportion of actions recalled from other episodes. For example, one story had a goal of trying to find a book on a university campus; one episode described a failed attempt to find the book in the library, and a second episode described a successful attempt in the university bookstore. Black and Bower created a "short" version of each episode by including the goal (looking for the book in the library), three actions in service of the goal (entering the library, looking in the card catalog, and finding the location), and the outcome (the book was not there). They also created a "long" version by including five other actions that probably occurred in each episode (e.g., asking the librarian). Adding these five other actions to a given episode increased the recall of the original goal, outcome, and three actions for that episode, but had no effect on the recall of statements in the other episodes. This study showed that episodes are indeed independent in recall and also that adding more statements that served to fill in the gaps between actions in episodes increases the recall of these actions.

Mandler (1978) and Glenn (1978) provided additional evidence that episodes act like separate units in memory. In particular, Mandler found that when she interleaved the actions from two episodes in a story, her subjects separated the actions into episodes during recall. That is, the actions of a given episode were recalled together even though they were separated in the original text. Glenn (1978) found that her subjects tended to elaborate short elliptical stories in recall. These elaborations were inferences that made the stories more coherent by linking the original statements. However, it was the lengths of the episodes, not the total length of the story, that was the critical determinant of whether elaboration would occur.

Haberlandt, Berian, and Sandson (1980) found reading time evidence for episodes as independent units. In particular, they found that readers spend a relatively long time reading the beginnings and ends of episodes. Each time their readers encountered a new episode, they spent time in the beginning determining what knowledge was relevant to understanding the rest of the episode (the relevant plan), and then they paused at the end to store the episode in memory as a unit. Thus, we have both reading time evidence and memory evidence that goal-based episodes are cognitive units in story understanding.

Plot Units

Another kind of higher level memory unit is the plot unit—a particular pattern of goals and outcomes that forms a standard thematic unit (Lehnert, 1981). Plot units are composed of causally linked mental states (goals), positive events (a positive outcome for a plan), and negative events (a negative outcome for a plan). For example, the competition plot unit consists of mental states between two characters with mutually exclusive goals where the same event results in the failure of one character's goals (a negative event for that character), and the success of the other character's goals (a positive event for that character). Thus, two people wanting to watch different programs on the same TV at the same time, or two teams each wanting to win a football game, are instances of the competition plot unit.

Reiser, Black, and Lehnert (in press) found that people use plot units when categorizing and writing stories. For example, people group stories involving competition, denied request, retaliation, and fleeting success (a story with four plot units) into the same story category regardless of specific content; while grouping stories involving competition, denied request, change of mind, and success born of adversity (another set of four plot units) into a different category. Similarly, when asked to write a story like one they are shown, subjects write stories with basically the same set of plot units as the model.

Schema-plus-Correction

My discussion of cognitive units thus far has dealt with cases in which the story statements fit standard expectations; but what happens when story statements deviate from the standard? Research has shown that the deviation becomes a salient part of memory because it is stored as a correction to the standard unit within the current context. This standard unit plus the correction then becomes a cognitive unit in its own right (Schank, 1982). In fact, this is probably how most new cognitive units are learned. For example, if one walks into McDonald's expecting to be seated and waited upon by a waitress, then one's expectation is not fulfilled and the deviation is stored as a correction to the standard restaurant script for the context of a fast-food restaurant. (These days, it is typically the reverse—one learns about McDonald's before standard restaurants.) This general notion of schema plus correction is actually an old one (e.g., Barlett, 1932; Woodworth & Schlosberg, 1954), but modern versions have been proposed by Graesser (1981) and Schank (1982).

The basic idea of a schema-plus-correction theory of memory is that what a person remembers of an experience is the general schema that applies, plus any deviations from that schema. For example, if a person reads a story about going shopping, then later the reader will be confused about which standard shopping actions were stated in the story but would remember deviations more distinctly. Graesser and his colleagues confirmed this notion by showing that even irrelevant actions were remembered better than the standard actions in the shopping script after the memory results have been corrected for guessing (Graesser, Gordon, & Sawyer, 1979; Graesser, Woll, Kowalski, & Smith, 1980).

While the results of Graesser et al. are consistent with a schema-plus-correction theory, such irrelevant deviations are a weak case in which the reader can do little more than tag the irrelevancies as deviating from the schema. Bower, Black, and Turner (1979) used stories requiring corrections in which the deviations were causally related to the schema. Specifically, they used such script deviations as obstacles that blocked standard script actions from occurring (e.g., the customer cannot find a sales clerk), errors in the standard actions (e.g., being charged more than the price), and distractions which interrupted the standard flow of the script (e.g., stopping to talk to a friend about a concert). The results showed that these causally related deviations were remembered much better than either irrelevancies or standard script actions. Causally related deviations are remembered best because they are distinctive information that had to be dealt with, rather than being merely another occurrence of commonplace information about this particular experience.

MEMORY RETRIEVAL STRUCTURES

I have discussed how the information contained in stories is represented in memory, but it is not sufficient to merely represent the information; it must also be organized and indexed in ways that allow one to access the information when needed. Three major kinds of memory retrieval structures have been investigated for stories—reference hierarchies, episode hierarchies, and plot unit networks.

Reference Hierarchies

Kintsch (1974) proposed that the memory representation of a text contains hierarchies of statements, where the statement that first contained a concept (or referent) is superordinate to any later statements that contain the concept and statements are propositions (i.e., predicate terms like verbs or adjectives and noun concepts related to them). For example, the statements

> The Greeks loved beautiful art. When the Romans conquered the Greeks, they copied them, and thus learned to create beautiful art.

could be linked in a reference hierarchy, such as that shown in Figure 10-1. The first statement (proposition) introduces the concept *Greeks* which is then repeated in two other statements, namely, Romans conquered Greeks and Romans copied Greeks. Thus these

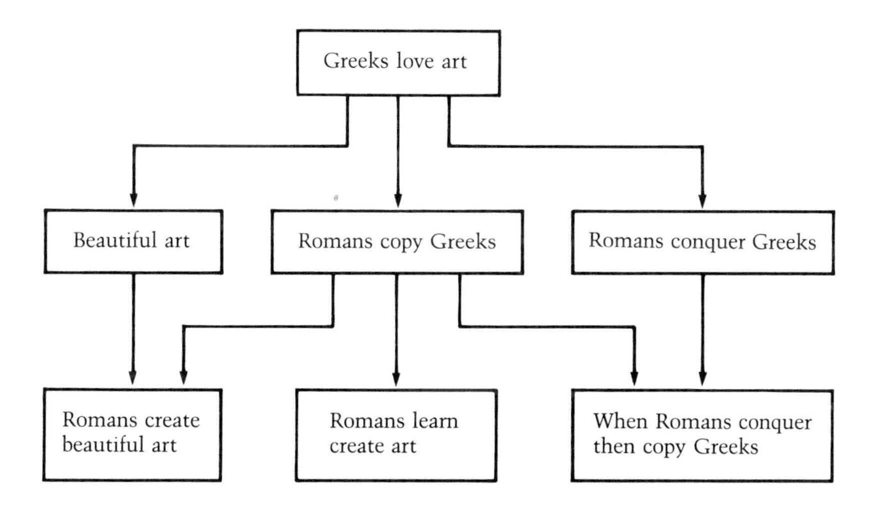

FIGURE 10-1 An example of a reference hierarchy. The arrows connect statements with common referents. The statement that first introduces a referent is superior in the hierarchy to any other statement that contains the referent.

latter two statements are subordinate to the first (and connected to it by a common reference link) because they repeat a concept introduced in the first. The figure represents this with statements (propositions) in boxes connected by arrows corresponding to the reference links. However, these statements also introduce *Romans,* which is then in other statements—e.g., Romans' learning to create art. Thus we have a three-level reference hierarchy with the first two levels being determined by the introduction of the concept *Greeks* and the last two by the concept *Romans.*

Kintsch, Kozminsky, Streby, McKoon, and Keenan (1975) showed that in such reference hierarchies, memory for a given statement depends on its position in the hierarchy. In particular, the lower in the hierarchy, the poorer the recall, a finding consistent with a memory retrieval process that starts at the top of the reference hierarchy and works its way down, searching for the needed information. Thus, the lower in the hierarchy a statement is, the more memory links that have to be traversed and the more likely it is that one will have been lost. Similarly, McKoon (1977) showed that the lower a statement is in the reference hierarchy, the longer it takes people to recognize that they read that statement in the text. Again the time is longer because the memory search starts at the top of the hierarchy and searches downward, so the lower the statement is in the hierarchy, the longer the search will take.

Episode Hierarchies

Most stories are composed of a hierarchy of episodes, another structure that is used to retrieve information from memory. When a story has a hierarchy of goals, attempts to attain the main goal evoke other subgoals that must be attained first; thus, the episodes for the subordinate goals are embedded in the episode for the overall goal. For example, if we revised the "book" story described earlier, so that the student in the bookstore needed to go to the bank to get money to buy the book, then the bank episode would be embedded in and subordinate to the bookstore episode, as shown in Figure 10-2. Numerous researchers (Black and Bower, 1980; Graesser, 1981; Thorndyke, 1977) have found that the more subordinate such episodes are (i.e., the lower they are in the goal hierarchy), the worse they are recalled. This finding is consistent with a memory retrieval process that starts at the top of the goal hierarchy and works its way down. Thus, the lower in the hierarchy an item is, the more likely that at least one link has been lost, so the more likely the item is unretrievable.

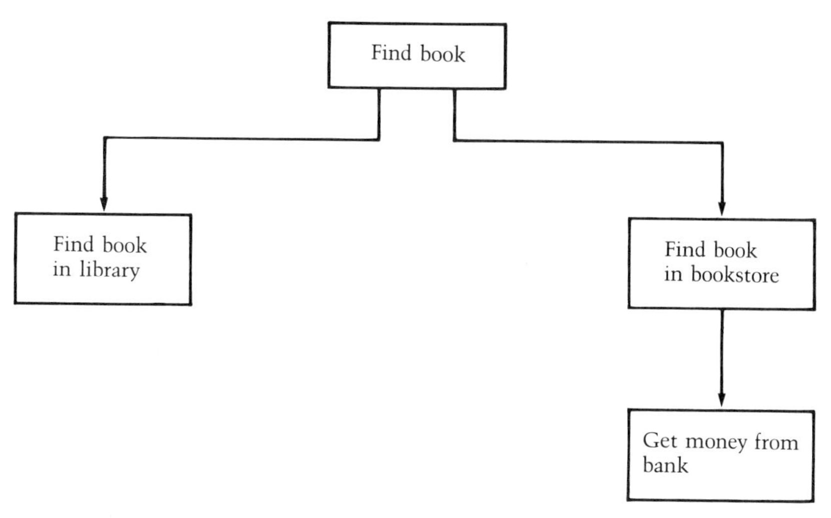

FIGURE 10-2 An example of an episode hierarchy. Each arrow points to an episode that was attempted in order to accomplish the episode at the beginning of the arrow.

Further evidence for such memory retrieval structures is provided by the finding that repeating the same structure in more than one text facilitates memory for the general outline of the text, although it may lead to confusion about the details (Thorndyke, 1977; Thorndyke & Hayes-Roth, 1979). For example, assume an individual first reads a story about a farmer who has to get hay for a cow in order to get milk from the cow for a cat in order to get the cat to scratch the dog so that the dog will bark at a donkey thereby scaring the donkey into the shed (which is what the farmer wanted to accomplish all along). Now, assume that the same person reads another story with a similar long chain of embedded subgoals (i.e., do *x* to accomplish *y* in order to accomplish *z*, etc.), but with a different content (e.g., a political party funds some scientific research in order to get a scientist to testify in favor of a project so that a union will support the project thereby pressuring the other political party to also support the project so that it will pass in the legislature). The overall memory for the second story will be facilitated because the readers realize that it has the same subgoal-embedded structure as the original story.

If people use such goal structures to retrieve information from memory, then adding such a structure to a story should improve memory. Owens, Bower, and Black (1979) introduced such a goal structure by adding a thematic statement (which conveyed a structure of related goals) near the beginning of one version of a story, leaving it out of the other version. For example, in the "no-theme" version, subjects read a boring, rambling story about a college student (Nancy) getting up in the morning, going to a grocery store, attending a class, being examined by a doctor, and going to a party. In the "theme" version, subjects read this same story, but with a brief introduction that said she had awakened feeling sick again, so she wondered if she were pregnant and how she would tell the professor she had been seeing. This statement seemed to electrify the boring story and tie together many otherwise unrelated statements (e.g., going to the doctor, seeing the professor in class and at the party, etc.). Owens, Bower, and Black found that readers later remembered the "theme" version much better than the "no-theme" version and that they remembered the statements related to the theme particularly well. Owens, Bower, and Black termed their results the "soap opera effect" because soap operas seemed like this—boring, rambling stories with just a little spice to galvanize them and make them "memorable." In a related study, Anderson (1980) found that recognizing one statement speeded up the recognition of others that were thematically related to it, even when the other statements came from a different script.

Similarly, Anderson and Pichert (1978) found that when subjects read about looking around a house with the goals of a prospective house buyer in mind, the subjects recalled the details related to house-buying best. However, Anderson and Pichert also found that if they later introduced a different goal structure, the subjects used that retrieval structure to remember details not remembered with the first goal structure. In particular, after the house-buyer subjects finished recalling the story, they were told that the story could also be viewed from the perspective of a burglar. Using a burglar-goal structure as a retrieval guide, the subjects were then able to remember details that they could not remember using the house-buyer retrieval structure.

Plot Unit Networks

The plot unit network functions as a memory retrieval structure that supplements the general episode hierarchy by representing patterns of specific episode content; that is, the plot units capture particular kinds of specific goal-outcome patterns. Lehnert (1981) and Lehnert, Black, and Reiser (1981) showed that plot unit networks also predict what readers would include in summaries of stories. With memory studies, one can always score for the gist of the statements in the text. Empirical research on summarization is more difficult because good short summaries include statements not in the original story. For example, a concise summary of

> Ann and Judy both tried out for a position in the first violin section. They both auditioned impressively, but Judy was hired in the end.

would be "Ann and Judy competed for a position, but Judy got it." Note, however, that the idea of competition here was not explicitly stated in the story. Plot units provide a solution for this research problem because these memory retrieval structures tell us under what conditions to look for particular kinds of generalizations in the summarizations.

Summarization research involving plot units has demonstrated that the more pivotal the plot unit is to a story (i.e., the more causal connections it has with other plot units), the more likely it is to be included in a summary. Also, the more of the plot units in a story that are included, the better the summary will be. For example, the plot unit network for the following story is shown in Figure 10-3.

> Paul wanted to date Susan, but she was going out with Ken. Paul asked Ken to stop seeing her, but Ken just laughed at him. Susan stopped seeing Ken when Paul told her that Ken was also going out with her worst enemy.

This story contains four plot units: competition (i.e., Paul and Ken both wanting to date Susan), denied request (Ken denying Paul's request to stop dating Susan), retaliation (Paul telling Susan that Ken was going out with another girl), and fleeting success (Ken originally gets to date Susan, but it doesn't last long). The pivotal plot unit here is the competition because it is causally connected (in the plot unit network) to all three of the other plot units while the others are connected to at most two others. Thus, if a subject gave a very brief

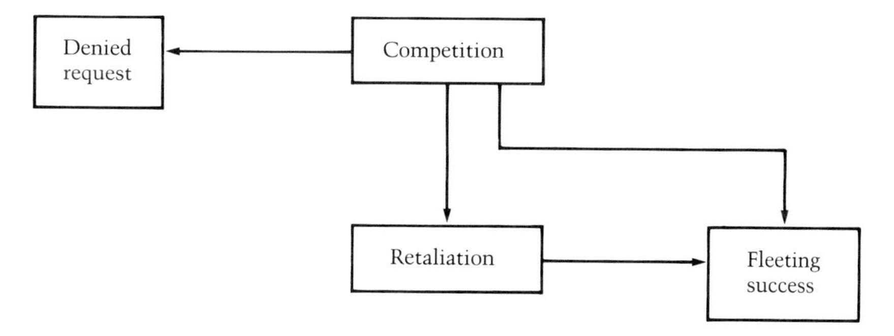

FIGURE 10-3 An example of a plot unit network. The arrows represent causal links between plot units. For example, competition causes the request to be denied.

summary, it would involve competition rather than the other plot units (e.g., Paul and Ken competed for Susan's attentions). However, the best summary would involve all four plot units (e.g., Ken refused Paul's request that he stop seeing Susan, so Paul stopped their dating by telling Susan that Ken was seeing another girl).

CONCLUSIONS

People understand stories by making inferences to establish coherence relations between story statements, to combine related statements into higher level units, and to construct structures appropriate for later retrieval of the story information from memory. There is evidence for four kinds of coherence relations being inferred during story understanding: referential inferences that link common referents in different statements, setting inferences that establish the background needed for the plot to take place, and causal and motivational inferences that link statements in the story plot. The two main higher level cognitive units in stories are goal-based episodes and thematic plot units. Also, new cognitive units are formed as needed by making corrections to the standard units and these corrections are particularly memorable. The linked statements and cognitive units are organized and indexed for efficient memory retrieval by reference hierarchies, episode hierarchies, and plot unit networks.

REFERENCES

Abbott, V., & Black, J. B. A comparison of the memory strength of alternative text relations. Paper presented at the meeting of the American Education Research Association, New York, 1982.

Anderson, J. R. Retrieval of propositional information from long-term memory. *Cognitive Psychology*, 1974, *5*, 451–74.

Anderson, J. R. Concepts, propositions, and schemata: What are the cognitive units? In J. H. Flowers (Ed.), *Nebraska Symposium on Motivation* (Vol. 18). Lincoln: University of Nebraska Press, 1980.

Anderson, J. R. & Bower, G. H. *Human associative memory*. Washington, D.C.: V. H. Winston & Sons, 1973.

Anderson, R. C., & Pichert, J. W. Recall of previously unrecallable information following a shift in perspective. *Journal of Verbal Learning and Verbal Behavior*, 1978, *17*, 1–12.

Bartlett, F. C. *Remembering*. New York: Cambridge University Press, 1932.

Black, J. B. Point of view and causal inferences in story understanding. *Cognitive Science Technical Report Number 20*, Yale University, 1982.

Black, J. B. and Bern, H. Causal coherence and memory for events in narratives. *Journal of Verbal Learning and Verbal Behavior,* 1981, *20,* 267–75.

Black, J. B., & Bower, G. H. Episodes as chunks in narrative memory. *Journal of Verbal Learning and Verbal Behavior,* 1979, *18,* 309–18.

Black, J. B., & Bower, G. H. Story understanding as problem-solving. *Poetics,* 1980, *9,* 223–50.

Black, J. B., Turner, T. J., & Bower, G. H. Point of view in narrative comprehension, memory and production. *Journal of Verbal Learning and Verbal Behavior,* 1979, *18,* 187–198.

Bower, G. H. Experiments on story comprehension and recall. *Discourse Processes,* 1978, *1,* 211–32.

Bower, G. H., Black, J. B., & Turner, T. J. Scripts in memory for text. *Cognitive Psychology,* 1979, *11,* 177–220.

Bransford, J. D., Barclay, J. R., & Franks, J. J. Sentence memory: A constructive versus interpretive approach. *Cognitive Psychology,* 1972, *3,* 193–209.

de Villiers, P. A. Imagery and theme in recall of connected discourse. *Journal of Experimental Psychology,* 1974, *103,* 263–68.

Glenn, C. G. The role of episodic structure and of story length in children's recall of simple stories. *Journal of Verbal Learning and Verbal Behavior,* 1978, *17,* 229–47.

Graesser, A. C. *Prose comprehension beyond the word.* New York: Springer-Verlag, 1981.

Graesser, A. C., Gordon, S. E., & Sawyer, J. D. Memory for typical and atypical actions in scripted activities: Test of a script pointer + tag hypothesis. *Journal of Verbal Learning and Verbal Behavior,* 1979, *18,* 319–32.

Graesser, A. C., Woll, S. B., Kowalski, D. J., & Smith, D. A. Memory for typical and atypical actions in scripted activities. *Journal of Experimental Psychology: Human Learning and Memory,* 1980, *6,* 503–15.

Haberlandt, K., & Bingham, G. Verbs contribute to the coherence of brief narrative passages: Reading related and unrelated sentence triplets. *Journal of Verbal Learning and Verbal Behavior,* 1978, *17,* 419–25.

Haberlandt, K., Berian, C., & Sandson, J. The episode schema in story processing. *Journal of Verbal Learning and Verbal Behavior,* 1980, *19,* 635–50.

Haviland, S. E., & Clark, H. H. What's new? Acquiring new information as a process in comprehension. *Journal of Verbal Learning and Verbal Behavior,* 1974, *13,* 512–21.

Hayes-Roth, B. Evolution of cognitive structures and processes. *Psychological Review,* 1977, *84,* 260–78.

Jones, E. E., & Nisbett, R. E. The actor and the observer: Divergent perceptions of the causes of behavior. In E. E. Jones, D. E. Kanouse, H. H. Kelley, R. E. Nisbett, S. Valins, & B. Weiner (Eds.), *Attribution: Perceiving the causes of behavior.* Morristown, N.J.: General Learning Press, 1971.

Kintsch, W., & van Dijk, T. A. Toward a model of text comprehension and production. *Psychological Review,* 1978, *85,* 363–94.

Lehnert, W. G. Plot units and narrative summarization. *Cognitive Science,* 1981, *5,* 293–331.

Lehnert, W. G., Black, J. B., & Reiser, B. J. Summarizing narratives. *Proceedings of the Seventh International Joint Conference on Artificial Intelligence,* Vancouver, B.C., August, 1981.

Lichtenstein, E. H., & Brewer, W. F. Memory for goal-directed events. *Cognitive Psychology,* 1980, *12,* 412–45.

Mandler, J. M. A code in the node: The use of a story schema in retrieval. *Discourse Processes,* 1978, *1,* 14–35.

Mandler, J. M., & Johnson, N. S. Remembrance of things parsed: Story structure and recall. *Cognitive Psychology,* 1977, *9,* 111–51.

McKoon, G. Organization of information in text memory. *Journal of Verbal Learning and Verbal Behavior,* 1977, *15,* 247–60.

McKoon, G., & Ratcliff, R. Priming in item recognition: The organization of propositions in memory for text. *Journal of Verbal Learning and Verbal Behavior,* 1980, *19,* 369–86.

Owens, J., Bower, G. H., & Black, J. B. The "soap opera" effect in story memory. *Memory and Cognition,* 1979, *7,* 185–91.

Reder, L. M. Plausibility judgments versus fact retrieval: Alternative strategies for sentence verification. *Psychological Review,* 1982, *89,* 250–80.

Reder, L. M., & Anderson, J. M. A partial resolution of the paradox of interference: The role of integrating knowledge. *Cognitive Psychology,* 1980, *12,* 447–72.

Reiser, B. J., Black, J. B., & Lehnert, W. G. Thematic knowledge structures in the understanding and generation of narratives. *Discourse Processes,* in press.

Rumelhart, D. E. Understanding and summarizing brief stories. In D. LaBerge & S. J. Samuels (Eds.), *Basic processes in reading: Perception and comprehension.* Hillsdale, N.J.: Lawrence Erlbaum Associates, 1977.

Schank, R. C. The structure of episodes in memory. In D. G. Bobrow and A. M. Collins (Eds.), *Representation and understanding: Studies in cognitive science.* New York: Academic Press, 1975.

Schank, R. C. *Dynamic memory.* New York: Cambridge University Press, 1982.

Schank, R. C., & Abelson, R. P. *Scripts, plans, goals and understanding.* Hillsdale, N.J.: Lawrence Erlbaum Associates, 1977.

Seifert, C. M., Robertson, S. P., & Black, J. B. On-line processing of pragmatic inferences. *Proceedings of the Fourth Annual Conference of the Cognitive Science Society,* Ann Arbor, Mich., 1982, 74–76.

Smith, E. E., Adams, N., & Schorr, D. Fact retrieval and the paradox of interference. *Cognitive Psychology,* 1978, *10,* 438–64.

Smith, E. E., & Collins, A. M. Use of goal-plan knowledge in understanding stories. *Proceedings of the Third Annual Conference of the Cognitive Science Society,* Berkeley, CA, 1981, 115–16.

Thorndyke, P. W. Cognitive structures in comprehension and memory of narrative discourse. *Cognitive Psychology,* 1977, *9,* 77–110.

Thorndyke, P. W., & Hayes-Roth, B. The use of schemas in the acquisition and transfer of knowledge. *Cognitive Psychology*, 1979, *11*, 82–106.

Trabasso, T., Seco, T., & van den Broek, P. Causal cohesion and story coherence. In H. Mandl, N. L. Stein, & T. Trabasso (Eds.), *Learning and comprehension of text*. Hillsdale, N.J.: Lawrence Erlbaum Associates, in press.

Woodworth, R. S., & Schlosberg, H. *Experimental psychology*. New York: Holt, Rinehart and Winston, 1954.

INDEX